WARHAMMER ARMIES

ORCS & GOBLINS

BY RICK PRIESTLEY

Cover art by Dave Gallagher, Story by Bill King
Black & white art by John Blanche,
Wayne England & Mark Gibbons.

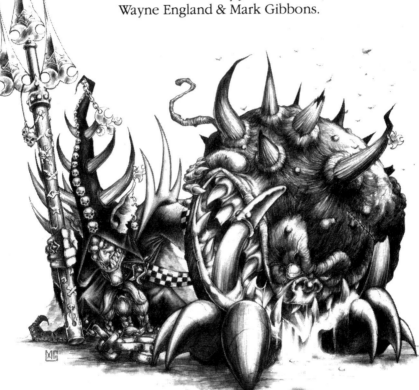

PRODUCED BY GAMES WORKSHOP

GAMES WORKSHOP LTD.
CHEWTON STREET
HILLTOP, EASTWOOD
NOTTINGHAM NG16 3HY

A

PRODUCT

GAMES WORKSHOP INC.
3431-C BENSON AVENUE
BALTIMORE, MARYLAND
21227 - 1072

PRODUCT CODE: 0131

ISBN: 1 872372 64 3

CONTENTS

INTRODUCTION

This is a book about Orcs and Goblins and their armies in the Warhammer game. Within its pages you will find background information explaining much about Orcs and their smaller cousins: where they come from, how they live and fight, and how their wars have helped to shape the Warhammer World. In addition you'll find all the rules you need to use an Orc or Goblin army in the Warhammer game, including rules for new creatures and troop types not covered in the Warhammer Bestiary itself.

Unfortunately we didn't have room to include the complete rules for war machines and chariots as they appear in the Warhammer rulebook, but you will find a summary for them at the end of the War Machines section.

The heart of this book is the Army List section which provides a full list and points values for the Orc and Goblin army. By means of the Army List you can choose your own Orc and Goblin force, equip your own warlord and his entourage of shamans and bosses, and descend upon your quaking foes with the awesome power of the Waaagh behind you!

Orcs and Goblins are one of the most popular and most effective armies in the Warhammer game. One of the reasons for this popularity is the tremendous degree of choice. For example, although we generally refer to 'Orcs and Goblins' you can perfectly well field a force that is all Orcs or all Goblins. You could go further and have an army made up entirely of Night Goblins, Savage Orcs or Forest Goblins if you wanted. We know of at least one person whose army consists entirely of Goblin wolf riders! However, such extreme examples are exceptional, and most players use the wide variety available to create an effective mix of different troops.

This variety is another reason why Orcs and Goblins appeal to so many players, as the number of different troops types enables you to tailor an army to your own style of play or to a particular opponent. For example, a player whose regular opponent fields High Elves might wisely decide to abandon any attempt to out-shoot his enemies in favour of a fast, hard-hitting attack force combined with long range artillery. Both these options are available in abundance with boar riders, trolls, and chariots for attack and rock lobbers or doom divers for long range destruction.

On the other hand, a player faced with an Empire army would probably adopt a different strategy altogether. With its knights and cannons the Empire army would soon sweep aside an army based around boar boyz, while Orc artillery and large creatures such as trolls would present excellent targets for cannons and Helblaster volley guns. In this case the Orc general might choose Night Goblin units with fanatics, backed up by units of Orcs to provide some backbone and either doom divers or flying monsters to take out cannons from the air. Woe betide those Empire knights when they tangle with the Night Goblin fanatics! The options are many and varied, and part of the challenge of the Orc army is to discover the combination of troops and equipment that works best for you.

In writing this book we have assumed that the reader either owns or has access to copies of both Warhammer and Warhammer Battle Magic. As far as possible we've attempted to provide references within the Warhammer rulebook, the Bestiary, or the Battle Magic rulebook so that you can find relevant sections more easily. Where practical we've chosen to repeat information or at least summarise pertinent details within this volume so that you shouldn't need to keep swapping from one book to another.

THE DOMINION OF THE ORCS

Orcs exist more or less everywhere in the Old World, in the lands to the east, and in the far north western realm of Naggaroth beyond the Sea of Chaos. Naturally there are places where Orcs are relatively concentrated and others where they are rare. In the realms of Men, for example, Orcs live only in the wildernesses, deep in the forests or high in the mountains. From their secluded hideouts they raid and rampage over the surrounding territory. There is nowhere in the Old World where the threat of marauding greenskins is completely unknown.

Beyond the realms of Men, Orcs and their small Goblin kin are far more numerous, and in some places they are the dominant intelligent creature. Orcs don't have kingdoms or countries in the same way as Men do, but there are nevertheless areas where Orcs or Goblins are very definitely in control.

The Troll Country north of Kislev is a barren wilderness inhabited by brigands and monsters including, as its name suggests, many wild and savage Trolls. Trolls are not the only monsters to be found there, but they are one of the few creatures able to thrive in this grim and hostile land. In the Troll Country Chaos warbands fight each other for supremacy and Orc armies gather their strength to invade south. On numerous occasions massive Orc armies have swept down from the north, destroying the towns and cities of Kislev and invading the northern provinces of the Empire.

Orcs and Goblins live in vast numbers between the Black Mountains and the Worlds Edge Mountains. This part of the Old World is known as the Badlands on account of it being dominated by interwarring Orc and Goblin tribes. It is from this battleground that many of the most successful Orc leaders have emerged. From the Badlands Orcs move northwards into the Border Princes, a violent and battle-torn land shared by Men and Orcs, and further north still through the Black Fire Pass and into the Empire.

The Worlds Edge Mountains themselves are riddled with old Dwarf mines and the cruder tunnels of Night Goblins. The ancient Dwarf hold of Karak Ungor has become so infested with Night Goblins that it is now known as Red Eye Mountain. Further south, the ancient hold of Karak Varn has become Crag Mere, infamous haunt of monsters and evil creatures of all kinds: its slopes home to Orcs and its deep tunnels the preserve of Night Goblins. Further south still the mountains between Mad Dog Pass and the

quiescent volcano of Fire Mountain are riddled with the lairs of Goblins and Orcs. Mad Dog Pass is overlooked by the crude forts of Goblins, while Black Crag is a vast Orc stronghold which guards the western entrance to Death Pass.

To the east of the Worlds Edge Mountains, over Mad Dog Pass and Death Pass, is the Dark Land, a region of desolation inhabited by all kinds of evil creatures including Chaos Dwarfs, Orcs, Goblins and especially Black Orcs. According to Orc lore, Black Orcs originate from the eastern side of the Dark Lands adjoining the distant Mountains of Mourn. Black Orcs are certainly more common in the eastern part of their territory, in the Dark Lands themselves, and in the Worlds Edge Mountains adjoining the Bad Lands.

In the far west, beyond the Old World and the Elven Kingdoms of Ulthuan, the Orcs and Goblins of Naggaroth are the descendants of captives taken by the Dark Elves many thousands of years ago. Orcs were forced to fight for the Dark Elves in their wars against the High Elves, although in truth the Orcs took little persuading. Since that time many independent Orc and Goblin tribes have taken root in the forests and mountains of that cold land. Sometimes the Orcs ally with the Dark Elves, but they are creatures of shifting loyalties, and are equally likely to attack their erstwhile allies and rampage through the Dark Elf lands.

ORC TRIBES

All Orcs and Goblins live in tribes. A tribe usually contains Orcs or Goblins of the same type, for example it might be a Night Goblin tribe, a Black Orc tribe, a Forest Goblin tribe, etc. However, most Orc tribes also include inferior Goblins of lower status. Tribes vary in size from a few hundred individuals to many thousands of warriors. A tribe is led by a chieftain called a Warboss or, if he is very powerful, a Warlord. If a chieftain is very successful other Orc and Goblins will flock to join his tribe and other tribes will place themselves under his command.

Green-skinned warriors will travel halfway across the Old World just to fight alongside a particularly powerful Warlord. The tribe of a successful Warlord will tend to grow in size and power, enabling it to fight other tribes or invade the realms of Men.

Orc and Goblin tribes are dependent for their fortunes on the abilities of their chieftain. Tribes grow and become powerful under brave and successful leaders, and then shrink or break apart when their chieftain is eventually defeated or slain. When a tribe breaks apart the main portion will probably continue under the old leader or under his successor if the original boss has been slain. The contenders for a tribe's leadership come from the group of especially large Orcs known as Big'uns – the closest that Orcs get to a ruling class. Every tribe has its own core of Big'uns waiting their chance to take over and becomes the tribe's chieftain. Of course there can only be one chieftain, so defeated rivals must either accept his supremacy or leave the tribe altogether and set up a new one of their own.

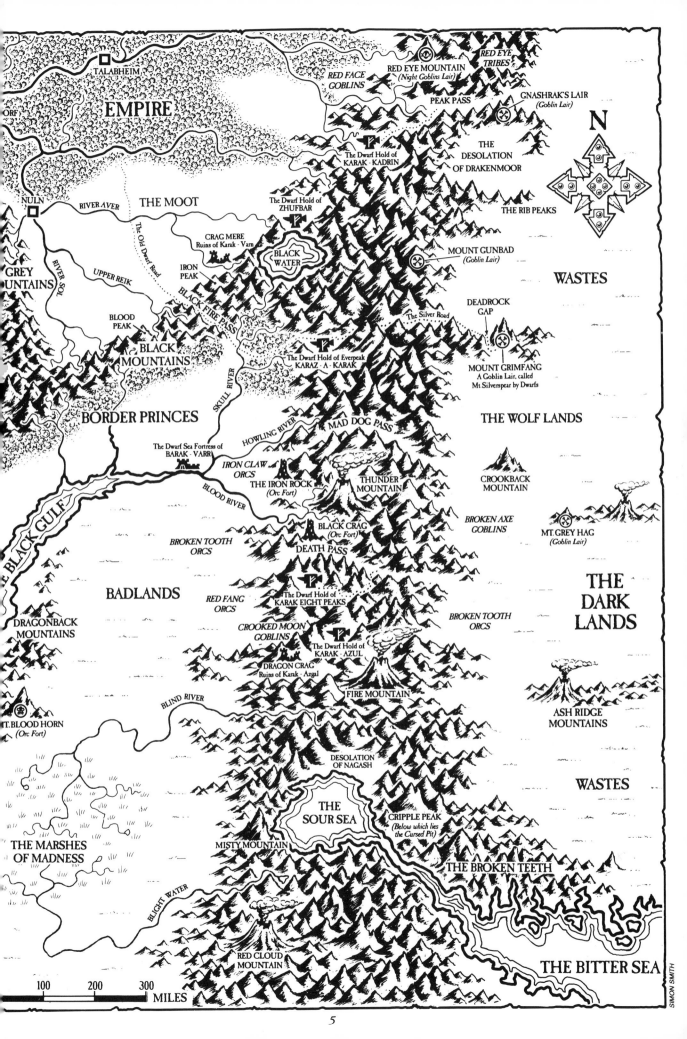

EMPIRE

TALABHEIM

RED FACE
GOBLINS

RED EYE MOUNTAIN
(Night Goblins Lair)

RED EYE
TRIBES

PEAK PASS

GNASHRAK'S LAIR
(Goblin Lair)

The Dwarf Hold of
KARAK - KADRIN

THE
DESOLATION
OF DRAKENMOOR

N

THE RIB PEAKS

THE MOOT

NULN

RIVER AVER

The Dwarf Hold of
ZHUFBAR

CRAG MERE
Ruins of Karak - Varn

BLACK
WATER

MOUNT GUNBAD
(Goblin Lair)

WASTES

UPPER REIK

IRON
PEAK

The Old Dwarf Road

RIVER SOL

GREY
MOUNTAINS

BLACK FIRE PASS

DEADROCK
GAP

The Silver Road

BLOOD
PEAK

BLACK
MOUNTAINS

The Dwarf Hold of Everpeak
KARAZ - A - KARAK

MOUNT GRIMFANG
*A Goblin Lair, called
Mt.Silverspear by Dwarfs*

THE WOLF LANDS

BORDER PRINCES

SKULL RIVER

HOWLING RIVER

MAD DOG PASS

CROOKBACK
MOUNTAIN

The Dwarf Sea Fortress of
BARAK - VARR

IRON CLAW
ORCS

THUNDER
MOUNTAIN

BROKEN AXE
GOBLINS

MT. GREY HAG
(Goblin Lair)

THE BLACK GULF

THE IRON ROCK
(Orc Fort)

BLOOD RIVER

BLACK CRAG
(Orc Fort)

DEATH PASS

BROKEN TOOTH
ORCS

RED FANG
ORCS

The Dwarf Hold of
KARAK EIGHT PEAKS

BROKEN TOOTH
ORCS

THE
DARK
LANDS

BADLANDS

CROOKED MOON
GOBLINS

The Dwarf Hold of
KARAK - AZUL

DRAGONBACK
MOUNTAINS

DRAGON CRAG
Ruins of Karak - Azgal

FIRE MOUNTAIN

ASH RIDGE
MOUNTAINS

MT. BLOOD HORN
(Orc Fort)

BLIND RIVER

DESOLATION
OF NAGASH

WASTES

THE
SOUR SEA

CRIPPLE PEAK
*(Below which lies
the Cursed Pit)*

THE MARSHES
OF MADNESS

MISTY MOUNTAIN

THE BROKEN TEETH

BLIGHT WATER

RED CLOUD
MOUNTAIN

THE BITTER SEA

100   200   300
MILES

SIMON SMITH

5

ORC HISTORY

The history of Orcs and Goblins, as recorded by Men, Dwarfs and Elves, is an account of the rise and fall of huge tribes which have fought against them. Only the really big and powerful tribes impinge upon human or Dwarf history. As such it is a fragmented account but a spectacularly bloody one, punctuated by occasions when the whole of the Old World stood on the brink of destruction.

THE BATTLE OF BLACK FIRE PASS

Before the time of Sigmar the lands west of the Worlds Edge Mountains were as much a realm of Orcs as they were of Men. The tribes of Men were divided amongst themselves, with embittered rivalries and long feuds leading to constant warfare and raiding. The Orc and Goblin tribes were engaged in their own wars against each other and against the tribes of Men, so the whole land was dangerous and strife torn. In the Worlds Edge Mountains the Night Goblins were multiplying deep within their tunnels, and most of the ancient subterranean realm of the Dwarfs was in the possession of Orcs and Goblins.

From out of this turmoil emerged Sigmar, a great leader of Men and the founder of the Empire. Sigmar united the human tribes and forged a mighty army to rid the land of Orcs and claim it for his own. After many battles the Orcs were driven north into the Forest of Shadows and deep into the Great Forest itself. In the east, many old Dwarf holds were cleared out, and the power of the Orcs was broken for many years. It was a terrible time for the Orcs, who suffered defeat after defeat and never found a leader of their own to equal Sigmar.

Eventually the Orcs sent to the east for reinforcements, and a huge Orc army headed up towards the Black Fire Pass from the Badlands, which in those days encompassed the whole of the area which would come to be known as the Border Princes. The Orc army destroyed a small scouting force of Dwarfs who were unlucky enough to be caught at the eastern end of the pass. Wild with their easy victory, the Orc army advanced quickly into the pass itself, taking little care to scout ahead or leave a rearguard to protect its line of march.

The ensuing conflict is the most famous battle in all of the history of Men, the Battle of Black Fire Pass. The Orc army was destroyed and Sigmar was ultimately victorious. It was not the end of the Orcs of course, and in the following years Sigmar took the battle deep into the forests and mountains, rooting out Goblin strongholds and driving his enemies ever deeper into the wilds.

GORBAD IRONCLAW

Gorbad Ironclaw was one of the most successful Orc leaders of all time: his campaign of destruction raged across the Empire and left the region of Solland so devastated that it has never fully recovered. He rose to power deep in the Badlands where his tribe, the Ironclaws, held the fortress known as the Iron Rock.

The Iron Rock is a core of molten iron vomited from the bowels of the earth during some incalculably ancient upheaval. It lies in the western shadows of Thunder Mountain, and was discovered by the Dwarfs who mined into it creating a labyrinth of tunnels, caverns and partially complete workings. The Orcs found the Iron Rock when they overran the Worlds Edge Mountains, establishing their own domain over all the peaks between Mad Dog Pass and Fire Mountain.

The Ironclaw Orcs lived around the Iron Rock for many years, and their fortunes rose and fell with the accustomed regularity of Orc tribes. The Ironclaw's chief rival was the Broken Tooth tribe, whose leader was the notoriously huge and brutal Crusher Zogoth. The Broken Tooths were currently in possession of Black Crag, the old Dwarf hold to the south. In a lightning raid Gorbad moved his army through the ancient Dwarf tunnels and smashed the Broken Tooth tribe before they realised what was happening. Crusher Zogoth escaped into the old Dwarf tunnels threatening revenge and Gorbad sent wild Cave Squigs after him. The squealing of the Cave Squigs echoed through the passages of Black Crag for several days, and Night Goblin Squig Hunters were sent in to retrieve them. Neither Squigs nor Goblins ever returned.

The Broken Tooths readily accepted Gorbad as their leader, as is the fashion of Orcs who know when they are beaten and who would much sooner be on the winning side. With the Broken Tooths under his thumb Gorbad soon conquered the surrounding Goblin and Night Goblin tribes. Waaagh Gorbad had begun! From all over the Badland tribes of Orcs and Goblins rushed to join the huge army as it gradually moved north.

As the growing Waaagh moved past Mad Dog Pass it was joined by the Goblin tribes that lived along its tunnel-strewn length. As the army swung westwards by the forest below the Dwarf Hold of Everpeak it was joined by Forest Goblin tribes riding giant spiders and whooping their savage war cries. The Waaagh crossed Black Fire Pass by night as the skies thundered and lightning crashed about the peaks of the Black Mountains. A small holding force of Empire troops was swept aside and the Orc army descended into the plains of Averland.

Gorbad Ironclaw took the old Dwarf road through Averland, looting and destroying the farms and small towns along its path. The Orc army made camp at the Three Towers, the ancient Elf ruins on the borders of the Moot. Here the Orcs feasted and fought amongst themselves while their loot lasted, and, after three days of drunken brawling, readied to invade the Moot. Forewarned of the Orc advance, the Halflings gathered to defend themselves, and the Count of Averland sent troops to support them. It was a futile gesture. Gorbad struck north through the Tower Hills and caught the Halflings and their allies on the Aver Down, the range of low hills in the southern Moot. The Halflings were cut down to a man, and only a few Knights Panther escaped to warn the Emperor Sigismund of the impending approach of the Orc horde.

The Orcs spent two more days looting the Moot and drinking the contents of its many inns. Halfling refugees poured down the river Aver in a convoy of boats, barges, and improvised rafts, and eventually took refuge in Nuln. Meanwhile, the Orcs advanced upon Averheim. Orc war machines battered the city's gates and broke its walls, and soon the Waaagh was inside the city itself, burning and destroying while the helpless citizens fled to the hills.

By this time Gorbad Ironclaw's reputation had spread amongst all the Orc and Goblin tribes of the Great Forest, and many more green-skinned warriors flocked southwards to join him. The Orcs began to loot and pillage in their usual fashion, but Gorbad had other plans. On his orders, the Ironclaw Big'uns prowled the burning streets gathering up the half drunken Orcs and dragging the Goblins back into the battlelines. This caused much grumbling and many heads were knocked together just to remind everybody who was boss.

Nuln was next to feel the power of the Waaagh. Gorbad advanced towards the city from the east, roughly following the line of the river Aver. Nuln was already crammed with Halfling refugees and people from eastern Averland who had taken shelter from the Orc horde. The Orcs barely slowed their pace at the town walls, but poured over the city gates destroying and killing in a repetition of the slaughter at Averheim. Brutus Leitdorf, the Count of Averland, ordered the retreat over the great bridge and rallied his troops in the western half of the city.

The Count ordered the centre section of the bridge to be raised as the Orcs approached, cutting off the Orc advance. However it was to no avail: the Orcs swarmed across the river floating on broken timber beams and other debris. At first the Orcs were beaten back and many drowned in the blood-filled river, but in the end sheer numbers prevailed and the Orcs gained a firm foot-hold on the western bank. By nightfall the whole city was burning and the few survivors were fleeing southwards towards Altdorf. Brutus Leitdorf was among them, leading the remnants of his army away from the disaster and towards Altdorf.

The destruction of Nuln was a great blow to the Emperor Sigismund and a mighty victory for Gorbad Ironclaw. The Empire's army was so weakened by the loss of its forces that Sigismund could do nothing but watch and wait while the Orc hordes devastated the surrounding lands. The whole of Solland and Wissenland were plundered and burned after the defeat of another army led by Count Eldred of Solland in what came to be known in the Empire as the Battle of Solland's Crown. Count Eldred was slain in personal combat by Gorbad and the Solland sword, the Runefang of Solland given to Sigmar's heirs by the Dwarfs, was taken by the Orcs. According to legend, Gorbad tore the crown of Solland from the Count's head and placed it upon his own, and wore it thereafter as a token of his victory. The Orcs rampaged through Solland for weeks, burned and looting, until turning north once more towards Altdorf.

An army was dispatched under the Count of Wissenland to intercept the advancing Orcs before they reached the capital. The Count of Wissenland, Erich Adolphus, was counted the best general in the Empire, the victor of several fierce battles against the pretender to the Imperial throne, Count Gerhardt Meister of Middenland. Adolphus's army was small but composed of the cream of the Empire's soldiery – the Reiksguard, Knights of the White Wolf, Knights Panther and Knights of the Blazing Sun. Soon, Wolf Riders began to report news of the Empire army's advance to Gorbad, who sent a large force of Orc Boar Boys, Wolf Riders, Forest Goblin Spider Riders, and chariots to meet it.

The resulting conflict, the Battle of Grunberg, was unusual in that it consisted almost entirely of mounted troops on both sides, the best of the Empire's knights versus the most mobile part of the Orc horde. Gorbad led his troops in person, wearing the crown of Solland upon his head and swinging his huge battle axe Morgor the Mangler. At first the Empire knights looked unstoppable as they drove the Goblin wolf riders from the field, but soon both sides became embroiled in hand-to-hand combat where the Knights' lances were hindered by the close press of warriors.

With their troops locked in combat both leaders rushed forward to add their weight to the battle. The Empire's greatest general and the mightiest Orc Warlord of the age fell upon each other with the fury of ancient enemies. Gorbad drove his wolf chariot straight at the Count, its three slavering wolves leaping as one for their enemy's throat. Adolphus swung his sword, one of the twelve mighty Runefangs, and brother to the Solland blade taken by Gorbad at the Battle of Solland's Crown. The three wolves fell dead, all three heads severed with one blow as the Runefang described a bloody arc through the air. Gorbad's chariot came to a crashing halt, throwing the Orc Warlord at Adolphus's feet.

The Count thrust his blade through Gorbad's massive chest and steaming green blood gushed over his armour. Gorbad bellowed in agony and swung Morgor wildly, catching Adolphus a glancing blow across the temple. Both mighty leaders staggered with pain as the battle swirled around them. As they prepared to strike again knights and boar boys rushed in from both sides and the two leaders were swept apart and caught in the maelstrom of carnage. It was a hard-fought battle on both sides, but eventually the Orcs began to gain the upper hand, and the knights fell back before them.

As night fell the Empire army was in full retreat with wolf riders snapping at their heels. Gorbad was too badly hurt to mount a vigorous pursuit, and many gallant knights were able to escape including the badly wounded Count of Wissenland.

In Altdorf the Emperor Sigismund prepared for the Orc invasion by fortifying the city's walls and gathering in the harvests. After every man, woman and beast within fifty miles was safely enclosed within the capital he ordered the lands about to be devastated. When the Orcs arrived they found fields already burned, wells poisoned, and inns empty. The Orc army therefore lost no time in its usual pillaging, but launched straight into its attack. The first assault was thrown back from Altdorf's tall walls with the loss of many Orc and Goblin warriors. The marshes around Altdorf made it difficult for the Orcs to group for the assault, and several mobs of Orcs disappeared forever when they strayed into the marshes.

Gorbad halted the attack and prepared for a long siege. At first his huge rock lobbers pounded the walls and dropped stones within the city, causing considerable damage. In response the city's cannons were trained against the Orcs and soon the rock lobbers were silenced. Gorbad, still weak from the wound suffered at Grunberg, was unprepared for a frontal assault. He began to collect together an aerial force to attack the city. Four wyverns from the Worlds Edge Mountains took to the air, swooping and marauding within the city while Goblin doom divers rained down causing panic and consternation. During the height of the fighting Sigismund was slain as he led a regiment of archers out to defend the palace against wyvern attack. Two wyverns fell on the same night and after the Emperor's death the aerial attacks gradually subsided and the siege settled down into a protracted stalemate.

As time ebbed away the wound inflicted by the Count of Wissenland did not heal but began to trouble the mighty Orc Warlord more and more. For days he would rage in fevered pain, screaming at his minions and cursing his underlings for failing to deliver Altdorf into his hands. Gradually his horde dissipated, the power of the Waaagh lost its impetus, and the tribes returned to the forests and mountains. Eventually even Gorbad had to give up, Altdorf had defeated him and the Waaagh was over.

The Ironclaws and the Broken Tooths were all that was left of the countless Orc tribes that had flocked to Gorbad's banner. There were more Goblin tribes still loyal or too afraid to desert, but even they were few compared to the great days of conquest. Gorbad Ironclaw withdrew to the east, following the river Reik back to the Worlds Edge Mountains. As his depleted army made its way home it was harried by Dwarfs and Men, and even attacked by Orc tribes that had once fought as part of the Waaagh. There was to be only one more pitched battle, the Battle of Blood Peak, fought in the shadow of the notorious red-coloured mountain south of Black Fire Pass.

It was here that the Orc horde was confronted by a large Dwarf army led by the Lord of Karaz-a-Karak. During his first march into the west Gorbad broke into many Dwarf tombs and stole the magic weapons they contained, an act of desecration that enraged the Dwarfs but which they were powerless to prevent at the time. As Gorbad headed back east, the Dwarfs saw their chance to revenge themselves and prepared a trap for the retreating Orc army. Although encircled by the Dwarfs, half starved and weary from the march, the Orcs gave a good account of themselves by fighting their way out of the trap and out-distancing the Dwarfs. Gorbad survived but his army was scattered. Divided into many small bands, the Orcs made their way east out of the Old World and recorded history.

As Orcs keep few records of any kind it is uncertain what happened to Gorbad. Perhaps he regained his old power in the Badlands and rebuilt his domain, or maybe he fell to the sword stroke of an ambitious young Orc Warboss before ever reaching the Iron Rock. It's impossible to be sure what fate befell the mightiest Orc Warlord of all time, but whatever became of him his reputation and memory lives on. To Orcs he has become a great hero whose spirit stands beside the gods Gork and Mork in battle. To Men he is a reminder of the terrifying destructive power of the Waaagh!

AZHAG THE SLAUGHTERER

After the particularly bitter winter that began the Imperial year 2512, a massive horde of Orcs and Goblins descended from the World's Edge Mountains and ravaged the eastern provinces of the Empire. The Orc Warlord that led them was Azhag the Slaughterer, and under his command were tribes of Orcs and Goblins from the highlands around Red Eye Mountain. In ancient times Red Eye Mountain was a mighty Dwarf realm called Karak Ungor, the Delving Hold. Since the fall of the old Dwarf Empire it has become the most powerful Night Goblin stronghold north of Mad Dog Pass.

Azhag's career of carnage began when he was chieftain of a small Orc tribe from the Troll country. His feet were firmly placed upon the road to power when he uncovered a magic artefact, the Crown of Sorcery, in the subterranean ruins of the daemon-haunted city of Todtheim on the edge of the Northern Wastes.

When attacked by marauding Chaos warbands Azhag and his Orcs were forced underground into the labyrinthine ruins of Todtheim. The Orcs spent weeks in the darkness, fighting off the monstrosities that lived in the cursed city. After fighting many monsters and uncovering countless ancient horrors, Azhag was confronted by a huge Chaos Troll. Azhag fought the Troll, and eventually chased it back to its lair where he slew it after a bloody struggle. Searching through the Troll's hoard of treasure he chanced upon the Crown of Sorcery. Unsuspecting of its true power, Azhag placed the metal band upon his head, and instantly its magic began to work. Strange and terrifying thoughts flooded his mind, and darkness overwhelmed him.

Azhag and his tribe fought its way out of Todtheim easily, indeed, Azhag seemed almost to know the way out. Azhag was changed. Sometimes the tribe's Big'uns recognised their old leader as he stomped up and down the battle lines bawling at his lads. At other times, and especially at night, he seemed disturbingly different. His eyes appeared dark and fixed, as if possessed of some terrifying secret.

At first he wore the crown he had found only occasionally, but later it was always on his scarred green skull and he became increasingly silent and brooding. Unknown to the Orcs, the crown was working its power upon Azhag, for it was an ancient and evil device that once belonged to the Liche Lord Nagash himself, and his power and his spirit still clung to it. Azhag was not entirely Azhag any more, the immeasurably strong personality of Nagash was gradually eating him away. But Azhag and Nagash had one thing in common, a lust for conquest and power that the Orc warlord was now in a position to fulfil.

Azhag's tribe struck eastwards, into the Worlds Edge Mountains and against the Orc and Goblin tribes that lived there. At first his challenges were met by rival warbosses, and there were several bloody battles, but after rumours of Azhag's victories became well known the tribes gave up any ideas of fighting and flocked to join the growing Waaagh. Moving southwards along the Worlds Edge Mountain chain he conquered tribe after tribe, and eventually all the Night Goblins of Red Eye Mountain joined the Waaagh. This greatly increased the size of Azhag's army, for there are more Night Goblin tribes living in and around Red Eye Mountain than anywhere else in the Old World.

After holing up for the winter of 2512 the horde descended into the eastern provinces of the Empire. At first the Orcs looted and pillaged through Ostermark, feasting upon the few beasts that the people had carefully nurtured through the winter and driving the impoverished population westwards through the snow. The towns of Kohlizt and the Temple of Sigmar at Nachtdorf were razed to the ground. The Count of Ostermark led a small army of local troops and Knights Panther to try and stem the Orcs' advance, but his troops were hopelessly outnumbered and soon driven from the field in rout.

The Count rallied his forces in Bechafen where the constant stream of refugees meant lean rations and poor quarters for all. The snows persisted until the second month of the new year, and many died of cold and hunger before the spring. The cold did little to hinder the Orcs, for Orcs and Goblins are hardy creatures, and, if needs must, will eat any flesh no matter how foul or what manner of creature it comes from. The Orcs were also provided with food and reinforcements by Forest Goblins who flocked to join them from the Great Forest.

Bypassing Bechafen the horde headed west, towards the Middle Mountains and Ostland, crossing the river Talabec by the old bridge at Rinn. The Imperial troops posted to defend the river gates from Kislev fled when they saw the green horde stretched out across the horizon and advancing at full speed towards them. In Ostland the horde began to loot and destroy with customary Orc efficiency, crushing the spring crops underfoot and gorging themselves on the hard won stores of the local people. Tough frontier folk that they were, the Ostlanders fought as hard as they could, and the Count of Ostland gathered an army to fight the green tide. At the Battle of Grim Moor the Count Valmir von Raukov won a temporary respite, putting to rout many of Azhag's Goblins before being forced to withdraw.

Azhag flew over the battlefield on his wyvern, swooping upon regiment after regiment and harrying the retreating army as it made its way to the refuge of Wolfenburg. After

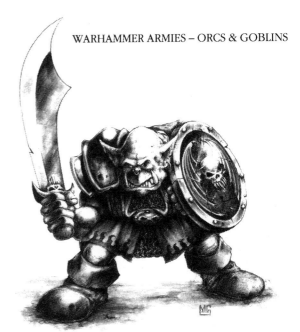

the battle Orc tribes came from the Forest of Shadows, swelling Azhag's horde still further, but the Count of Ostland built his defences well and Wolfenburg held out. Frustrated at this set-back Azhag headed south, where the horde wreaked havoc, destroying the town of Forstich before turning back east through the Great Forest and into Ostermark once more. By now the Emperor's army was approaching from the south, led by one of his most able generals, Marshal Otto Blucher.

The two armies met near the village of Osterwald, where, after a long and close fought battle the Orcs were driven from the field. Early in the battle Azhag was struck from the back of his wyvern while fighting against the Knights Panther, leaving the Orc army leaderless and demoralised in the face of a fierce Empire attack. It was the end of Azhag and of the Waaagh – with a single blow the Orc horde had been defeated, and after the battle it would disperse into the forests and hills. As for the Crown of Sorcery, it was recovered and taken back to Altdorf by the Grand Theogonist of Sigmar who placed it in the deepest vault of the Temple to be guarded for eternity by powerful spells and iron locks.

GROM THE PAUNCH OF MISTY MOUNTAIN

Most of the warlords whose campaigns of destruction have shaken the world and threatened the destruction of the realms of Men have been Orcs rather than Goblins. Orcs are bigger than Goblins, more dangerous, and more brutally ambitious. Grom was to prove the exception, a Goblin who was not only as dangerous and ambitious as the best Orc, but vastly bigger as well! It was not that Grom was especially tall, certainly not as tall as an Orc, but he was enormously and infamously fat. In fact he was so huge that he became known as the Paunch of Misty Mountain, or simply as Grom the Fat.

If tales are to be believed his improbable bulk was due to his eating raw Troll for a wager. Apart from being enormously tough, Troll flesh has the unusual property of being able to regenerate itself quite quickly. If a Troll suffers harm his flesh will almost instantly re-grow. It is this as much as their stubborn stupidity and iron-hard muscle which makes Trolls very hard to fight. It also makes Troll flesh virtually impossible to eat unless it is very thoroughly cooked.

Determined to out-eat his challenger, Grom consumed a plate of raw Troll steaks only to discover the meat regenerating inside his stomach. As the churning mass swelled within him his resilient Goblin digestive system got to work on the over-abundance of raw material. For days Grom lay moaning and groaning as at first the Troll's regenerative abilities outpaced his own ability to digest it and then his stomach gradually gained ground. Eventually an equilibrium was reached, and although the Troll flesh was still there Grom was digesting it as fast as it was regrowing.

After several weeks of fevered indigestion and almost terminal flatulence Grom emerged triumphant. He was also quite a bit fatter. Although he ate nothing afterwards he continued to gain weight thanks to the presence of the Troll flesh. He was to suffer from bouts of explosive flatulence for the rest of his life.

Grom's tribe was the Broken Axe, a tribe of Goblins that lived at the eastern end of Mad Dog Pass. The tribe occupied one of the countless tumble-down fortresses that line the craggy and tunnel strewn pass. Some time around the Imperial year 2400 Grom engaged in the infamous eating contest described above. The effect was to be startling and highly visible. To Orcs and Goblins size is power and by any reckoning Grom was looking to be very powerful indeed. Within ten years he had conquered the other tribes along the Mad Dog Pass and subjugated the Night Goblin tribes that lived around and under Thunder Mountain. It was the beginning of Waaagh Grom and the birth of a legend amongst Orc kind.

For a number of years the Broken Axe tribe wandered west and north, conquering the Orc and Goblin tribes of the southern Worlds Edge Mountains and the Badlands. Some time around the year 2410 Grom led his horde over the Black Fire Pass and then northwards along the Dwarf-held highlands. Destroying several small Dwarf holds and looting the tombs of Dwarf ancestors, his forces roamed unopposed whilst the Dwarfs gathered their forces.

At the Battle of Iron Gate, the site of one of the old Dwarf gateways into Karak Varn, the King of the Dwarfs and his army met a part of Grom's Horde led by Grom himself. After a long and hard fought battle the two sides retreated leaving many dead on the field but no clear victor. None-the-less the battle ultimately favoured Grom who could afford to lose vast numbers of troops without affecting his horde's strength. For the Dwarfs it was a disaster. Many of

the King's best warriors lay dead and all hope of driving the horde away were gone. In desperation the Dwarfs sent to the Empire for help.

Unfortunately for the Dwarfs and for the Empire the reigning Emperor was Dieter IV, the Elector Count of Stirland, perhaps the most ineffective and self serving individual ever to sit upon the Imperial throne. For years Dieter had diverted resources away from the army and into his own pocket. Nothing had been spared to turn the city of Nuln into a spectacular metropolis with marble fountains, golden statues, and dazzling gardens. Dieter had razed nearly half the city to build his awesome Palace of Gold with its surrounding temples and public gardens.

When the Dwarf King's messenger reached Dieter the Emperor reacted immediately, not by sending help (for the army was so starved of funds there was no help to send) but by removing his entire court westwards to Altdorf in order to be as far as possible from the threat of Grom's horde. Disgusted, the Dwarf messenger returned to Karaz a Karak where the King received the news of the Emperor's decision with typical Dwarf stoicism. Unable to contain the Goblin Warlord's ambitions, the Dwarfs resolved to shut their stout doors and defend their fortresses from within. For the next few years the horde ravaged at will through the mountains, desecrating shrines, despoiling tombs, and waylaying travellers, but Grom was unable to take any of the Dwarf holds or bring them to battle.

As the Waaagh roamed freely over the Worlds Edge Mountains it was joined by multitudes of Goblins including the Night Goblin tribes of Red Eye Mountain and many Forest Goblin tribes from the Great Forest. As his armies grew in number and strength Grom ventured further and further west, devastating much of Stirland, Talabecland and even going as far as Hochland in the shadow of the Middle Mountains. Empire armies were met and defeated. The human population retreated to the towns and much of the countryside was abandoned. The Great Forest became a virtual Goblin realm where not even an Imperial army was safe. Nuln, whose city defences had long been neglected in favour of marbled magnificence was attacked and burned. Dieter's marvellous Palace of Gold and all his great buildings and fountains were destroyed.

The horde moved westward until the whole Empire became a land under siege. Communities driven from the countryside huddled behind heavily defended walls while outside the horde roamed and plundered at will. Seeing the humans abandoning their lands, the tribes of the deep forests and high mountains flocked to join the Waaagh. The end of the Empire seemed inevitable, for no land was being tilled or crops sown, beasts were slaughtered and seed grain ground into flour to feed the hungry. The Emperor seemed unable or unwilling to even raise an army, but skulked behind the walls of Altdorf and dreamed of better days.

While the Emperor did nothing, his cousin, Wilhelm Prince of Altdorf, was to prove the saviour of the Empire. He organised the defence of Altdorf and raised a new army from amongst the beleaguered citizens. Although Wilhelm's army was no match for the total power of the Waaagh, Grom's forces were split up all over the Empire into many small armies. By avoiding the largest concentrations of Orcs and Goblins Wilhelm was able to fight several successful holding actions and prevent Grom from completely devastating the Reikland.

JOHN BLANCHE

Meanwhile Grom's attentions had turned to the west and to the coastal regions of the Empire. After wreaking havoc throughout the Middenland and defeating an army led by the Count of Middenheim, Grom reached the shores of the ocean. According to Imperial records the horde gathered at the coast and began to construct a huge fleet. Acres of forest were felled to provide the timber, and whole tribes of Goblins were sent to forage for materials amongst the ruins of the Empire. For weeks the forges bellowed and Goblins sweated as Grom's fleet took shape. It was a fleet whose like had never been seen before, vast hulks of crudely fashioned wood propelled by massive tread wheels and gigantic sails. The world watched as the fleet took shape. Riders from the Empire sent word to Bretonnia, Kislev, and the southern kingdoms warning them of the inevitable approach of the armada. Rulers throughout the Old World trembled and waited, hoping that the path of the Waaagh would pass them by.

When the fleet put sail outriders from the Empire followed its progress along the coast. At Marienburg the Orcs fought a massive and bloody sea battle against the Empire fleet, sending half the Imperial ships to the bottom of the sea and scattering the rest to the four winds. Marienburg lay open to the plundering Orc and Goblin horde and the sturdy Marienburgers prepared to defend their city. As fortune would have it the weather turned for the worse, and Grom's fleet was blown westward before a devastating storm. The Goblins, unused to the sea and ignorant of navigation, could do nothing but ride out the storm. At least one ship was broken up and its wreckage cast upon the coasts of Bretonnia, but of Grom and the rest of the Waaagh nothing was ever seen again in the realms of Men. Only years later did the full story of Grom's voyage to the Elven land of Ulthuan emerge, and did Men learn of the final defeat and destruction of the Waaagh before Tor Yvresse

WAAAGH SKARSNIK

After the collapse of the Dwarf empire almost three and a half thousand years ago the Dwarf stronghold of Karak Eight Peaks lay in ruins. Its deep caverns and tunnels were taken over by Night Goblins and Skaven. Deeper still nameless horrors crawled into the old Dwarf mines and settled in the long-abandoned depths. Within a few years of Karak Eight Peaks' fall the Night Goblins had settled permanently in the ruins and split into many tribes based around the adjoining mountains and the tunnels that ran beneath them.

Although the Dwarfs often tried to recapture Karak Eight Peaks they did not succeed until about the Imperial year 2470, when Belegar established a fortified bridgehead in the old citadel. Though the Dwarfs were forced to live in a virtual state of siege, they gradually managed to clear the Night Goblins and other evil creatures out of the upper levels. Today Belegar and his kinsfolk still live amongst the ruins of Karak Eight Peaks, and hope one day to reconquer the whole realm of their ancestors.

Belegar's Dwarfs face constant raiding by the Night Goblin tribes that live in the surrounding eight peaks of the old Dwarf kingdom. The most powerful of these tribes is the Crooked Moon tribe under its leader Skarsnik. Skarsnik is a cunning and observant leader who has grown to understand the Dwarf mind. When Belegar arrived he watched the Dwarfs rebuild their citadel but did not attack at first. Instead he waited until stragglers ventured outside

the walls and then picked them off one by one, capturing the Dwarfs alive if possible and tormenting them for days within earshot of the citadel walls.

Over the years Skarsnik has amassed a large collection of Dwarf beard scalps which he displays on long wooden stakes driven into the mountain side. The Dwarfs are forced to watch the number of beard scalps grow day by day, while by night the pounding war drums of the Night Goblins and the screaming of captives haunts their sleep. Skarsnik's fame has grown amongst the other tribes, and today all the Night Goblins of Karak Eight Peaks, and many others besides, hail him as their undisputed master.

About forty years before the present day, Belegar attempted to break the deadlock with aid from the north. The Dwarfs sent word to the Dwarf capital of Karaz a Karak high in the Worlds Edge Mountains, explaining that the Night Goblins were virtually holding them prisoners within their own citadel and that without reinforcements it could only be a matter of time before the Dwarfs were defeated. Duregar, a kinsman of Belegar from Karaz a Karak, immediately gathered an army and marched southwards along the western flanks of the mountains.

By this time Skarsnik's horde had grown into a huge Waaagh. The Night Goblin warlord's forces were fighting every Dwarf and Orc between Thunder Mountain to the north and Fire Mountain to the south. In the Badlands several Orc tribes joined the Waaagh. Even Barak Varr, the Sea Fortress of the Dwarfs by the Black Gulf, was under attack. As the Dwarfs from Karaz a Karak marched south they saw the rising plumes of smoke in front of them. Messengers from Barak Varr brought news that the western approaches to Karaz Eight Peaks were held in strength by the Red Fang Orcs led by Gorfang Rotgut. It was at this point that Duregar made an important decision. Rather than enter Karak Eight Peaks from the west, he would cross the Worlds Edge Mountains and move south along the eastern edge, entering Karak Eight-Peaks from what he hoped would be the more lightly held eastern gate. With the sun ebbing in the sky and the smoke of Thunder Mountain drifting across the horizon, the Dwarf army camped at the entrance to Mad Dog Pass.

The following day the Dwarfs advanced into the pass. Mad Dog Pass is notoriously dangerous. Its steep sides are thronged with Goblin strongholds and its rocky slopes overlay caves and tunnels that are riddled with evil creatures. Duregar pinned his hopes on Dwarven determination to keep the army safe. As the Dwarfs advanced into the mouth of the pass they were attacked by a large army of Orcs and Goblins that had apparently been waiting to attack them from behind once they had moved south. The Dwarfs were hard pressed at first, but eventually saw the Orcs off with the help of their formidable cannons. This battle became known later as the Battle of the Jaws, an apt name considering the manner in which the Orc attack closed in on the Dwarfs, like the jaws of the Mad Dog itself.

During the battle five Troll Slayers distinguished themselves by attacking and destroying three Trolls which were perilously close to crushing Duregar himself. Only two of the Troll Slayers survived. One was heard to complain that there were insufficient Trolls to go round.

Although the Orcs and Goblins were beaten they accounted for only a small part of Skarsnik's horde. When he heard of his army's defeat he proclaimed a huge mushroom feast and ordered his shamans to brew up a fresh batch of Mad Cap fungus liquor for the Fanatics. Squig Hunters were dispatched into the deep tunnels to fetch more Cave Squigs, while Netters were sent off to hunt down Stone Trolls amongst the mountains. As the Dwarfs moved south Goblins watched them from the hills, reporting their movements by means of oily smoke signals and throbbing war drums.

Skarsnik sat upon his iron throne and waited. In the meantime he amused himself by feeding Dwarf captives to Gobbla, the enormous, malodorous and psychopathically vicious Cave Squig which he kept firmly chained to his left leg. Why the demented creature never bit Skarsnik was a matter of some mystery. It certainly bit everything else.

Duregar's army moved steadily southwards until it reached the eastern entrance to Death Pass. The East Gate of Karak Eight Peaks lay several miles inside the pass through a broad side valley paved with ancient stones and studded with the ruined tombs of Dwarf ancestors. The Dwarfs advanced in battle formation fully expecting an attack from the steep mountain slopes which towered ominously above the old Dwarf road.

The East Gate had been built thousands of years before at a place where a long ridge ran down into the valley causing it to narrow to a hundred yards or less. Here the Dwarfs of antiquity had built their gate, once a vast and impregnable fortress but now little more than a pile of stone through which the road still led. In front of the gate and connected to it by a high causeway was a tall grey watchtower whose summit commanded the approach down the valley. Although partially ruined, the watchtower had been rebuilt and fortified by Skarsnik's Goblins. Now it was crammed with Night Goblin archers, and on top there was a huge rock lobber crewed by fierce Orcs.

As the Dwarfs marched forwards Orcs and Goblins closed in from their hiding places in the slopes to left and right. Behind them a huge force of Orcs moved to block their escape. The Dwarfs were surrounded by foes on all sides. Stones from the rock lobber began to fall amongst their densely packed ranks. Duregar pushed forward, pinning his hopes on breaking through the East Gate. As the Dwarfs approached the first ranks of Night Goblins a massive whoop went up amongst the greenskins, and from out of their formation charged Night Goblin Fanatics whirling balls and chains. Like spinning tops they lurched crazily towards the Dwarfs. Many were shot down with crossbow bolts, some whirled away and missed the Dwarfs altogether, but some hit the Dwarfs killing many before collapsing with exhaustion.

The Dwarfs advanced. The Night Goblins in front were easily driven away, but just as soon as a gap appeared and the Dwarfs caught sight of the gate more Night Goblins charged in to hold them. Night Goblin archers rained arrows down from the watchtower. Black-fletched arrows hit Dwarf and Night Goblin alike, but the archers carried on shooting regardless, ignoring the hurt done to their fellows.

Things looked bleak for the Dwarfs. Over half of their army had been destroyed during the initial rush towards the gate. The Goblin horde seemed hardly diminished. With typical Dwarf stubbornness Duregar led his troops up onto a small mound, the remains of an ancient Dwarf tomb, to make his last stand. As the Dwarfs steeled themselves for the inevitable assault, there was a loud explosion and the gateway burst apart in a cloud of dust.

As the dust cleared Duregar saw Dwarfs pouring through the gateway towards them. The confused Night Goblins scattered leaving piles of dead in their wake. It was Belegar and the Dwarfs of Karak Eight Peaks. They had advanced eastwards from the other side of the gate and destroyed the unsuspecting Night Goblin rearguard before blowing the gates with gunpowder.

The Night Goblins and Orcs were thrown into disorder. Skarsnik, watching from his vantage point on the mountain slopes, saw his army waver. For the Dwarfs it was a much needed respite. The Dwarf forces met across a sea of blood and green bodies. Forming into a huge and solidly packed square the combined army began to move steadily back towards the gate. Before they were half way there the Orcs and Goblins regrouped. When they saw how few Dwarfs there were their confidence returned. Stones from the rock lobber smashed into the Dwarf column and arrows fell amongst their ranks.

Many Dwarfs stumbled to the ground dead with Goblin arrows embedded in them, but more still made the gate. Cave Squigs were unleashed upon the Dwarfs, but several were killed by Troll Slayers while others ran wild snapping at the Night Goblins, biting off limbs and heads before vanishing into the mountains. Smashing through the few Night Goblins that remained to oppose them, Duregar and Belegar headed west. The Night Goblins continued to harass the Dwarf column all the way to the Citadel, but thanks to their heavy armour and natural toughness there were few more casualties. As night fell Skarsnik was master of the battlefield, but Duregar and Belegar had escaped his net.

Although not as catastrophic as it might have been, the Battle of East Gate was a resounding defeat for the Dwarfs. Over half of the Dwarf force had been slain and although Skarsnik had lost many good warriors they were losses he could easily afford. The Dwarf army was bottled up inside the Citadel and, although not destroyed, the Dwarfs were not going anywhere. Skarsnik had other enemies to crush, and would launch huge attacks against Karak Azul, Barak Varr and throughout the Badlands over the course of the next three summers. Gobbla, his hugely bloated and eternally hungry Cave Squig would feed well. Although repulsed time and time again, Skarsnik's power continues to grow even today, and his grip over the mountains around Karak Eight Peaks is just as tight.

IMPORTANT EVENTS IN ORC HISTORY

Imperial Year

NOTABLE EVENTS IN ORC HISTORY

-c1500 At about this time the Elves abandon the Old World and the declining Dwarf empire is destroyed by earthquakes and volcanic eruptions. Orcs and Goblins pour over the lands, looting the remaining Elf cities and destroying Dwarf holds. Karak Ungor is the first Dwarf hold to fall to the Goblins, it becomes the Night Goblin stronghold of Red Eye Mountain. The Dwarfs refer to the following five hundred years as the time of the Goblin Wars, as Dwarfs and Goblins fight for possession of the old Dwarf empire.

Karak Varn is flooded and then occupied by Skaven and Goblins. The isolated Dwarf mines at Ekrund in the Dragonback Mountains fall to Orcs who rename the place Mount Bloodfang. Goblins take over the Dwarf watch towers and forts throughout the Mad Dog Pass. The Dwarf gold mines at Gunbad fall to the Night Goblins. Gunbad was the richest and largest mine in the Worlds Edge mountains as well as a source of precious gems and the brilliant blue crystal rock *Brynduraz* or 'Bright Stone'. It is taken over by Goblins and fortified.

-1387 The Silver Road Wars begin between Dwarfs and Goblins. After twenty years the Dwarfs abandon the mines at Mount Silverspear to the Orcs. The mines are occupied by Warlord Urk Grimfang and known ever after as Mount Grimfang. With the loss of Gunbad and Silverspear, the Dwarfs lose their most important mines in the east and within five years they abandon the eastern fringes of the Worlds Edge Mountains altogether.

-c1250 The Troll Wars. Trolls are driven north by fresh eruptions of Thunder Mountain, attacking Dwarf miners and prospectors and overrunning several small Dwarf settlements south of Karaz a Karak.

-1245 From this time the Dwarfs launch a series of attacks against Goblin-held territories. They drive the Orcs from the mountains and gain control of the whole area between Karak Kadrin and Mad Dog Pass. Mount Gunbad is temporarily recaptured by the Dwarfs but then lost again. Mount Grimfang is attacked but the Dwarfs are beaten off by Orc Chieftain Nurk Ard'ed. For the next 250 years the Dwarfs consolidate their hold over the mountains, gradually reopening many of their old mines and rebuilding countless tombs of their ancestors.

-c1200 Nagash the Black excavates the Cursed Pit. Goblins and Orcs flee west to escape the necromantic evil that grips the south.

-1185 Kadrin Redmane the Dwarf Runesmith leads an expedition into the ruins of Karak Varn where he discovers a rich vein of Gromril. The Dwarfs continue to mine the vein for several years and even talk of resettling the old hold.

-1136 Kadrin Redmane killed by Orcs above Black Water leading a muletrain of Gromril ore. The Dwarf miners pull out from Karak Varn under renewed pressure from Skaven in the depths.

-975 Battle of a Thousand Woes. A Dwarf attempt to recapture Red Eye Mountain fails when the Dwarf army is ambushed somewhere north of Karak Kadrin. Many Dwarfs are slain and the Dwarfs give up their attempted reconquests. The Dwarfs concentrate on fortification and consolidation, so few records are made of Orc activity for the next few hundred years.

-750 The Red Cloud Goblin tribe attacks Karak Azgul and are repulsed. They then go on to attack and partially occupy the hold of Karak Azul. Ten years of hard fighting follow before the Goblins are eventually expelled.

-513 After hundreds of years of embattled resistance the Dwarf city of Karak Eight Peaks falls to attack by Orcs, Goblins and Skaven. Its ruins and the surrounding mountains become infested with Goblins and Skaven who fight each other for possession of what remains.

-469 Orc Warlord Dork leads a huge army of Orcs and Goblins to take the Dwarf hold of Karak Azgal which he destroys and abandons, leaving the secrets of its depths unexplored. Three years later he attacks and captures the Dwarf hold of Karak Drazh which is occupied and renamed Black Crag. Within fifty years of the fall of Karak Eight Peaks the Dwarfs have lost all of their major holds south of Karaz a Karak with the exception of Karak Azul, which is under constant siege. All the mountains between Mad Dog Pass and Karak Eight Peaks are Orc or Goblin controlled.

-370 According to Dwarf tradition the rampages of Urgok the Beard Burner occur about this time. Orcs and Goblins almost overwhelm the remaining Dwarf holds but are finally beaten back at the Battle of Black Water.

-15 to 50 The time of Sigmar sees the Orcs and Goblins driven out of the lands west of the Worlds Edge Mountains. Orcs take refuge in the deep forests or travel north into the Troll Country. Goblins flee to the mountains. A massive Orc army is defeated at the Battle of Black Fire Pass (in the year -1), a resounding defeat which paved the way for the accession of Sigmar as the first Emperor.

977 Gilles le Breton conquers all the lands west of the Grey Mountains and creates the land of Bretonnia. Orcs and Goblins retreat to the Grey Mountains and northern forests under pressure from the new Bretonnian armies.

1142 Guillaume, the third Bretonnian King, defeats a large Orc army at the Battle of Armandur and drives out the last of the Orcs from northern Bretonnia.

c1705 Around this time Gorbad Ironclaw defeats Crusher Zogoth and unites the Ironclaw and Broken Tooth tribes at the fortress of Iron Rock.

1707-1712 The greatest Warlord of all time, Gorbad Ironclaw, leads a huge Waaagh into the Empire. Averland and the Moot are devastated. Averheim and Nuln are taken and burned. At the battle of Solland's Crown Eldred Count of Solland is slain and his magic sword the Runefang of Solland taken by the Orcs. Solland is devastated. Gorbad is badly wounded at the Battle of Grunberg, but the battle is won and the Empire army flees back to Altdorf.

Altdorf is besieged. The Emperor Sigismund is killed in the fighting. Gorbad's wound causes him to become weaker and weaker, until the Waaagh gradually loses impetus. The Orc army breaks up leaving the eastern half of the Empire in ruins.

2201 The beginning of the Errantry Wars when Louen Orc Slayer, the King of Bretonnia, declares his intention to rid Bretonnia of Orcs. Over the next century Bretonnian territory is gradually cleared of Orcs who take to the mountains and forests to escape the king's knights.

2302 The Great War Against Chaos in the north forces many Orc tribes southwards into the Empire and Worlds Edge Mountains. Some join Chaos but others attack the Chaos armies as they pass.

2420 Bretonnian King Charlen announces his intention to carry the Errantry Wars east into the Border Princes and beyond. Bretonnian knights win a huge victory against Orcs at Blood River, and more settlers move east into the Border Princes.

2420-2424 The Goblin Warlord Grom leads a coalition of Orc and Goblin tribes into the Worlds Edge Mountains. After defeating the Dwarfs at the battle of Iron Gate the Waaagh moves into the Empire. Much of the north and east is devastated and Nuln is burned to the ground. Grom leads his armies to the sea where he builds a huge fleet and sails into the west, never to be seen again in the Old World.

Years later it is discovered that Grom reached the Elven Kingdoms of Ulthuan, causing great destruction until finally defeated by the High Elves.

2488 The Battle of Death Pass. A Bretonnian army is defeated by Morglum Necksnapper. The Bretonnian king declares the Errantry Wars at an end.

2498 The Battle of the Jaws. An Orc army is defeated at the western end of Mad Dog Pass by Dwarfs led by Duregar. Dwarfs subsequently beaten at the Battle of East Gate by the Night Goblin Warlord Skarsnik. The partially resettled Dwarf hold of Karak Eight Peaks is under constant pressure from surrounding Goblin tribes.

2500-2510 Orc Warlord Gnashrak unites the Orcs and Goblins of the eastern Worlds Edge Mountains and leads a huge army along the Silver Road towards Karaz a Karak. The Orcs rampage through the mountains for years, causing considerable destruction and even threatening to capture the capital. Eventually Gnashrak is defeated and captured at the Battle of Broken Leg Gulley by a Dwarf army led by Lord Ungrim Ironfist of Karak Kadrin.

2503-7 An Orc army under Gorfang Rotgut besieges Barak Varr and later joins up with Orc and Goblin tribes led by Morglum Necksnapper to attack Karak Azul. The Orcs briefly take possession of parts of the Hold and Gorfang captures many kinsfolk of Lord Kazador.

2512-2515 Orc Warlord Azhag the Slaughterer leads a huge army of Orcs and Night Goblins into the northern Empire. He is finally met and defeated at the Battle of Osterwald.

ANIMOSITY

Because they argue and fight amongst themselves even in the thick of battle, Orcs and Goblins are affected by a special *Animosity rule*. The Animosity rule is explained below in complete detail. Although basically the same as that given in the Warhammer rulebook, we have made a few additions and included more explanation, so we suggest you read through these new rules even if you are already familiar with the original ones. In particular, note that Mobs already fighting in hand-to-hand combat are not affected by Animosity – they are too busy bashing the enemy to worry about bashing each other.

Orcs and Goblins argue and fight amongst themselves continually. Even at the best of times fighting in the ranks can cause disarray and confusion in the army. The behaviour of Orc and Goblin units (Mobs) can be rather unpredictable. One moment a Mob is striding purposefully towards the enemy, and the next it is suddenly brought to a halt while two warriors settle their differences. This wayward tendency is a great drawback to an Orc warlord. Inevitably you will hear the cries of squabbling amongst your forces and realise that, once again, your best laid plans have been laid low by some dispute in the ranks. A good Orc warlord takes such things into account when he draws up his battlelines, but even the best commander will be lucky to avoid the effects of Animosity altogether.

WHO TO TEST

At the start of his turn the Orc player must test amongst his troops to determine if Animosity has taken effect. You must test separately for each of the following:

1. EACH ORC OR SAVAGE ORC MOB

This means you must make a test for every Orc infantry or cavalry unit. Black Orcs are not affected by Animosity so no test is necessary for Black Orc units. Big'uns **do** have to test as they are an Orc Mob.

2. EACH GOBLIN, NIGHT GOBLIN, OR FOREST GOBLIN MOB

This means you must test for every Goblin infantry and cavalry unit. This includes Night Goblin Netters and Squig Hunters.

A Mob which is already engaged in hand-to-hand combat at the start of the turn is not affected by Animosity and no test is necessary.

Characters are not affected by Animosity unless they join a Mob, in which case they are affected along with the unit itself. A shaman will be unable to use his magic if the unit he is with fails its Animosity test.

War machines and chariots are not affected by Animosity.

Night Goblin Fanatics are not affected by Animosity at all. Obviously the unit they are hiding in can be affected, but the Fanatics are too crazed to realise what is going on.

Squig Hoppers are not affected by Animosity.

Trolls, Snotlings and other creatures in your army are not affected by the Animosity rules.

WHEN TO TEST

At the start of your turn you must test for each Orc and Goblin Mob as described above. Starting on one side of the table and working through your army, roll a D6 for each unit. If the dice roll is 2 or more the unit passes the test and may fight normally this turn. If the dice roll is a 1 then the unit has been affected by Animosity.

THE EFFECT OF ANIMOSITY

To determine what the affected unit does roll a D6 and consult the Animosity Table.

LIVING WITH ANIMOSITY

Animosity is just one of those things. If you command a horde of Orcs and Goblins you will suffer from its effects now and again, and sometimes it will be a real pain in the neck. There are a few things you can do to make sure that when Animosity strikes the effect is minimal. When you choose your army remember that the more Mobs you have the more likely they are to fail an Animosity test. If you have six Mobs, for example, then on average one unit will fail its test each turn; if you have twelve Mobs then two units will fail, and so on. To minimise the chances of failure, make sure you have a few big Mobs rather than lots of small ones. Goblins need to be in big units to fight well anyway.

When you deploy, bear in mind your Mobs' tendency to fight amongst themselves. If you place two Mobs beside each other, then there's a chance they might attack each other. This is an acceptable risk up to a point, but remember that Mobs don't attack chariots, characters on their own, war machines, or units of Trolls, Snotlings, Black Orcs, etc. This means you can reduce the risk by positioning, say, some Black Orcs between two Orc Boyz Mobs. Of course, this doesn't stop a Mob squabbling amongst itself, but at least this only halts one unit for a turn rather than bringing two units to a standstill and inflicting casualties.

The classic mistake to make when deploying Orcs is to put one Mob directly behind another. This is a recipe for disaster, because you have placed both Mobs where they are in an ideal position to charge each other. Furthermore, if the Mob in front starts to squabble the unit behind is stuck, and won't be able to take advantage of a *We'll get 'em* result to get an extra move. If you must place one unit directly behind another, make sure it is a unit that doesn't suffer from Animosity.

The other thing to remember is that Mobs already engaged in hand-to-hand combat are not affected by Animosity and can't be attacked by another Mob that fails its Animosity test. So don't hang around... get stuck in! If you just stand around waiting for the enemy to come to you then of course your ladz will get bored, and naturally they'll start to get a bit fractious, then inevitably they'll end up failing an Animosity test probably just when you don't want them to. You can get stuck in faster with a *We'll get 'em* result on the Animosity Table of course, and sometimes this can really work in your favour, much to the dismay of your enemy.

ORC & GOBLIN ANIMOSITY TABLE

1   Get 'em

Them other greenskins is asking for trouble! Pulling faces, shouting rude insults, hurling dung. They deserve a good bashing!

If your Mob is armed with bows, crossbows, or other missile weapons, then this turn it will halt and shoot at the nearest other Orc or Goblin Mob. Note that the target must be an infantry or cavalry Mob of the kind that has to take an Animosity test itself – not a chariot, war engine, etc and not a Mob that is already engaged with the enemy. Although the Mob doesn't move, individual models may be turned in the ranks in order to shoot at their target. Work out the effects of shooting immediately – this means that shooting due to Animosity is worked out before normal shooting. The Mob cannot do anything else that turn, it will not move and it cannot shoot. If there are no other Orcs or Goblins to fire at, the affected Mob *squabbles* instead (see below).

If your Mob is not armed with missile weapons then it will *charge* the nearest other Orc or Goblin Mob if able to do so. Note that the target must be an infantry or cavalry Mob of the kind that has to take an Animosity test itself, not a chariot, war engine etc, and not a Mob which is already engaged against the enemy. If unable to charge (for example if it is too far away) then the Mob *squabbles* instead (see below). Assuming it is able to charge, the Mob is immediately moved against its target and a huge brawl breaks out. Immediately work out hand-to-hand combat with all models in base contact fighting. Once both sides have fought, casualties are removed and the two rival units spend the rest of the turn unable to do anything while they dust themselves down. There is no further effect – the two Mobs do not continue to fight in following turns.

2-5   Squabble

Ratgut is a filthy lyin' git and he spat on my favourite boots. He needs teaching a lesson!

An internal squabble amongst the ranks soon grows into a minor riot with fists and curses flying. This throws the Mob into disorder and prevents all moving and shooting this turn. The unit does nothing this turn while the Bosses crack heads together to restore order.

6   We'll Show 'em

The rest of the army is just softies compared to us. We'll show 'em how it's done. Charge!

Determined to show that they are best, the Mob dashes forward towards the enemy, cheering, waving weapons, and jeering at their foes. The Mob immediately moves forward a full normal move towards the nearest visible enemy unit, deducting the usual penalties for terrain. You must move the full distance possible. You cannot move less unless there is another unit or an uncrossable obstacle in the way. If you move into an enemy unit you count as having charged it.

This extra move is an exception to the normal movement sequence. Once the Mob has moved it may still move in the movement phase, shoot and fight just as normal. If the extra move brings you to within charge range of an enemy unit then you may declare a charge and attack it in your movement phase if you wish.

SHAMANS

Orc and Goblin wizards are called shamans. The power of a shaman comes from the the raw Waaagh energy radiated by all the Orcs and Goblins near him. The more greenskins there are crowded around a shaman the more easily he can cast spells. However, a shaman can handle only so much Waaagh energy. If there are too many Orcs and Goblins jostling around him, all excitedly generating raw unconscious power, then the shaman can suffer dizzying sickness, horrendous injuries or even death. For this reason Orc and Goblin shamans must take a special Waaagh Test during the magic phase as described in Warhammer Battle Magic.

As an Orc shaman gains in power and experience he learns how to handle the Waaagh energy better, hence Orc shamans are allowed to add their magic level to their Waaagh Test dice roll (D6 + magic level, as explained under Waaagh Magic in Warhammer Battle Magic). Goblin shamans, however, are more delicate: their minds are keener and more receptive than those of Orcs, they are more intelligent and definitely more imaginative. This makes them more susceptible to the effects of Waaagh energy.

Night Goblin and Forest Goblin shamans have special rules which make them different from other Goblin shamans. Night Goblin shamans are allowed to gobble pieces of mushroom to give them extra power, while Forest Goblin shamans are immune to 'Eadbangin' thanks to the spider venom flowing through their veins.

NIGHT GOBLIN SHAMANS

Night Goblins eat vast quantities of the multi-coloured fungi that grow in the dank caves where they live. Some of these fungi contain toxins that are either hallucinogenic or downright poisonous – but Goblins have tough digestive systems and can cope with this sort of thing. Night Goblin shamans are especially well-versed in fungus lore – they know which mushrooms can be eaten safely, which to avoid, and which to use for their potions and brews. It is the Night Goblin shamans who brew up the Mad Cap mushroom brew which sends the Goblin Fanatics drink into a whirling frenzy.

Because he is constantly handling, tasting and eating fungi the spores tend to work their way into the shaman's skin, penetrating his bloodstream and saturating his body. These spores take root in the Night Goblin's flesh and gradually start to change him. If the shaman is exposed to the insiduous effects of the fungus for too long he may eventually turn into a giant shaman mushroom. A magic-saturated shaman mushroom is very potent indeed, containing the essence of the shaman's magical power. If another living shaman eats a portion of shaman mushroom then it dissolves inside him and releases vast amounts of magic energy.

SPECIAL RULES

All Night Goblin shamans begin the game with one piece of shaman mushroom per magic level. A Shaman has one piece of mushroom, a Shaman Champion two, a Master Shaman three and a Shaman Lord four. Each piece of mushroom can be used once during the game.

The Night Goblin shaman may consume a single piece of mushroom at the start of any magic phase, before the Winds of Magic are determined. The shaman automatically receives D6 extra magic cards to use during that magic phase. These extra cards can only be used by that shaman – they cannot be used by other shamans.

Normally a Goblin shaman must be within 12" of at least one Orc or Goblin Mob to use his magic. However, if a Night Goblin shaman eats a piece of mushroom he can use magic even if there are no other Orcs or Goblins near. As there is no other source of Waaagh power within 12" the Shaman receives no magic cards from the Winds of Magic, he only gets the D6 cards from consuming the mushroom.

There is, however, a price to be paid for such power. As the energy of the mushroom surges through the Night Goblin shaman there is an enormous risk of his brain overloading and dribbling out of his ears. Make the Waaagh Test as normal (see Warhammer Battle Magic) but if you fail deduct -1 from the D6 roll on the 'Eadbangerz Chart. This penalty only applies when the mushroom has been eaten; at other times the shaman rolls normally.

FOREST GOBLINS

The Forest Goblin tribes share their domain with a great variety of spiders. Some of these creatures are eaten, others are kept as pets or ridden to war, while the very biggest are worshipped as gods. Forest Goblin shamans encourage small poisonous spiders to nest in their robes and live upon their bodies. These gaily coloured little creatures run all over the shaman's body, and often live in convenient crannies such as in his ears and in between his toes.

When a shaman opens his mouth dozens of tiny spiders skitter between his teeth and run up his nose. As a result of the spiders' poisonous bites the shaman becomes immune to their toxin and his flesh becomes almost completely numb. Orcs and Goblins feel little pain anyway, but Forest Goblin shamans feel none at all. Because of the build up of venom in their system the Forest Goblin shamans inhabit a dream-like world haunted by strange spider gods and shadowy eight-legged daemons. Their oddly twisted vision of reality is reflected in their wide-eyed stare and slavering tongue stained purple with spider venom. Although plainly crazy, the shamans are possessed of great power, for the spider venom that addles their mind also stimulates the part of their brain that controls magic.

SPECIAL RULES

Thanks to the intoxicating venom that floods his brain the Forest Goblin Shaman has great powers of mental control. He must take a Waaagh Test just like any other Goblin shaman, but he automatically adds +1 to his dice roll on the 'Eadbangerz Chart. If he rolls a 6 then he is completely unaffected just as if he had passed his Waaagh Test. This means that the worst score a Forest Goblin can get on the 'Eadbangerz Chart is 2 ("I fink I'm gonna...") and it is impossible for him to 'Eadbang.

Unfortunately, while his powers of mental control are impressive, this cannot be said of his ability to control his physical body. Forest Goblin shamans are prone to run off dizzily, or just blunder about, unable to distinguish fact from venom-induced fiction. Therefore, every time a Forest Goblin shaman fails a Waaagh Test he automatically staggers D6" in a random direction. Use a scatter dice to determine which direction he moves in. This happens even if he subsequently rolls a 6 for his 'Eadbangerz Test.

Move the shaman before applying the 'Eadbangerz results. If he walks into something he will stop. If he moves into an enemy then he is engaged in hand-to-hand combat and must fight in the following hand-to-hand combat round (he counts as charging in the first round as is also the case with magically induced movement). If already in hand-to-hand combat then he won't move away, but counts as charging again in the next round (the shaman dashes around with insane vigour much to the astonishment of his foes).

SAVAGE ORC SHAMANS

Savage Orc shamans are renowned for their extraordinary powers and their ability to make magic potions. When the Savage Orcs go to war their shaman marks them with tribal tattoos using a strong magical concoction. These tattoos protect the Savage Orc Boyz like armour. If a Savage Orc shaman is with a Mob of Savage Orcs then the power of their tattoos is enhanced still further, while the wild energy of the Mob increases the Savage Orc shaman's own power.

SPECIAL RULES

If a Savage Orc shaman joins a Mob of Savage Orcs (Boyz or Boar Boyz) then he gets +1 extra magic card when the magic cards are dealt at the start of the magic phase. This extra card can only be used by that shaman – the card cannot be used by other shamans. In addition, his protective tattoos now confer a saving throw of 5 or 6 rather than a 6.

If a Savage Orc shaman joins a Mob of Savage Orcs (Boyz or Boar Boyz) then the Boyz' protective tattoos give them a saving throw of a 5 or 6 rather than 6. This means a Mob of Savage Orcs with shields will have a save of 4, 5 or 6, for example. Remember that the protective value of a tattoo is not affected by weapon modifiers. However, if a weapon allows no save (eg, a cannon) then a protective tattoo does not save either.

SUMMARY

NIGHT GOBLIN SHAMANS

1. A Night Goblin shaman may consume a piece of mushroom at the start of the magic phase. This gives him +D6 magic cards.

2. Even if they are more than 12" away from Orcs/Goblins, Night Goblin shamans may use magic by consuming mushroom. If they do this, they receive no other magic cards.

3. When they consume mushrooms Night Goblin shamans deduct -1 from their dice score when they roll on the 'Eadbangerz Chart.

FOREST GOBLIN SHAMANS

1. Forest Goblin shamans add +1 to their dice score when rolling on the 'Eadbangerz Chart.

2. Whenever they fail a Waaagh Test they move D6" in a random direction.

SAVAGE ORC SHAMANS

1. A Savage Orc shaman receives an additional magic card if he is with a Mob of Savage Orcs.

2. Both shaman and the Savage Orc Boyz have a save of 5 or 6 from their protective tattoos when a shaman is with the unit.

WAR MACHINES

GOBLIN DOOM DIVER CATAPULT

By far the majority of Goblin tribes are partly nomadic. They journey from plain to forest, or along the river valleys and mountain passes, where they buy, sell, or steal things that they can re-sell to other Orcs and Goblins later on. Goblins make a living bartering and trading with Forest Goblins, Night Goblins, as well as Orcs, Ogres and other creatures. They particularly enjoy dealing with Orcs as it gives them a chance to outwit their larger and more brutal cousins. This they accomplish fairly easily as Orcs are rather dim.

Goblin tribes often include huge caravans of scrap metal, captured monsters in crude wooden cages, as well as captive men, Elves and Dwarfs. The lumbering carts and chariots are protected by outriders mounted on giant wolves who patrol the area in front of the advancing tribe, probing for enemies and scouting for small settlements to loot. As the outriders can only move so fast, their ability to reconnoitre ahead is limited. To overcome this shortcoming the Goblins have developed a unique machine known as the Doom Diver Catapult, more often referred to as the bat-winged loony lobber.

This machine, a small but powerful catapult, lobs Goblins high into the air, from where they can spy out the land ahead. Of course, the information they glean is of little value if the Goblin is pulverised as he impacts with the ground. To help keep the Goblin alive, if not exactly intact, a whole variety of life preserving techniques were originally developed. These included tying lots of cushions to the Goblin, making parachutes, and kitting

him out with wings. Although none of these methods have ever proved completely successful, the idea of having wings appealed to the Goblins best of all and the other methods rapidly fell out of favour. In any case, Goblins have a marked tendency to bounce so casualties are probably fewer than one might reasonably expect.

It didn't take long for some bright spark to try out the Doom Diver Catapult in a battle. It was probably whilst flying high over an approaching enemy that one Goblin got a bit carried away, and steering himself as best as he could with his crude wings, crashed right down onto the enemy army. So impressive was the damage, and the mess, that willing Goblins soon began to take this form of warfare quite seriously. It does not seem to bother them that their chances of survival are low, but then only the most crazed Goblins would want to be propelled high into the air anyway. These Goblin are known as Doom Divers, although it is usual for other (saner) Goblins to call them bat-winged loonies.

The Doom Divers themselves care not a jot about such criticism, they know that the ultimate excitement of diving through the air at high speed is well worth the considerable risks. In the dirty, brutal and often painfully short life of a Goblin the chance of swooping through the air and smashing right through their enemies is just too good to miss. Doom Divers take their opportunity very seriously, practising for weeks by jumping off increasingly taller rocks, strengthening their arms by flapping their wings as they run about in circles, and getting trolls to throw them into the air.

When the big day comes the Doom Diver prepares by strapping on his wings which he makes himself (no Doom Diver trusts any other Goblin to make his wings and gets very angry if anyone else should even so much as touch them). Next he straps on his spiked helmet. The spiked helmet is intended to spear his chosen target, but in reality the huge splat the Goblin makes as he hits the ground is what tends to cause the damage. Finally he hooks his belt onto the Doom Diver Catapult and braces himself for sudden acceleration.

The catapult is powered by a huge piece of stretchy sinew and the height the Goblin reaches is largely dependent on how far back the Doom Diver can force the catapult. It has been known for Goblins to get so ambitious that the entire catapult springs from its mounts and hits the Goblin splat in the face, putting paid to the whole device. When he just can't stretch the catapult any further, the Goblin emits a frantic whoop and lets go. With a loud twang the Doom Diver is propelled high into the air, his exulted cries and excited squeaks gradually dimming as he becomes a tiny speck above the Goblin army.

The Doom Diver rips through the clouds like a bullet until he reaches the pinnacle of his ascent. The lands below are a patchwork quilt across which armies of ants march and countermarch. Using his wings he begins to glide downwards, and by dropping one wing tip and then the other he guides himself towards the enemy army and his chosen target. It can take several minutes for the Goblin to pick his target, at which point he folds his wings back and starts to plummet, yelling wildly as the speed of his descent drives his small Goblin brain wild.

Down on the ground the first thing to be heard is a distant squeal, and a sharp-sighted man might just discern a black dot like a bird high in the sky. With worrying rapidity the dot expands into the silhouette of the Doom Diver, and the squeal expands into a terrifying roar of ecstatic destruction. The screaming exultation of the descending Doom Diver is enough to scatter troops who are not particularly steadfast.

When the Goblin finally impacts his spike drives straight through whatever he lands upon. If this is an enemy he will almost certainly be slain. If he lands on a tree or on the ground he sticks in like a dart, and even if he survives the impact he won't be able to free himself easily. It is more likely the Goblin will be smashed apart – which although sad is considered a good way to go for a Goblin and infinitely better than being eaten by a peckish troll. Alternatively the Goblin might survive the impact and bounce around two or three times, possibly breaking a few bones but definitely causing considerable damage to the enemy he lands on.

DOOM DIVER RULES

The catapult and Doom Diver model constitutes the Doom Diver Catapult war machine. Although there is only a single Doom Diver model it is assumed that there is an infinite supply of would-be Doom Divers ready and waiting to be thrown into the air. The catapult works very much like a stone thrower as described in the Warhammer rules except that the Goblin is able to steer himself to his target and is therefore more accurate than a stone.

The catapult may be fired in the shooting phase. You will need the smaller 2" diameter template supplied with Warhammer – the catapult is much smaller than a regular stone thrower so the template is smaller too.

Firstly pivot the catapult on the spot so that it is pointing in the direction you wish to shoot. Now declare how far you wish to throw the Doom Diver. As with stone throwers you must do this without measuring the distance to your target, so you must guess the range as accurately as you can. There is no limit to the distance you can guess other than the confines of the tabletop. Once you have made your guess place the template directly over the spot where you have guessed.

DOOM DIVER MISFIRE CHART

1-2   **DESTROYED.** The catapult gives way when the Doom Diver attempts to stretch it back too far. With a resounding crack the frame breaks apart and smashes right into the Goblin, flattening him. The launch is unsuccessful and the machine is destroyed. Remove the catapult and Doom Diver from play.

3-4   **DISABLED.** The catapult elastic gives way leaving the Doom Diver helplessly earthbound. The catapult must be fixed before it can be used again, which takes all of next turn. To help you remember it is a good idea to turn the catapult around to show that you must miss a turn.

5   **BOUNCE.** The Doom Diver miscalculates his shot entirely. He is propelled more or less horizontally forward, bouncing along on his stomach until he hits something solid. The Goblin travels straight forward D6 x 10" and hits the first target in his path causing D6 strength 5 hits. Note that no template is used – the Goblin hits the first target in his path be it an individual, a unit of troops, a building, or whatever. If he hits a wood, wall, or other terrain that would block his path he stops. The machine itself is unaffected and may be used normally next turn.

6   **WILD SHOT.** The catapult slips in its mountings, spinning around and projecting the Goblin randomly into the air. Determine where he lands as follows. First roll a scatter dice to determine which direction he goes in, note that the HIT results also have direction arrows indicated at the top of the 'I' in 'HIT'. The Goblin comes down D6x10" in the direction indicated. There is no need to roll further dice to determine where the Goblin lands and the Doom Diver may not attempt to correct his approach as he is totally out of control. Position the template and work out casualties as normal. The machine itself is unaffected and may be used normally next turn.

To decide if the Goblin lands where you have aimed it roll both the scatter dice and the artillery dice. The scatter dice is marked with arrows on four sides and the word HIT on two sides. If you roll a HIT then you have hit, and the Goblin lands bang on target. If you roll an arrow the Goblin Doom Diver has missed and veered off in the direction indicated by the arrow.

The artillery dice is marked 2, 4, 6, 8, 10 and MISFIRE. If you roll a misfire then something has gone wrong – roll a D6 and consult the Doom Diver Misfire Chart. A misfire result automatically cancels out the shot even if you also roll a HIT. If you roll a number on the artillery dice and an arrow on the scatter dice then this is the distance the Goblin veers off target: reposition the template the distance indicated. If you roll a HIT on the scatter dice and numbers on the artillery dice then the numbers are ignored – they have no effect – the Doom Diver has landed smack on target.

Because the Doom Diver can steer himself as he dives downwards, he can attempt to correct his flight path should he veer away from his target. If the template veers off target, you may attempt to bring it back towards the original target. Roll a D6 and move the template back the number of inches indicated. If the D6 roll is more than the distance you have veered away then the Doom Diver has over compensated and the template is moved over and beyond the target the full distance roll.

DAMAGE

Once you have worked out where the Goblin lands you can work out damage. The model that lies directly under the centre point of the template is automatically hit and suffers a strength 10 hit. Note that this direct hit can only ever affect one model. If your roll to wound is successful the individual receives not one wound as normal, but D6 wounds. If the creature has only one wound this further dice roll is, of course, unnecessary, as it will be slain whatever the result. However, it does mean that you can take out big monsters with a direct hit from a Doom Diver, which makes them very useful indeed.

No saving throw is ever allowed for armour. The spike on the Goblin's head can pierce even the thickest dragon-hide and armour.

Models whose bases lie under the rest of the template are hit on the D6 roll of 4+. As with stone throwers you will have to use your judgement to decide how many models are caught. The rule of thumb is that a model is a potential target if at least half of its base area if covered by the template. Any models hit are not struck by the Goblin's spike, but caught by pieces of flying debris, smashed weapons, and broken armour. This is nowhere near as dangerous as the spike itself, but still causes a strength 5 attack on any targets hit. This further damage inflicts only 1 wound and saving throws apply as normal.

	Maximum range you may guess	Strength	Wounds	Save
Doom Diver	Anywhere on the tabletop	10	D6 for direct hits	None
		5	1 for other hits	-2

The catapult itself is fairly solid and difficult to destroy. There is no crew as such because the Doom Diver effectively launches himself, although it is assumed that there are a number of Doom Divers ready and willing to step forward and be catapulted into the air. The Doom Diver has the same profile as an ordinary Goblin. Should the Doom Diver be slain then the catapult cannot shoot in its following turn while another Doom Diver steps forward to replace him – the model can therefore be removed and replaced in its following turn.

The catapult may be moved by the Doom Diver up to 4" which is the Goblin's normal move. If the catapult is moved other than to pivot to face the target, then it may not shoot that turn. The catapult itself has a profile as follows.

MOVE	TOUGHNESS	WOUNDS
4" – as Goblin	7	3

LOSS OF DOOM DIVERS

As discussed above there are assumed to be a number of willing Doom Divers ready and waiting to step forward and be catapulted into the air. The Doom Diver model is not removed when he is shot, but remains in place to indicate that the catapult has a crew of Doom Divers standing ready. If the model is slain by enemy missile fire or similar then the catapult may not shoot next turn, but the model may be returned to indicate that another Doom Diver has stepped forward. If the catapult is destroyed, or if the catapult and crew are broken either in hand-to-hand combat or as a result of a psychology test, then the catapult is removed from the game.

DOOM DIVER CATAPULT SUMMARY

1. Declare target and guess range

2. Position template and roll the Scatter and Artillery dice.

3. If the Artillery dice is MISFIRE refer to Misfire Chart. Otherwise see below.

4. If the Scatter dice is a HIT the Doom Diver has struck home.

5. If the Scatter dice is an arrow the Goblin has landed in the direction shown 2, 4, 6, 8 or 10" from his aiming point as shown by the Artillery dice. However, the Goblin may attempt to correct his flight path by D6".

6. The single model in the exact centre of the template is hit. Remaining models beneath the template are hit on a D6 score of 4+.

7. Work out hits as normal. The single model which suffers a direct hit has no saving throw.

SNOTLING PUMP WAGON

The Snotling Pump Wagon is very much like a chariot in that it consists of a wooden fighting platform, rather like a ramshackle wooden hut on wheels, and it moves under its own power. In the case of the Pump Wagon this power is provided not by horses, wolves or some other beast, but by the frantic pumping of Snotlings which drives a simple mechanism and keeps the Pump Wagon moving. The Pump Wagon is also equipped with a spiked roller at the front, which crushes and pierces any foes (and Snotling crew) unfortunate enough to fall beneath it.

The rules described for chariots apply to the Pump Wagon as well with a few exceptions which take into account its unusual construction and crew. As the Pump Wagon has no horses pulling it any hits must be distributed amongst the crew or machine only, as shown on the chart below.

SHOOTING		HAND-TO-HAND	
1-2	Snotling	1-2	Pump Wagon
3-6	Pump Wagon	3-6	Snotling

The Pump Wagon is heavily constructed and has the same basic profile as a chariot. This is shown here again for convenience. Like a chariot, the Pump Wagon causes a great deal of damage as it charges but the effect is even more extreme due to the destructive power of the crunching roller at the front.

PROFILE	M	WS	BS	S	T	W	I	A	Ld
Pump Wagon	2D6"	-	-	7	7	3	1	-	-
Crew	-	2	2	1	1	3	3	3	4

HITS INFLICTED
CHARGING 2D6
OTHERWISE .... NONE

The pump wagon is crewed by stand of Snotlings.

The speed of a Pump Wagon tends to be somewhat unpredictable as its crew are continually squabbling over which of them is going to operate the pump. An enthusiastic Snotling will fight his way forward and pump like crazy for a while until he is completely exhausted when another will shove him aside and take over. This means the machine tends to go forward in fits and starts, sometimes quite quickly but at other times embarrassingly slowly.

Because the machine's speed is reliant upon the whim of its rather dim-witted crew, the player has little control over its speed at all. To represent this the Pump Wagon has no fixed move rate. It automatically moves 2D6" and is moved along with compulsory movement before other troops can move.

The player can control the direction which the machine moves in, representing the efforts of its crew to steer the thing by leaning precariously to one side or the other, but he has no say over the speed. If the machine's speed is sufficient to bring it into contact with a target then it is considered to have charged. No formal declaration of charge is necessary. The target may make the usual response just as if it had been charged in the normal manner.

It sometimes happens that the Pump Wagon's move means it has to traverse terrain which it cannot cross. For example it might be forced into a river, bog or straight through a wall. In these situations the Pump Wagon sustains D6 strength 6 hits due to damage sustained as it crunches and smashes its way through.

It can also happen that a Pump Wagon is obliged to move into friendly troops, although this is rare as you can move the machine as you wish. A foolish general might surround his Pump Wagon with friendly units only to see the machine crunch through his own lines in the first turn! When this happens work out the effect just as if it were an enemy unit. Even the Snotlings will fight as they are far too excited to care what they are doing. The Pump Wagon does not abandon the fight until the combat is complete and one side broken or destroyed.

A Pump Wagon is dependent on its crew for mobility, so once its crew are all slain it cannot move. It does not rampage around like a chariot for example. The model may be removed once the crew are slain, as it is of no further value.

ROCK LOBBER, BOLT THROWER & CHARIOT RULES SUMMARY

ROCK LOBBER SUMMARY

Orcs call stone throwers rock lobbers, but in all other respects they are exactly the same. The rules for rock lobbers are summarised below, but see pages 75-76 of the Warhammer rulebook for the complete rules.

	Maximum Range You May Guess	Strength	Wounds	Save
Small Rock Lobber	48"	7	D3	None
Big Rock Lobber	60"	10	D6	None

MOVE	TOUGHNESS	WOUNDS
As crew	7	3

1. Declare target and guess range.

2. Position template and roll Scatter and Artillery dice.

3. If the Artillery dice is MISFIRE refer to Misfire Chart, otherwise...

4. If the Scatter dice is a HIT the stone has struck home.

5. If the Scatter dice is an arrow the stone has landed in the direction shown 2, 4, 6, 8 or 10" away from the aiming point as shown on the Artillery dice.

6. The single model in the exact centre is hit. Remaining models under the template are hit on the D6 score of a 4+.

7. Work out hits as normal. Models are allowed no saving throw from a rock lobber.

BOLT THROWER SUMMARY

For the complete bolt thrower rules, please refer to page 79 of the Warhammer rulebook.

RANGE	STRENGTH	DAMAGE	SAVE
48"	5 -1 per rank	D4	No save is allowed

MOVE	TOUGHNESS	WOUNDS
As crew	7	3

1. Align bolt thrower on target and roll to hit.

2. Resolve damage at strength 5. No save is allowed for a bolt thrower.

3. If the target is slain roll damage against the second rank at strength 4.

4. Continue rolling for damage until you fail to slay the target or run out of ranks. Deduct -1 from the strength for each rank already pierced.

CHARIOT SUMMARY

The complete chariot rules can be found on pages 72-73 of the Warhammer rulebook.

1. Chariots move individually in the same way as large monsters or characters. If grouped together (within 5" of another chariot) they may be treated as a unit for leadership tests testing on the value of the highest.

2. A chariot moves at the speed of the creatures pulling it. Casualties reduce this speed in proportion, eg a chariot pulled by three Giant Wolves moves 9". If one Giant Wolf is slain the chariot moves 6", if two are slain it moves 3", if all three are slain it is immobilised. If all of a chariot's crew are slain it will move 2D6" up to its maximum speed in a random direction, collapsing on a double.

3. Chariots cannot move over obstacles or difficult terrain except to cross a river at a bridge or ford. If obliged to do so it suffers D6 S6 hits.

4. In hand-to-hand combat the enemy fights against the highest WS of the chariot crew. All hits against the chariot in hand-to-hand or shooting are randomly allocated as shown below. Remember that chariots are large targets and so +1 to hit. If a chariot has crew with differing profiles hits may be randomised between them.

SHOOTING		HAND-TO-HAND COMBAT	
1	Crew	1	Chariot
2-3	Creature	2-3	Creature
4-6	Chariot	4-6	Crew

5. Chariots have their own profiles as shown below. Once a chariot has taken its full quota of wounds it is destroyed. Surviving crew may continue to fight on foot if the player has models to represent them.

6. Crew may fight all round. Creatures pulling the chariot may fight to their front. The chariot itself may attack only as it charges causing D6 hits plus +1 per scythe if scythes are fitted on the model.

7. Chariots flee and pursue exactly like other troops. If forced to flee and subsequently caught by their pursuers they are destroyed.

8. In the case of stone throwers and other war machines with a template, treat each individual part of the chariot as a separate target.

PROFILE	M	WS	BS	S	T	W	I	A	Ld
Chariot	-	-	-	7	7	3	1	-	-

TACTICS

The Orc and Goblin army is a real gambler's army, an army with many, many different choices, but ultimately an army that favours aggressive play. Your troops are not completely predictable – when they're good they're brilliant, but when they're bad they're the worst!

Even the best generals sometimes lose with this army just because that's the way it is. On the other hand, if the dice roll in your favour you'll thrash your opponent no matter how good he might be. That's not to say it's just a question of luck whether you win – nothing could be further from the truth. Like any good gambler you have to understand how the odds work and how to stack things in your favour.

When you start to put your army together you'll be confronted with a bewildering amount of choice because there are so many kinds of troops. At first the very quantity and variety of troops can be confusing. It is important to realise that you can't hope to include every type of warrior and machine in your army... there are just too many! Instead, build your army around a core of reliable troops such as Black Orcs, Big'uns, or Boar Boyz. This core doesn't have to be very large, it could be a single Mob, but it is necessary to give some solidity to the army.

Once you have decided on your core force you can elaborate upon it by adding more troops, war machines, and monsters. When choosing your army bear in mind that some types of character model, war engines, or special troops are only available if your army includes Mobs of corresponding Orc or Goblin types. For example, you need at least one Goblin Mob to include Doom Divers. If you want to include specific special troops or machines you'll have to tailor your army appropriately.

If you play against a particular army a lot then you'll naturally try to assemble your own force so that it stands the best possible chance against that foe. Your own preferences will also make a difference to how aggressively you play, and what tactics you use. Ultimately it's up to you to decide for yourself what works best for you. There are some things that hold true whatever you do. These are the first principles of Orc generalship... the things that everybody learns pretty quickly. The following notes embody these principles and guide you through the pros and cons of the different troops.

BASIC PRINCIPLES

It is a good idea to make your units fairly big. A bigger unit can take more casualties before its combat worthiness is eroded. Remember that a unit which takes 25% casualties from shooting must take a panic test, and the bigger your unit the more casualties it will be able to sustain before having to test. War machines can crumple up small units easily. You must be able to take casualties so make sure your units are big enough to take a serious hit without depleting their effectiveness.

Arrange your units as deeply as possible. The more ranks a unit has the better its combat result bonus. If your units are four ranks deep you receive a +3 bonus (the maximum). If your units are five ranks deep you receive the maximum bonus and you can afford to take some casualties before you start to deplete the all important fourth rank. Remember, if you have relatively few models in your frontage compared to your depth the advantage of the rank bonus is accentuated because neither you nor your enemy can inflict many casualties. It is therefore to the advantage of poor troops (Goblins) to have as much depth and as little frontage as possible.

Give all your units bosses and standards wherever you can afford it. If you cannot afford it consider dropping the unit altogether. Goblin units must be led by Big Bosses, or else you need to find some other way to improve their leadership or combat resilience with magic items or standards. The reason for this is that Goblins, with their leadership of only 5, are very fragile, which means they are virtually certain to fail any break or psychology test they have to take. Remember that an Orc Big Boss can be placed with a Goblin unit to lead it. By including bosses you will be improving your chances of inflicting casualties and reducing the number of casualties sustained. By including a standard you add +1 to your combat result score. All these are important to any unit and vital to Goblins.

Attack! Your army contains troops which are very good in hand-to-hand combat – use them to spearhead your advance. Your army also contains troops which are good at pinning or delaying the enemy, for example large Goblin units, Fanatics, pump wagons, Snotlings, etc. If you can bog down one of your enemy's top units with Snotlings, or keep him pinned down by landing Fanatics in front of him, then you are free to win the game with your core units.

THE CORE UNITS

The very first decision to make is what core units to include in your army. Think of these as the troops who will do most of the real fighting. The rest of your army is there purely to support these guys and tie down the enemy while your core units get to work. Your choices are between Black Orcs, Big'uns, Boar Boyz and Boyz.

Black Orcs are the most reliable because they are not affected by animosity and they have an extra point of leadership over both Big'uns and ordinary Orcs. If you go for a Black Orc Mob you'll be able to include Black Orc characters too and this is well worthwhile if you're worried by animosity or by your army's generally low leadership levels. On the down side Black Orcs are expensive.

Big'uns are cheaper than Black Orcs but lack the benefit of the extra point of leadership. They do have an extra point of initiative instead, which puts them on a par with Men and gives them an advantage over Dwarfs. Big'uns are good fighters for the points and with a strength of 4 and toughness 4 superior to ordinary Orcs. They are very good value for the points.

Orc Boar Boyz are the best troops you can get. The war boar is a dangerous beast whose charge puts him in the same category as a fully armoured, lance-armed knight. Orc Boar Boyz are the most expensive choice for a core unit. Savage Orc Boar Boyz are marginally cheaper with a lower WS and no armour but have the advantage of their protective tattoos. The Orc Boar Boyz option really does commit you to the attack, and things can go wrong if animosity strikes or if the supporting troops don't perform up to par. In other words it's a relatively high risk gamble, but if your army holds together you will probably win. This is even more true of Savage Orc Boar Boyz because they are subject to frenzy, which means they have to charge enemy within reach whether you want them to or not.

Orc Boyz are powerful enough to be considered core units but it is doubly important to beef them up by including a powerful character. They are obviously not as powerful as Black Orcs, Big'uns or Boar Boyz, but they are much cheaper and still better than most opposition.

The number of core units you can afford will depend on the total points value of the army. You will need two core units as a minimum and of these at least one should be Black Orcs, Big'uns or Boar Boyz. A third unit would be useful but this would start to eat into the army's points value in a big way. Orc Boyz units work out cheapest per model, so it makes sense to include extra Boyz units if you are going to increase the size of your core. To be of any real value core units have to be fairly big for the reasons discussed. Generally speaking, ten is an absolute minimum for a core mob of Boar Boyz, and infantry units need to be at least sixteen, preferably twenty, and bigger if you can manage it. All the earlier comments about characters and standards apply, and it is well worth mentally putting aside some points for magic standards and magic weapons for your characters (more on magic later).

Decide on what core units you're going to have before even thinking about the rest of your army. You have to imagine how your supporting troops are going to help the core units do their job. You have plenty of choices, some are more reliable but potentially less effective, while others are completely unreliable but devastating. This is where the gambler's instinct comes to the fore!

INFANTRY

Once you have chosen your core it is time to consider the rest of your army. One immediately obvious solution is just to expand your core until you have an entire army, ignoring all the least reliable and more chancy troops altogether. This is certainly an option, but one has to ask why choose an Orc and Goblin army if you don't like taking chances? You'll be affected by animosity regardless and without supporting troops of some kind you'll be out-shot by bows and crossbows, crushed by war machines, and given the run around by skirmishers.

Putting aside the option of expanding your army with more core troops, the choices are basically between Goblin Boyz of different types, mounted Goblins, and various special troops such as chariots, trolls, giants, and ogres. Other troops which have a supporting role, and which can be considered in this category are Orc and Savage Orc Boyz armed with bows or crossbows.

Orcs and Savage Orcs are good fighting troops and can therefore be thought of as core units, but they can also be used as quality supporting troops if armed with missile weapons. With bows or crossbows you can shoot up the enemy before your core units get to grips with them, or you can attempt to draw enemy missile troops into an exchange to divert fire from the core units as they advance. Once the core units are engaged you can pile in alongside them or form them up beside the core units to block enemy attacks from the sides. In this supporting role your Orc units don't need to be so large and there is less need to provide standards or characters.

Goblins are a different story altogether. Some players find Goblins hard to use because they imagine they are fighters and commit them to combat as if they were Orcs. This is very rarely successful. Goblins are primarily support troops – their role is to ensure that your core troops get into combat against their chosen target. The different sorts of Goblins can do this in different ways but the objective is the same: either attack an enemy unit and bog it down in a protracted combat, or stand in the way of an enemy unit to prevent it attacking your core units. In either case you will need to gear the unit up to fight. The basic principles of large units, deep ranks, and good characters doubly apply to Goblins.

Goblins are so weak and vulnerable that small units are all but useless, while the principle of deep ranks and narrow frontage is essential for combat survival. If you include a

Boss and Big Boss in your front rank this will reduce the number of vulnerable Goblins fighting and cut down on the number of casualties you suffer. At the same time you might score a few wounds on the enemy, and with a huge rank bonus and bonus from your standard you stand as good a chance as you're going to get. Consider upping the effect with magic weapons if you can afford it. Remember, an Orc or Black Orc Big Boss can be placed with a Goblin unit to lead it, raising your deplorable leadership value as well as stiffening your front rank. A Black Orc will give you invulnerability to animosity too. A Goblin Big Boss has the advantage of being cheap and he will do almost as good a job, especially if you give him the Crown of Command to raise his leadership to 10.

When it comes to fighting it is best to think of Goblin Mobs as characters with a +4 combat resolution bonus (+3 from the ranks behind and +1 from the standard). Don't assume the Goblins will hit anything – if they do it's an unexpected bonus! Assuming the Boss and Big Boss can score a few wounds you are in with a good chance of winning the combat. If your Big Boss ends up against an enemy character then the two will tend to cancel out. This is good because it prevents the enemy character wiping the floor with your Goblins. It also accentuates the value of your rank bonus by reducing the overall number of casualties caused. Give the Big Boss a magic weapon if you can. Remember – anything that reduces the casualty count will work in your favour because of your fixed rank bonus.

Night Goblins are the most effective type of Goblin infantry because you can include Fanatics within their ranks. Fanatics are potentially battle winning troops as your opponent will quickly learn. You will find he will go to immense trouble to avoid Night Goblin units if he even thinks they might contain Fanatics. Regard the Night Goblin Mobs as a vehicle for carrying Fanatics. The Fanatics are the real weapon, the Mob is just a means of deploying them close to the enemy lines. The threat of Fanatics can often be a more powerful weapon than the Fanatics themselves, because although their potential for causing carnage is great the actual effect can sometimes be disappointing.

There are two good ways to use Fanatics. If you place the Night Goblin unit close to your best core unit the enemy won't dare to charge the core unit with knights or other precious troops – if he does the Fanatics will come out and whap him as he moves. If he freezes that's fine, your core unit can attack where it wants while the enemy units are dithering. Your other option is to press ahead with your Night Goblins and release your Fanatics in front of his best unit. If a Fanatic ends up in front of the unit (and it probably will) this effectively pins the unit in place and stops it moving. If your Night Goblins have bows they can add further insult by taking pot shots at the enemy while he squirms.

On the subject of Fanatics you should always buy the full allowance. You need to do this because they are inherently random. As the ultimate gambler, you will therefore play the odds by having the maximum number. While one may whizz straight through the enemy, and another might stall in front of your Mob, the other one is bound to end up somewhere where you want him. After the first turn it's down to luck, the Fanatic could go anywhere, but the chances are you'll either block the enemy or hit him hard for at least one more turn. Some enemy will try to draw your Fanatics from their Mobs by

sending out a small unit of fast cavalry to gallop past, forcing you to release your Fanatics before you are ready. There isn't much you can do about this other than vengefully shoot up the sacrificial unit in your following turn.

When considering the armament of your Goblins remember arming them up with light armour and fancy weapons makes them expensive for what they are. Spears are probably a good buy, the extra fighting rank helps to stiffen the Goblins a little bit, and shields are well worthwhile too. Bows are an option which can work well in the right circumstances, but with a range of only 16" don't expect anything too dramatic. Even archer units have to be fairly big, and they need the Bosses, standards and all the trimmings just like other units. If you arrange your archers on the slopes of a hill the rear ranks can shoot over the heads of the ranks in front, enabling you to take advantage of large numbers. Although your Goblin archers are feeble compared to Men or Elves, bear in mind the comparable points cost. If you can occupy a unit of Elf archers for a few turns then the exchange can sometimes be worth it. Watch out for the 25% casualty level panic test though. If your Mob is taking high casualties you could be forced to take a panic test, resulting in your archers fleeing and panicking other Goblins.

Squig Hunter and Netter units are an entertaining variation with some specific advantages over ordinary Night Goblins. You can get away with slightly smaller units of these than of other Goblins. With Netters you can get away with about twenty, but you'll still need a Boss, standard, drummer/horn blower, and a Big Boss if possible. With Squig Hunters nine Squigs and three Hunter teams is about right. Squigs are unpredictable and in many way the best thing that can happen is for them to go wild once they are near the enemy. You can't put standards or Bosses with Squig units because the Squigs tend to eat them, or you have to put the Bosses at the back where they can't do anything.

CAVALRY

When it comes to choosing cavalry you have fewer options than with infantry but you are still spoiled for choice compared to most armies. In addition to the core-type Boar Boyz you have Wolf Riders and Spider Riders.

Although described as core troops, you might consider including smaller units of Boar Boyz in a supporting role. You can deploy such a unit beside a core unit to prevent an enemy attacking its flanks and, to a degree, to draw fire away from the main unit. A Mob of even five Boar Boyz is potentially very strong and can get stuck in once your core units are committed. The disadvantage of using these troops in this way is that they are very expensive, and it's easy to lose such a small unit to a hit from a war machine or good archery. Although this might seem a 'safe' option compared to buying Goblins, this isn't really the case.

Remember that if your Orc units panic and flee they will spread panic amongst your other Orcs and Goblins, whereas Orcs will ignore fleeing Goblins altogether.

Wolf Riders are not as powerful as Orc Boar Boyz but then again they are nothing like as expensive either at 9 points against 27. The Wolf has WS4 and can put up a pretty good show against most enemy. It is tempting to buy a small unit of Wolf Riders and use them to race ahead of your army, move around the enemy's flanks, and maybe to attack his war machines before he has a chance to use them on your main force. This plan usually falls down because the Wolf Riders are vulnerable to shooting and because small units of Goblins are very fragile.

For example, two casualties on a unit of five models causes a panic test and the chances of passing that with a basic leadership value of 5 are remote to say the least. A far better option is to treat the Wolf Riders in the same way as Goblin infantry Mobs – go for a fairly large unit, deploy in deep ranks, and include at least one worthy character. Used in this way the Wolf Riders can move in fast to pin your chosen enemy unit, taking the heat off your Boar Boyz and other core units. How long the Wolf Riders last once they are fighting depends to an extent on the characters and magic you put with them. Don't expect much from the Goblin riders themselves!

Spider Riders are similar in principal to Wolf Riders and the same comments apply. Spiders have a better strength than wolves (4 as opposed to 3) and although their WS is lower it is still better than the Goblin rider's. Their big advantage is that they ignore difficult ground and obstacles. This means they can move straight through woods and debris and such like. They can also go straight over obstacles, which is very useful if your enemy is defending a wall or hedgerow.

CHARIOTS AND OTHER SUPPORTING TROOPS

Chariots are relatively expensive models and the added protection they offer is useful for your Warlord and maybe your best Shaman. A group of several chariots is certainly powerful but suffers all the disadvantages of large monsters. They become instant targets for enemy war machines! If you can get them into combat they stand a good chance of winning, but you can guarantee the enemy will do his best to shoot them up first. If your battle plan is to charge headlong at the enemy and engage him as soon as possible chariots are ideal. If your enemy has a preponderance of missile weapons or lots of war machines then chariots are vulnerable.

Snotlings are an oddball troop type with more to recommend them than their profiles might suggest. True, they have feeble strength and toughness, but with three wounds they are more resilient than the same frontage of Goblins or Orcs. Because they are unaffected by psychology and don't take break tests they can be used to pin down a much more powerful enemy, diverting attention away from the core units. The only problem with Snotties is that they take casualties fairly quickly. This means that if they fight alongside other troops their vulnerability will drag down your overall combat result score. To counter this make sure you keep a narrow frontage and rack them up deep, and make your attack slightly away from other units.

You need a four base width formation to get your rank bonuses, but it is better to sacrifice the bonus in favour of avoiding being dragged into a broader combat. By keeping the Snotties slightly apart they won't get involved in a larger combat and the casualties they suffer will be of no account. Because they don't need leaders Snotties are a good way to spend a few extra points to round off your army – at 15 points a base they're cheap too.

Trolls are extremely powerful and because they regenerate damage they are very hard to kill. As they are stupid they are unreliable, and with a leadership of only 4 they will almost always fail their test. The only answer is to buy an Orc Big Boss to look after them. Apart from that get them into combat as soon as possible. At least they stand a fifty-fifty chance of fighting if they go stupid.

Ogres are good solid troops with plenty of of muscle, high wounds value, two attacks, and a basic leadership as good as Orcs. They also cause fear. Double-handed weapons are a good option because Ogres have such a low initiative they usually end up striking last anyway. Their toughness and wounds are high enough to enable them to get away without a shield. If you can afford it a unit of Ogres will provide you with another tough unit to rank alongside your Black Orcs or Boar Boyz as part of the army's core. Because they are so tough, and have three wounds, you can have a relatively small unit, say five. This will still cost you two hundred points even without standard and musician. Two hundred points buys an awful lot of Goblins! If your idea of an ideal army is compact and tough then Ogres are a good choice. As with all small units you have to be wary of war machines and magic.

A **Giant** is good fun but frighteningly unreliable. It also makes an ideal target for every enemy war machine in sight. A Giant will have the same effect on your enemy as a big monster. Your opponent will tend to fixate on the Giant and divert a lot of his resources against it while the Boyz get on with winning the battle (hopefully!). The best reason for including a Giant in your army is that they are very entertaining! It's worth having one just to see the expression on your enemy's face as the Giant jumps up and down on his cherished troops.

WAR MACHINES

You have two good options for long range artillery in the form of Orc Rock Lobbers and Goblin Doom Divers. In both cases you need to include an appropriate Mob before you can have these war machines in your army. Both are comparably effective – the Rock Lobbers being more destructive while the Doom Divers are more accurate. Either or both will do a fine job of picking off enemy war machines or lobbing missiles into the middle of key enemy units. Neither are completely reliable, and the only way to be sure of landing an effective shot is to play the odds – buy several machines! A group of, say, four machines gives you a pretty good chance of hitting where you want at least once every turn. Try to make every shot count and concentrate on hitting important targets. If you can take out enemy war machines early on with Doom Divers then you will protect your core units and you can lob a few shots at the enemy's best troops before the Boyz get stuck in.

Bolt Throwers are more like super-archers than the other two machines. They need a clear line of sight to shoot and will tear through several ranks of an enemy unit. Bolt throwers work well if they are positioned on a hill or facing an open line of advance, preferably behind a hedge or a wall. If your tactics are basically to run straight towards the enemy and hit him hard then a bolt thrower isn't really going to do you any good. For one thing your own troops will probably end up blocking the line of sight. If you're fighting Dwarfs, who you know will stand around a lot waiting for you to come and get them, then a few rounds of bolt fire from two or three machines can soften them up nicely. Always concentrate your fire if you have several machines – ten casualties on one unit is better than two casualties on five units.

Snotling Pump Wagons are fun, difficult to control and occasionally deadly. Like big monsters and chariots they will become the target of every bowman and war machine that can fire at them, so it's no use sending a Pump Wagon out on its own as it will just get shot up. Because its potential to cause damage is huge the Pump Wagon will unnerve your enemy and force him to divert resources towards destroying it. At least while the enemy is shooting up your Pump Wagon he's ignoring the rest of your army as it storms forward, and at 40 points each that's a small price to pay for keeping your core units intact. You can use several Pump Wagons together, or advance them with chariots or big monsters, but their random move means you can't rely on them to hit the enemy at the same time. Bear in mind that if you deploy a Pump Wagon right in front of one of your Orc or Goblin units there is a good chance it will get in the way of their advance – the average Pump Wagon move is 7" while a march move for Orcs or Goblins is 8".

CHARACTERS

The amount of points you can spend on characters is restricted and you need to spend a lot of points on Bosses and Big Bosses to accompany your Mobs. That won't leave a lot to spend on your Warlord or Shamans. In practice, the number of Bosses and Big Bosses you can afford will determine how many infantry and cavalry units you have. There is no point at all in buying Mobs of Goblins without putting a half way decent leader with them, and a Goblin Boss isn't enough on his own

(leadership 5). You really need to raise the leadership to at least 7 for your Goblins and that means either an Orc Big Boss or a Goblin Big Boss with a magic item to increase his leadership such as the Crown of Command (Ld 10). If you can afford a magic standard then you can use this to increase the leadership or add to your combat result which amounts to the same thing for the all important break test. In any case, you have to make sure all your Mobs have sufficient characters to ensure they can fight properly. The bottom line here is a Boss for every unit, and a Big Boss of some sort for every Goblin unit (preferably an Orc). Black Orc Big Bosses are best, as a unit led by a Black Orc is not affected by animosity, but at 91 points each you won't be able to afford many. A Goblin Big Boss may have a leadership of only 6, but he still has 2 wounds and 3 attacks, can carry two magic items and costs only 33 points. If you feel tempted to field Mobs without proper leaders think again! Better to drop the unit and spend the points on increasing the size of your other Mobs. A Mob without a proper leader is just a liability.

When it comes to choosing a Warlord as your army's leader you have plenty of choice and all of it pretty good. A Goblin Warlord is cheap, but with a leadership of only 7 this is a risky option even with an accompanying Battle Standard Bearer. You could buy him the Crown of Command as one of his magic items, which at 50 points still makes him marginally cheaper than an Orc or Black Orc Warlord. A good option for the Goblin Warlord is to ride a chariot. If you buy Grom you get the army's Battle Standard in the same chariot. If you do decide to have Grom take his full allowance of magic items to protect the chariot as much as you can. An Orc Warlord riding a war boar accompanied by the Battle Standard Bearer also riding a war boar can both accompany your Boar Boyz

core unit, assuming you have one. If you have taken the sensible option of a Boar Boyz Boss this gives you a formidable front line with eight Orc and three Boar attacks concentrated into three models, not to mention the effect of magic weapons or the war boars' charge. This is a good option for those who like to get stuck in. Of course, if the enemy lands a magic attack or a war machine hit on top of this lot you're in trouble, but you can avoid this with careful protective magic and a bit of luck. The other option for a Warlord is to put him on a wyvern or other big monster, but this isn't recommended. You need your Warlord near his troops to pass on the benefits of his leadership and to get stuck in alongside the Boyz. If you put him on a wyvern there is a temptation to spend half the game flitting about behind the enemy lines or stuck up in the air.

By the time you've bought a Warlord, a Battle Standard Bearer, Bosses for your units, and Big Bosses for vulnerable Goblin units, plus magic weapons and armour for the most important characters, the chances are you won't have many points left. In fact, the chances are you'll have to go back and pare down your heroes to give you enough points for Shamans. This is where you find yourself trading in those Black Orcs for something more realistic!

You need at least one Shaman, and if you can only afford one he should be an Orc or Forest Goblin (assuming you have Forest Goblins in your army to allow you to choose him). Forest Goblins don't 'ead bang while other Goblins are prone to fail their Waaagh test. Other Goblin Shamans need to be kept towards the flanks or placed so that there are not too many Orcs and Goblins about, otherwise they will 'eadbang. Low level Goblin Shamans are cheap and, to a degree, disposable, so don't worry too much when they fail their Waaagh test. Orc Shamans are better and it's worth going for a Shaman Lord if you can afford it. Remember, Shamans have to be within 12" of Orcs or Goblins to cast spells. If you put your Orc Shaman on a wyvern and fly him to the other end of the battlefield he won't be able to use his Waaagh magic. See comments on monsters below.

MONSTERS

If you mount up your Warlord or Shamans on big monsters you will substantially increase their fighting potential but they become easy targets for the enemy. If you can keep your characters partially obscured, or fly them behind the enemy lines and out of his fire arcs then so much the better. However, you really need your Warlord to be with the troops, and your Shaman has to be within 12" of at least one sizeable Orc or Goblin unit to use his magic. This certainly makes a big monster a less favourable option as a mount for these characters.

You could buy a spare Big Boss, load him up with magic items, mount him on a wyvern and use him to pick off the enemy's general or other vital pieces early in the game. This tactic does sometimes work, but it's quite risky for Orcs because it ties up a lot of character points which you could well use elsewhere.

A wyvern without a rider can be employed either to launch an early attack on your enemy's artillery or on a powerful character. Alternatively, let him fly high to act as a aerial patrol to intercept an enemy trying the same thing. Some sort of flying creature is definitely a good idea, as otherwise you are vulnerable to attack from the air. You can use the magic item Orb of Thunder to darken the skies and spoil high level flight altogether, but you can't count on this working. You can also use magic to fend off attacks from the air, taking advantage of the magic phase during your enemy's turn.

MAGIC ITEMS

It is well worth putting aside a portion of your points to buy magic standards, for those units that are permitted them, and magic items for your leaders. When choosing your magic try to anticipate your troops' shortcomings and compensate for them. To a degree this depends upon your enemy – some enemies require a slightly different approach than others. In the case of Undead and Elves you will have to take into account that they cause fear, especially the Undead, and with generally low leadership values this is bad news. To compensate, choose as many magic items as possible that either boost leadership or negate fear. A good choice here is the Dread Banner which actually causes fear and makes the unit carrying it immune to fear too – this is very useful against any opponent. The most obvious choice is the Crown of Command, which gives you a unmodifiable leadership value of 10 which is very useful for a Goblin leader.

You can boost your hand-to-hand fighting effectiveness with banners (Battle Banner, War Banner, Banner of Courage, Banner of Might) or by equipping characters with appropriate magic weapons. Another useful device here is the Potion of Strength, a cheap item at only 10 points, and well worth giving to a character with lots of attacks already. If you're planning a risky aerial attack with a high-ranking character the Healing Potion might be a good idea. At 50 points it's quite expensive, but if it saves your Warlord's life it's obviously worth it.

Magic can protect your army as well as enhance it. Always take at least one Dispel Magic Scroll for every Shaman, and use them carefully. Remember you can only use a Dispel Scroll once, so it's important not to waste any. The Amulet of Fire is a good investment at 25 points. It will protect the wearer and unit he is with from a single magic attack per turn, but only works on a 4, 5 or 6 (ie, as a standard Dispel card). Another useful item is the Orb of Thunder which you can use to darken the skies and prevent the enemy flying high into the air. This is a good way of stopping early aerial attacks against your Warlord or artillery. The Black Amulet is good for reducing your own wounds and shifting them onto the enemy, pushing up your all important combat result.

Magic swords are a good investment because anything that improves your hand-to-hand fighting abilities is a good idea. If you have a Goblin character he often works best as a 'spoiler' to cancel out the enemy's characters by absorbing attacks. In this case, weapons which work defensively are best. Aanything that lowers the overall casualty count will work in the favour of your deep Mobs. A sword which improves your toughness (Swords of Resilience, Defiance, and Unyielding) are therefore good although expensive. A Warrior Bane or Parrying Blade are useful too as they reduce your enemy's attacks. Swords which affect psychology are extremely useful and a Sword of Fortitude is a must for any Orc or Goblin army, as it makes the bearer and the unit he is with immune to fear, terror and panic.

ANIMOSITY

As an Orc and Goblin player animosity is something you will have to learn to live with. You can do things to limit its effects, but ultimately you can't stop it so you might as well not worry about it too much. You have to assume that Mobs will occasionally fall prey to animosity come what may. If you like, go back to playing the odds to ensure success – if you need to rely on a unit to do something then send two units!

While it is important not to fixate on animosity it is wise to take it into account. Black Orcs don't suffer from animosity and units led by Black Orcs don't suffer from animosity either. So if you can afford them Black Orc Big Bosses can be very useful. Also, a *Get 'em* result will only result in fighting between Mobs if there is a suitable target nearby to attack. As an Orc or Goblin Mob will only attack another Mob that is also liable to animosity, it makes sense to avoid putting these units next to each other. Certainly don't put them one in front of the other, as this is asking for trouble. If you deploy with a unit of Orcs you could put a unit of Black Orcs next to them, then Goblins, then Trolls, then more Orcs, and there will be no two animosity-suffering units next to each other. That way the worst that can happen is you will miss a turn. That is bad enough of course, but infinitely better than two Mobs scrapping.

Note also that the fewer units you have the less likely you are to suffer from animosity. This is another reason to avoid small units – far better to have a single big unit than two small ones.

TACTICS

Remember that your prime objective has to be to advance quickly with your core units and hit your enemy hard. At the same time use your supporting troops to tie up the enemy units you want to keep out of the way. Don't get drawn into committing your supporting troops into combat if they can just as easily pin down the enemy from a distance. Night Goblin units with Fanatics are good for

this. Even if the Fanatics don't hit the enemy they will block his line of advance while you get stuck in elsewhere with your best troops. As a general point, you should try to tie down the enemy's best unit while you use your core troops to see off his second best troops. In practice, you will have to judge the enemy for yourself. If you're very confident of beating his best units with your core troops go ahead and attack.

Enemy artillery will probably be better than your own, so try to counter it early on. You could take it out with a flying monster. Alternatively, use Doom Divers to zap the enemy's artillery before it can damage your core units. Use your own artillery to soften up the enemy units that you wish to attack.

Always use the principles of size, depth, and narrow frontage to maximise your combat value. Don't deploy onto a larger frontage than you have to with Goblins. Anything you can do to gain the advantage in combat is worthwhile.

With Goblins watch out for panic. Buy magic items to keep panic in check if you can. A good leader is essential.

Your magic is well suited to aggressive play so don't hold back. Heads will explode but don't worry about Goblin Shamans as they are cheap. Put Night Goblin and Goblin Shamans where they are least likely to 'eadbang. Savage Orc Shamans and Forest Goblin Shamans are the most reliable and effective. Savage Orc Shamans are best placed with units of Savage Orcs where their protective tattoos will be enhanced.

Against specific opponents you might have to vary your approach – but this is something that players learn as they go. Dwarfs are a bit slow so you might prefer a more steady advance with more war machines to pound the stunties before you go in. Against a mobile enemy such as Bretonnian knights you must be careful of their charge – a unit of Goblins will be swept away in one turn if caught like this. Against Elves you have to be careful of the fear rule, as Goblins *fear* units of Elves they don't outnumber two to one. Increase the size of your Goblin units if you have to, even drop the number of units to a bare minimum to counteract the effect. Fighting the Empire you have to look out for the Helblaster volley gun. Try to take it out before you get close to it otherwise it'll blow a big hole in your advancing army. Cannons can cause considerable damage on your deep ranks too, but this is less worrying.

Expect to take casualties as you advance, especially Goblins. Don't let this dishearten you, the little greenies are there to soak up the enemy's attention after all. Remove Goblin casualties with a deliberately contemptuous gesture or casual lack of concern if it makes you feel better. Remember, while your Goblins are soaking up casualties your real troops are getting closer to the enemy. If your enemy is good he will realise where your real strength lies, and he'll probably leave your Goblins alone. This isn't necessarily a good thing, but at least it gives you the opportunity to advance those big blocks of troops close to his army.

ORC AND GOBLIN BANNERS

These black and white banner designs have been provided for you to photocopy then paint. Some designs you may wish to photocopy twice, once for each side of the banner, eg Grom's banner. Use the colour photographs shown elsewhere in this book as guides for colour schemes.

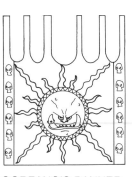

GORFANG'S BANNER

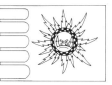
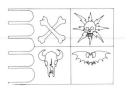

ORC SHAMAN BANNER

ORC GLYPH BANNER

ORC BOAR RIDERS

ORC BANNERS

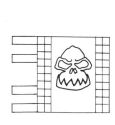

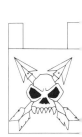

ORC BANNERS

ORC BANNERS

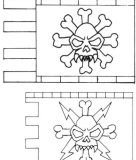

SAVAGE ORC BANNERS

GROM'S BANNER

FOREST GOBLIN BANNERS

GOBLIN BANNERS

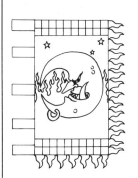

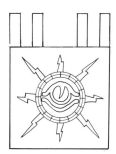

NIGHT GOBLIN BANNERS

Wyvern are ferocious winged beasts which attack with huge rending claws and gaping jaws full of barbed teeth. Ridden by an Orc Shaman, the War Wyvern circles the battlefield and swoops down on the enemy, sending them fleeing in terror.

ORC SHAMAN RIDING WAR WYVERN

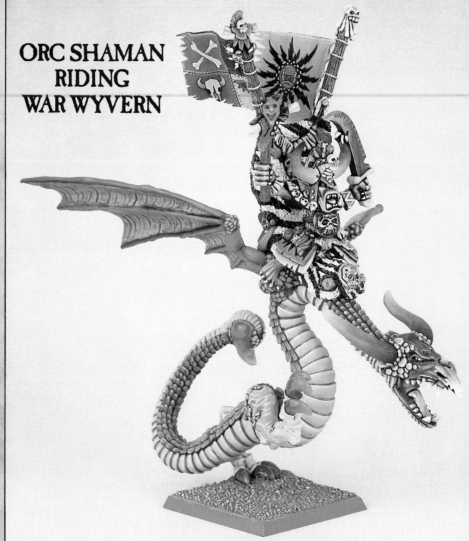

ORC ROCK LOBBER

ORC BOYZ

There are many tribes of Orcs in the Old World from the northern wastes beyond Kislev to the southern Badlands. The vask bulk of every tribe is made up of Orc Boyz, ferocious fighters armed with wicked edged blades, spiked clubs, and other deadly weapons. They are led by vicious Boss Orcs who are even bigger and meaner than the Boyz themselves. Orc Boyz form the backbone of the Waaagh!

SWORD AND SHIELD

ORC BOYZ WITH SWORDS AND SHIELDS

AXE AND KNIFE

SPIKED CLUB

AXE AND SHIELD

ORC BOYZ WITH SWORDS AND SHIELDS

FOREST GOBLINS

Forest Goblins are found in the dark forests of the Old World. These ancient forests are full of all kinds of horrifying creatures including giant spiders. Forest Goblins are experts at capturing these creatures and large ones are ridden into battle while the smaller ones are kept as pets.

Forest Goblins decorate themselves with brightly coloured feathers, bits of bone, and warpaint. This adds to their frightening appeerence when they emerge from the forests to carry out raids on surrounding villages and farms.

STANDARD BEARERS

LEADER

SHAMAN

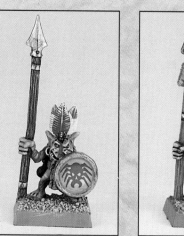

FOREST GOBLIN SPEARMEN

LEADER

FOREST GOBLIN WARRIORS

DRUMMER

FOREST GOBLIN ARCHERS

FOREST GOBLIN REGIMENT

SPIDER RIDER BANNER BEARER

FOREST GOBLIN SPIDER RIDERS WITH SPEARS

CHAMPION ON SPIDER

FOREST GOBLIN SPIDER RIDER

LEADER ON SPIDER

THE BATTLE OF IRON PEAK
By Jervis Johnson and Bill King

With a thunderous crash the support beams collapsed. Tons of rock tumbled downwards sealing the entrance to the old dwarf mine completely. From within came the squeals of the trapped gobbo boyz. Borzag shrugged: if the lads were stupid enough to go into a stunty mine and start chopping at the supports with their axes, then they got what they deserved. Plenty more where they came from, reflected the old orc shaman, patting the head of his wyvern and feeding him some more stunty fingers.

"Borzag, mate, Great fight! We certainly gave those stunties a good seein' to. Me trolls was great, eh? See the way they did my brilliant plan fing." Gorblum clapped Borzag matily on the shoulder. The shaman fought down the urge to cuff the over familiar little gobbo round the ear.

Gorblum had become ever more cocky and self-confident since Borzag had lent him the Crown of Command. He had gone from calling himself Gorblum Yellowstreak to calling himself Gorblum the Magnificent. What cheek! By Mork, he would never even have had the nerve to get within 50 feet of those trolls if it wasn't for the confidence the crown lent him. And the trolls would probably have eaten Gorblum and his spider if it wasn't for the crown's aura of command. Be calm, Borzag told himself. He still needed the little creep and his trolls and his gobbos and his fanatics. They were a central part of his great masterplan, the core around which he would assemble his army.

"Yez. It woz a great plan you thought ov, Gorblum," said Borzag, gently disengaging Gorblum's paw. The shaman wanted to spit. The entire plan had been his, giving credit to the goblin went completely against the grain. Still, the effects of the crown meant that Borzag had to feed the goblin chieftain's overweening ego. The old shaman moved over to the edge of the cliff. Gorblum followed. Borzag fought down the overwhelming urge to push the chieftain over the edge, just to see him fall, but instead he gave his attention to the panoramic view.

Far below at the foot of the mountain, the lands of the south eastern Empire were spread out for Borzag like a map. He could see the long silver trail where the little river flowed into the bigger one, the one the captured stunties always called the Reik. He could see the tiny boats that bobbed on the water like toys. The village was there and this meant more stunties to kill. Good. Borzag hated stunties, had done ever since he was knee high to a giant spider.

"Boss! Boss!" gibbered Sleekid, Gorblum's chief lackey. "Dis isn't gold. It's rocks!"

The gobbo threw a sack down in front of Gorblum. The little chieftain pretended to study it intently, as if a long hard stare would transmute the grey stuff to gold and pretty trinkets.

"Nar, ain't gold," Gorblum said eventually. "Unless it's dat funny grey gold. Dose stunty gitz has fooled us."

Borzag winced. Gorblum was as stupid as he was vain. "I fink I see what da Boss means," he said.

"You do?" said Gorblum, a trifle amazed.

"Yer. Dose stunties couldn't fool yer. Youse seen right through 'em."

"I 'ave? I mean I 'ave."

"Yer day has 'idden it. Down dere. In dat mantown. You saw it right away. No wonder dey calls you Gorblum da Magnificent."

"Yere. Dat's right. Wot woz my brilliant plan again?"

"Well, we should go down dere and give da stunties a taste of bootlevver. Den we'll find da 'idden gold."

"Mork's teef. I comes up wiv some brill plans, don't I mate?"

"Yer," muttered Borzag between gritted teeth. "Lez go."

At Gorblum's howled command, the orcs and goblins formed up in slovenly ranks. Sleekid's boyz began to spit and make faces at Wa-Kurran's ladz. Within moments a great scrap had broken out. Gorblum stood around and watched, amused by the great ruck. Borzag began to get a sore head, and his eyes began to glow as they always did when the ladz got into a bit of violence. Now was not the time though.

"Dat's enough!" he bellowed. Wading into the ruck he picked up Sleekid and Wa-Kurran by the scruff of their necks and tossed them out of the melee. The two rival gobbo leaders landed in front of Borzag's wyvern. It hissed and they fell quiet, petrified with fear. Slowly the melee abated.

"Save it fer da stunties," shouted Borzag. "Now, lez go!"

Chanting and gibbering, the greenskin army marched down towards the unsuspecting village.

On the day after Geheimnisnacht 2510 it was business as usual in the sleepy little village of Eisenhof. The mixed population of Dwarfs and Men loaded barges with iron ore destined for the great cannon works at Nuln. From the docks the heavily laden craft pushed out onto the Veiss, a minor tributary of the mighty Reik, and made their way down river towards the distant city. A caravan of ore had just arrived and the stocky Dwarf miners heaved the heavy sacks of raw metal from the backs of their pack mules and stacked them neatly on the wharves.

In the market square traders haggled over the price of a hundredweight of rock. The village drunk lurched from the tavern and loudly sang an old sad song. For the folk of Iron Mountain it was a typical day, in a typical month, in a typical year. Little did they know that a terrible doom was fast approaching the little hamlet.

From the bleak, desolate mountains to the east, a horde of Goblins had marched relentlessly down the windswept valleys to arrive at the outskirts of the village. To the fore was Gorblum the Magnificent, mounted on his great spider. Behind him marched his regiments of red-eyed Night Goblins and to the rear of the column, sweating gobbos tugged a huge rock lobber. Standing tall amidst the green mass, three giant river trolls grumbled and yawned, revealing endless rows of serrated teeth in their huge gaping maws. Overhead, mounted on his mighty wyvern, the dreaded Orc shaman Borzag soared on the wind, scanning the horizon with his malevolent keen-eyed gaze.

They had already destroyed two of the isolated Dwarf mines, and slaughtered dozens of Dwarf miners. Now they were drawn by the chimney fires of the town of Eisenhof and the prospect of considerable loot.

A single pedlar making his way up to the mines spotted their approach and fled back down the slopes to give warning. Hastily the innkeeper and the merchants packed their families into their carts and fled. The dock labourers took to the barges and headed down river taking all that they could carry.

When the Goblin horde arrived they were enraged by the absence of plunder. Cursing with frustration, they swiftly put Eisenhof to the torch. Drunk on the last sour ale, they rioted through the streets, looting the burning buildings and scavenging scraps and debris from the dungheaps.

Meanwhile, other eyes had spotted the blaze. Thorgrim Greybeard, clan lord of the Dwarfs of Iron Mountain had received word of the Goblin marauders and hastily summoned his warriors to battle. Thorgrim had sworn an oath to avenge his fallen kindred and every Dwarf with him had pledged to aid him in this task. Grunnir Thorbalson and his band of Troll Slayers, who'd been feasting in Thorgrim Hall, joined the band, for Borzag seemed a mighty foe to test their fates against.

So it came to be that late in the afternoon the forces of Thorgrim and Borzag confronted each other outside the burning remains of the village of Eisenhof.

CHOOSING THE ORC ARMY
(Jervis Johnson)

Fighting Dwarfs with an Orc and Goblin army is never easy. The Dwarfs have two significant advantages over Orcs which you must do your best to neutralise if you want to have any chance of winning. The first of these advantages is the quality of their infantry. A typical Dwarf warrior has a higher weapon skill than an Orc, is just as tough, and comes on a smaller base (20mm as opposed to 25mm). Formed four ranks deep and with a banner, it is next to impossible for Orcs (let alone Goblins!) to beat a Dwarf infantry unit. This problem is compounded by the Dwarfs' second advantage, which is that they *hate* Orcs and Goblins. This means that even if you do by some miracle win a round of combat it is very unlikely that the Dwarfs will break.

My knowledge of the fighting ability of Dwarf infantry had been learnt through bitter experience in the other games that I'd played against Bill's Dwarf army. In that game I fielded a fairly typical Orc and Goblin army and tried to counter the Dwarfs' superior skill with my larger numbers. It simply did not work. The Dwarf infantry soaked up all the casualties my fairly limited selection of ranged weapons were able to inflict, leaving them with the same rank bonus as my big blocks of troops. My superior numbers made no difference under such circumstances and my army was soundly thrashed.

Smarting from my defeat, I determined to come up with an army that could defeat the Dwarfs. In this I did have one very significant advantage over Bill. I knew that in order to field a 2,000 point army, he would have to use more or less exactly the same troops that he had in the previous game, as these were just about all of the models that were available. The Studio's Orc army, however, is considerably larger than 2,000 points, so I would be able to tailor it to suit my plans.

And what were my plans? Well, they rested on a two-pronged strategy. First of all I wanted to whittle down the size of Bill's large infantry blocks *before* I had to fight them. This would reduce their rank bonus considerably and give my infantry a better chance of winning. Because Dwarfs are tough and protected by good armour, missile fire from bows and short bows is unlikely to do them much damage. No, what I needed to ensure maximum damage to Dwarf infantry was artillery and of course, Goblin fanatics. I took as much of each as I could lay my hands on: an Orc man mangler, two Goblin doom divers and six Goblin fanatics.

Now I turned my attention to the more tricky part of choosing my army. The second 'prong' of my strategy was to pick fighting units that could battle head-to-head with Dwarfs. To create such units would cost me a lot of points, but I was determined to go for quality rather than quantity. However, before I could pick my elite units, I needed two regiments of Night Goblins so that I could field the six Goblin fanatics (you may not take fanatics on their own, but you can add up to three to each regiment of Night Goblins). I decided to take two regiments of 20 Night Goblin archers. These had the dual advantages of being cheap (78 points including champion and standard!), while being large enough to soak up a few casualties. In addition, as Night Goblins *hate* Dwarfs I could use them to tie up a Dwarf unit in hand-to-hand combat if necessary – the Goblins wouldn't win, but they probably wouldn't run away either!

I could now concentrate on buying my elite troops. First of all I selected my major characters. I would like to have had an Orc general and standard bearer, but unfortunately the models aren't ready yet, so I had to make do with my Goblin general 'Gorblum the Magnificent' mounted on his gigantic spider

and my trusty Goblin standard bearer 'Mikira'. I gave Gorblum the *Crown of Command* magic item card in order to increase his leadership characteristic to ten, and resolved to keep both these characters out of the front line, to ensure they both survived the battle. You need the general's leadership bonus and the army standard's dice re-roll when you field an Orc and Goblin army, believe me!

The fact that Gorblum and Mikira were so cheap allowed me to spend 542 points on Borzag, an Orc Shaman Lord riding a war wyvern and armed with a *Blade of Darting Steel* – an elite fighting unit if ever there was one, and obviously the power behind Gorblum's throne. Hopefully Borzag's spells would help to whittle down the Dwarfs, while his power in hand-to-hand combat would certainly help to finish them off!

Borzag could not deal with the Dwarfs on his own however, and I was determined to include one really tough unit of Orc Boyz to take on the Dwarfs and show them what for. I picked a unit of 20 Orc Warriors, and strengthened it considerably by adding a magical *Battle Banner*, a unit champion and an Orc Big Boss armed with a *Shrieking Blade*. The *Battle Banner* would add 1D6 to the number of wounds I scored in combat, thus greatly increasing my chance of winning a melee. The *Shrieking Blade* causes fear, which means that if I win a round of close combat against a unit of the Dwarfs that were outnumbered by my Boyz, the Dwarfs would *automatically* rout. Because Dwarfs *hate* Orcs and Goblins, they take a break test on an unmodified roll of 10 if they lose a round of combat. Without the *Shrieking Blade*, I would have next to no chance of routing them even with the *Battle Banner*.

I was now left with just over 200 points to spend. Now to me, an Orc and Goblin army just doesn't seem right unless it includes a few trolls, so I took as many as I could afford with the points I had left (three, to be precise). Trolls can be extremely effective in close combat as long as they don't go 'stupid' on you. However, by using Gorblum with his leadership of 10 to direct the unit, I was fairly certain that this wouldn't be a problem.

I now had a few points left over, which I used to buy a *Potion of Strength* for Skargash (the Orc Big Boss with the *Shrieking Blade*). An extra +3 to your strength can be very useful, even if it is only for one round.

All that now remained was to choose the spell cards for Borzag. As a Shaman Lord, Borzag was entitled to four cards selected from the *Waaagh!* deck of spell cards. When you choose magic, the ability to discard any of the spell cards you are first dealt for replacement cards is vitally important. This allows you to try to make sure that you get the spells that you feel are most important. The only card that I really wanted to get was *Hand of Gork* and I would have been willing to discard all four cards I was first dealt to try and get it. As it turned out, I was dealt *Hand of Gork* along with *Da Krunch*, *Gaze of Mork* and Waaagh!, and so was quite happy with the first four cards I received. With the selection of Borzag's spells, my army was complete.

THE ORC BATTLEPLAN

Although my overall strategy was already decided – pound the Dwarfs with artillery, spells and fanatics, then finish them off with the Orcs, trolls and Borzag – there were a number of important decisions to be made before I could put it into effect. The first of these was where I was going to set up. In the end I decided to set up on the right hand side of the table for the simple reason that it allowed me to set up Borzag under cover! The way we play, flying units must set up on the table, so you can't begin the game with them flying high above the battlefield where they will be safe from attack. If I placed

GORBLUM'S ORC AND GOBLIN HORDE

Borzag: Orc Shaman Lord riding a War Wyvern armed with a *Blade of Darting Steel.*

Gorblum the Magnificent: Goblin General riding a Gigantic Spider wearing the *Crown of Command.*

Mikira: Army Standard Bearer

3 River Trolls

Sleekid's Boyz – 20 Night Goblins: armed with short bows plus 3 Goblin Fanatics.

Wa Kurran's Boyz – 20 Night Goblins: Armed with short bows plus 3 Goblin Fanatics.

2 Goblin Doom Divers

Orc Regiment: 19 Orc Boyz armed with swords, light armour and shields and carrying a *Battle Banner.* Skargash: Big Boss Orc – heavy armour, *Potion of Strength* and *Shrieking Blade.*

Man Mangler: Orc stone thrower with 3 crew armed with hand weapons.

Total Points   **2003**

Borzag where Bill could see him and the Dwarfs got the first turn, I could almost guarantee that a Dwarf cannon ball would be whizzing towards my shaman before I had the chance to get him airborne. With just a little bit of luck Bill could wipe out over a quarter of the points in my army on the first turn and that I could live without! Fortunately, there was a large house behind which I could place Borzag where the Dwarfs couldn't see him. He could remain here until my first turn, when he would be able to fly up to safety. Once airborne, he could hover above the battlefield until I was ready for him to dive back down to deal with Bill's cannon!

The rest of my army set up on and around the large hill close to Borzag's lair. My artillery was positioned on the hill itself, from where it would have a commanding view of the battlefield. When it was set out, my battleline consisted of the trolls and Gorblum on the right, then a regiment of Night Goblin archers. Next to them were the Orcs, and finally the second regiment of Night Goblins on the left. The trolls were on the right of the line so that they could work round the Dwarfs' flank if they got the chance. Trolls are almost as fast as cavalry, and can be used to threaten an opponent's flank in much the same way as mounted troops. The Night Goblin archers were set up evenly along the line to make sure that I

would be able to launch some Goblin fanatics at the Dwarfs wherever they might set up. In addition, as they were subject to *hatred* of Dwarfs, the Night Goblins on the left flank should hold out against any enemies that might attack them as they hopefully wouldn't break even if they were beaten in hand-to-hand combat. The Orcs simply fitted into the gap left between the Night Goblins. The final model I set up was 'Mikira' – my army standard bearer, who I carefully positioned to be within 12" of all of my troops (with the exception of Borzag, who was quite capable of looking after himself).

When I saw Bill's set up I was more than pleased as it fitted in perfectly with my plans. Hopefully I would be able to ignore the Troll Slayers, Crossbows and Thunderers off to my left, and concentrate all of my attention on the three regiments of Dwarf Clansmen to my front. The only exception to this would be Borzag's quick flight to the Dwarfs' rear to deal with their single cannon, after which he would be able to return to the main attack. The bolt thrower didn't bother me very much, as it was not quite powerful enough to do much damage to Borzag and his lizard mount. However, as anyone will tell you, there's a big difference between having a plan and putting it into action, especially with an Orc and Goblin army...

CHOOSING THE DWARF FORCE
(Bill King)

My choice of units was pretty much dictated by the forces we have available in the Studio. Not that I'm complaining, I have long admired Wayne England's Dwarf army and was thrilled at the chance of using it on the field of Warhammer Battle.

For my confrontation with Jervis I chose to build my force around three large units of infantry. I would have liked units of Veterans or Clansmen armed with spears, but we just did not have the painted models. I wasn't too worried though, even the most basic Dwarf infantry are a match for the best combat units of most other armies. To improve them further, I upgraded each unit so that it was equipped with heavy armour as well as a shield. I then organised my troops into blocks of twenty models, including standards and champions, to enable them to get the maximum possible rank bonus. I was pretty confident that my stalwart warriors would be able to look after themselves, after all they had good armour, a weapon skill of 4 and a toughness of 4. With the addition of a few good magical items I was sure they could do the business.

My next choice was a unit of 10 Troll Slayers. They are among the most colourful and characterful of Dwarf troops and I like the look of them on the tabletop. I also fancied that their complete immunity to almost every form of psychology would come in handy when faced with any fear-causing monsters such as a wyvern or trolls.

Given a choice, I would have taken more than 10 each of Crossbowmen and Thunderers but here again I was limited by the painted models available. Missile-equipped Dwarf troops often come as a nasty surprise to their foes. Typically they are

equipped with weapons that cannot move and fire but since Dwarfs tend to fight in a stolid fashion, this is less of a disadvantage than for other races. The fact that both the guns and crossbows hit with a strength of 4 and have nasty saving throw modifiers can make them deadly when used en-masse. Tragically I just did not have sufficient miniatures available to demonstrate this fact.

Lastly I took the cannon and the bolt thrower. These were chosen on the grounds that they were the only artillery pieces available. My own preference would have been for a massed battery of cannons to pound the oncoming foe and a bolt thrower to snipe at large enemy units or models. Once again, alas it was not to be. Still, as has been pointed out before, real generals rarely have the choice of what forces to take against an enemy. I was just going to have to make do. It also has to be said that I'd fought Jervis's Orc and Goblin horde once before using this same army and given them a good sound thrashing.

As we are currently in the process of revising Dwarf Rune Magic for the Dwarf army book, we decided not to use it. Magic systems are notoriously prone to being unbalanced during the testing stage and we wanted a fair and even battle. We therefore agreed to use the tried and tested system from Warhammer Magic for this conflict. No doubt astute readers will have noticed that there is no Dwarf magic in the Battle Magic box. Could it be that I had been subtly tricked by my devious opponent? Actually no. Due to their innate resistance to magical energies, Dwarfs are able to use any dispel cards they pick up on a die roll of 4+, no matter what the magic level of the opposing wizard. While I couldn't have any spellcasters, I was allowed to choose any magical items from the Battle Magic set. And in theory, I am as capable of picking decent magic items as Jervis so although I wasn't too thrilled by the prospect of having no offensive spellcasters on my side, I consoled myself with the thought that the points I saved by having no magician could be well spent elsewhere.

Since I didn't have enough missile troops to begin a long range exchange with the greenskinned scum, I reckoned that my doughty longbeards should advance upon the Orc lines as fast as their stumpy legs could carry them. Their objective would be to carry the war straight to the enemy. I therefore picked my magic items accordingly. My general Thorgrim Greybeard was given *Armour of Protection*. and a *Giant Blade* This magic weapon gave him a strength of 7, which would enable him to damage even the largest of monsters. The magic armour, which allowed him to re-roll any failed saving throws with a 4 or better chance of success, would also help to keep him alive.

The army standard bearer was given a *Banner of Arcane Protection*. Since I lacked a magic user and consequently any dispel scrolls, I was a little paranoid about magical attacks from any Orc or Goblin Shaman. I intended to keep this standard with Thorgrim and his Guards to ensure that I would have at least one unit with a good chance of surviving any devastating magic. It later turned out that this was a wise decision. The standard bearer was also given a *Hydra Blade* which meant that any successful hit became D6 hits. Given a warrior with 2 attacks, a weapon skill of 5 and a strength of 4, this seemed like a good bet. For the more statistically minded among you it would usually manage around 4 strength 4 hits per round of close combat. This should put paid to most foes.

I decided on a *War Banner* for Borri's Iron Helms, to give them that slight edge in battle and a *Rending Blade* for Borri himself. This doubles any damage inflicted and would give him that extra bit of killing power.

THORGRIM'S DWARF COMMAND

Thorgrim's Guard: 20 Dwarf Clansmen – heavy armour, shields and hand weapons, including a champion and standard bearer.
Thorgrim – Dwarf General, *Giant Blade, Armour of Protection.* **Army Standard Bearer** – *Hydra Blade.*

Gharth's Oakshields: 20 Dwarf Clansmen – heavy armour, shields and hand weapons, including a champion and standard bearer.

Iron Helms: 20 Dwarf Clansmen – heavy armour, shields and hand weapons, including **Borri** – Dwarf champion armed with a *Rending Blade* and standard bearer carrying a *War Banner.*

Dwarf Cannon: 3 crew armed with hand weapons and light armour.

Dwarf Bolt Thrower: 3 crew armed with hand weapons and light armour.

Thunderers: 10 Dwarfs armed with arquebus, hand weapons and light armour.

Crossbowmen: 10 Dwarfs armed with crossbows, hand weapons and light armour.

Troll Slayers: 10 Dwarfs armed with hand weapons.

Total Points   **2000**

THE DWARF PLAN

The plan was reasonably straightforward. The hill on my table edge would provide a sound firing position for my missile troops and enable them to see and hit anything advancing across the open ground towards my army. More to the point, it would enable me to bring the maximum number of missile troops to bear with the Crossbows firing over the heads of the Thunderers placed at the foot of the hill. The Thunderers were the most advanced because they have the shortest range. The cannon and the bolt thrower were also positioned on the hill in an elevated position.

I placed the Troll Slayers in front of the hill to block any enemy that might advance on my vulnerable missile troops. These fearsome warriors could be expected to tie up almost any foe for a fair amount of time.

The remaining bulk of my infantry units were positioned to the left of the hill, in the centre of my table edge. They formed a compact mass that would enable them to swivel and face any threat. My general and the army standard bearer were also positioned centrally where their influence would be felt by my entire army.

As mentioned above, my plan was quite simple. I didn't have enough troops to fight a missile duel with Jervis so I planned on advancing my infantry into battle as fast as I could. Gharth's Oakshields, the central unit of the three infantry regiments, was assigned the unenviable task of drawing out any fanatics. It was to be moved slightly in advance of the rest of my army in order to do this. I did not have any cheap troops available to lure out those demented gobbo fiends, so sadly it fell to these doughty warriors. They lived only to die in droves. This was why I did not give them any magic items.

I felt that if I could actually get into battle with Jervis without taking too many casualties, then my stout Dwarf soldiers were more than capable of overcoming his force in a straight fight. Warrior for warrior we were more than a match for those greenskinned scum. That was it then. Given a choice it was not the force or the plan I would have chosen but…

DEPLOYMENT MAP

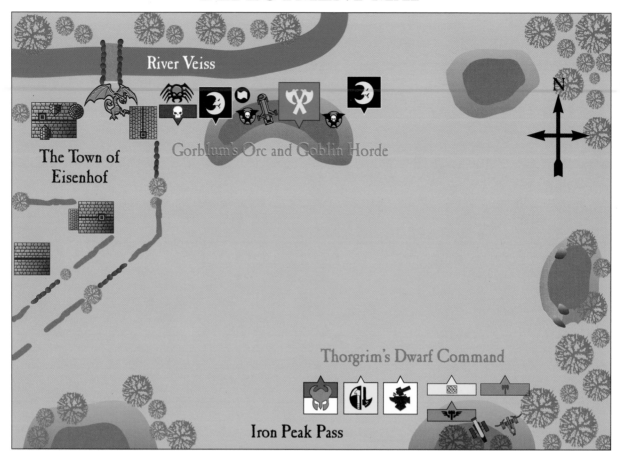

River Veiss

The Town of
Eisenhof

Gorblum's Orc and Goblin Horde

N

Thorgrim's Dwarf Command

Iron Peak Pass

THE TWO OPPOSING ARMIES LINE UP FOR BATTLE.

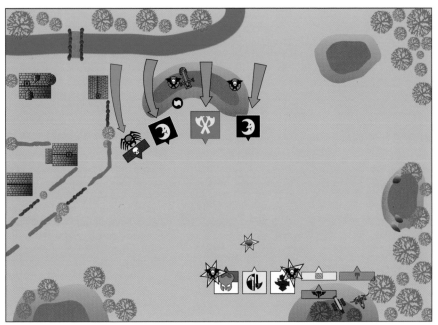

ORC TURN 1.

ORC AND GOBLIN TURN ONE

The Orc and Goblin army began its attack with unnerving calm and efficiency, untroubled by the animosity that so often disrupts an Orc general's plans before they have even begun. The Orcs, trolls and both regiments of Night Goblins marched forward and formed a solid battleline in front of the large hill, screening the army's valuable artillery. With a triumphant yell and the slap of leathery wings, Borzag took to the air on his war wyvern, climbing high above the battlefield and circling round his advancing forces.

Meanwhile, the crew of the Orcs' man mangler had been carefully estimating the range to Gharth's Oakshields, and gleefully released the first of their rain of rocks onto the Dwarfs' heads. Unfortunately, their range estimation proved to be somewhat out and the rock landed a good dozen yards short of the target. Then with a mighty 'twaaaaang!', the first two Goblin doom divers hurtled high into the sky. The tiny shrieking figure spiralled through the air before plummeting back to the ground in a terrifying dive. Steering themselves as they fell, the doom divers proved far more accurate than the Orcs' stone thrower. Thorgim's Guard and Borri's Iron Helms were both struck and several Dwarfs were killed outright. A mighty Waaagh! echoed across the battlefield. First blood to the Orcs!

From his position high above the battlefield, Borzag could just hear the distant cries, and smiled grimly. Although he was too far away to draw on the Waaagh!

energy of the Boyz, they seemed to be doing well enough without him. In any case they would have to do without his magic until he had destroyed the only thing in the Dwarf army he feared – the Dwarfs' ancient but extremely deadly cannon…

DWARF TURN 1

With a metallic clatter of wargear, the Dwarf army advanced, the bold Oakshields forming the centre point of a powerful wedge. As they marched forward their banners fluttered proudly in the breeze but their grim expressions told of the struggle to come.

Thorgrim's heart swelled as he surveyed his troops ranged out on either side. His keen eyes scanned the sky watching the circling wyvern. He knew that given a chance he would deal death to the great lizard and its sorcerous rider. At the end of the line, with much jeering and shaking of fists, the Troll Slayers began their long trot towards the distant foe.

From the hilltop the cannon belched forth a cloud of smoke and flame, sending a giant granite ball bouncing through the Orc regiment's lines. The shrieks of dying Orcs filled the air. The surviving Orcs ducked as a bolt from the bolt thrower slashed through the air above their heads. Coughing and spluttering, their eyes watering from the cannon's gout of powdersmoke, the Dwarf crossbowmen and Thunderers opened fire and hit not a single thing. The Night Goblins flinched and gibbered at the sound of musket fire but their leaders drove them forward.

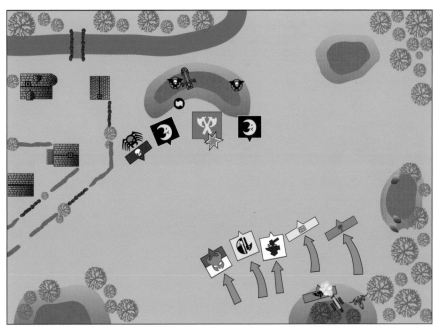

DWARF TURN 1.

ORC TURN 2.

ORC AND GOBLIN TURN TWO

The Orc advance, which had been working perfectly so far, suddenly ground to a halt. An almighty ruck broke out amongst the Orcs, bringing the regiment to a standstill until Skargash bashed a few heads together and restored order. Unfortunately the wild cries emanating from the Orcs confused the trolls, who stopped their march to scratch their heads and watch the Orcs fight amongst themselves. The two regiments of Night Goblins, desperate to inflict some harm on their hated enemy, carried on with the advance. As Sleekid's Boyz closed with the Dwarfs, three crazed figures broke from their ranks, dragging heavy ball and chains behind them. Slowly at first, and then with ever increasing speed, they spun the balls round their heads and launched themselves at the Dwarfs. Two of the Goblin fanatics smashed into the Oakshields, hurling broken and bloodied Dwarf bodies in the air and destroying the entire front rank at a stroke. The third fanatic headed towards Thorgim at the head of his Guards.

Wa-Kurran's Boyz also continued their advance, firing at the Iron Helms as they marched. However, the puny arrows of the Goblins' short bows proved no match for the stout Dwarfs and their thick armour, and not a single Dwarf warrior fell to the hail of Goblin arrows that rained down upon them. The Orcs' artillery proved equally as ineffective, the stone thrower and one doom diver being wildly off-target, while the second doom diver suffered a catastrophic accident at take-off which destroyed the doom diver catapult.

Then, like a thunderbolt from the blue, Borzag plummeted down from the sky onto the Dwarf cannon. The crew tried to defend their beloved gun, but two were ripped apart by the wyvern and the third hacked down by Borzag. With a horrible squawk of triumph the wyvern grabbed the ancient cannon and effortlessly flipped it over, crushing the bodies of the Dwarf crew under the weapon they had tried to protect. Borzag chuckled as he glanced over his shoulder back towards the Orc army's battleline. He was still too far away to use the power of the Waaagh! just yet, but with the Dwarfs' cannon destroyed he could safely rejoin the Boyz. How the despised Dwarfs would suffer when they felt the power of his mighty Orc magic!

DWARF TURN 2

Gasping and panting the Troll Slayers continued to trot forward, more determined than ever to get to grips with the hated enemy. Seeing the wyvern wreaking such havoc on the cannon crew the Thunderers turned about, hoping for a clear shot at the rampaging beast. Menaced by the oncoming fanatics the Dwarfs held fast, showing stalwart bravery in the

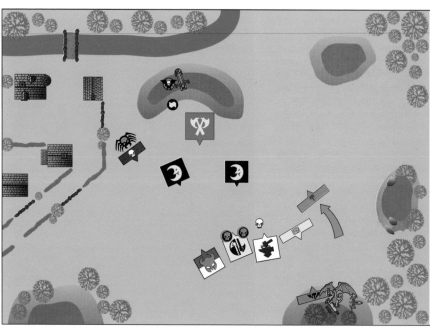

DWARF TURN 2.

THE WAR WYVERN SWOOPS DOWN TO ATTACK THE DWARF CANNON.

face of such a deadly threat. Knowing that the gaze of their general rested upon them, not a Dwarf showed any sign of unsteadiness.

Their stalwart bravery struck fear into the Goblins' hearts. The greenskins knew that here was an enemy who stood firm in the face of near certain death.

Hastily the bolt thrower commander bellowed his frantic orders and the crew swivelled their weapon to face the wyvern. The musty leathery stench of the great beast filled his nostrils, the baleful howls of the power-drunk shaman assailed his ears, but calmly he took aim. The mighty bolt hissed through the air and for a moment the Dwarfs' hearts leapt as the bolt flew straight and true. Strong enough to tear through massed ranks, the mighty missile glanced off the beast's iron-tough hide as gasps of dismay rasped from the Dwarf lines.

Despite the sounds of battle coming from behind them, the crossbowmen held fast. Ignoring the screams of the dying and the awful inhuman din of rending metal, they took careful aim at the fanatic whirling towards their leader Thorgrim. On their sergeant's bellowed command they let fly their missiles. The fanatic fell, pin-cushioned by black feathered bolts. A ragged cheer went up from the Dwarfs.

DEADLY GOBLIN FANATICS HURTLE TOWARDS THE DWARF ARMY.

ORC AND GOBLIN TURN THREE

Having restored order among his command, Skargash marched his Orcs forward to join the rest of the battleline. To their right, the trolls moved up to advance alongside the Wa-Kurran's Night Goblin archers and on the left flank, Sleekid

and his Goblins stood firm, anchoring the Goblin line. As Wa-Kurran's Night Goblins closed in on the Dwarfs, three more Goblin fanatics burst from their ranks and hurtled towards the Dwarf lines. No less than five Goblin fanatics were now whirling around and amongst the embattled Dwarfs.

The first of them smashed into Borri's Iron Helms, crashing through their ranks and killing six Dwarf warriors. To their right, a second crazed Goblin tore through both the Oakshields and Thorgrim's Guard, but with iron discipline, the stout warriors opened ranks to create a path for the delirious Goblin and only one warrior fell to his death-dealing ball and chain. Two other fanatics failed to reach their targets and the last one span off back towards the Goblin lines in demented confusion.

Meanwhile, up on the hill to the rear of the Orc lines, signs of disipline were sadly lacking amongst the crew of the Orc stone thrower. It all started when Grotsnak (in charge of the rocks) attempted to tell Korglum (in charge of the firing lever) how to do his job. Before Korglum or the weapon's Big Boss could

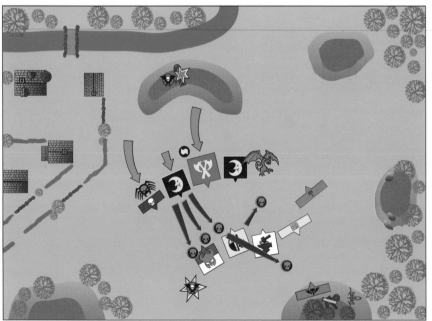

ORC TURN THREE

DWARF TURN THREE

wreak revenge with axe and hammer and blade.

Seeing the wyvern alight in front of them, the Troll Slayers let out a great cry and redoubled their efforts to close the gap with the foe. On the shouted command, the Thunderers turned smartly on the spot to bring their weapons to bear once more on the Night Goblins and Borzag. Soon their guns would spit death at the Goblins!

Determined to avenge their fallen kinsmen, the Crossbows and bolt thrower crew opened fire on the wyvern. A hail of bolts buzzed through the air around the shaman, but some evil god protected him and not a single missile found the mark. Propelled from the war machine, a great bolt buried itself deep into the hide of the wyvern but failed to bring the beast down. Bellowing with pain and anger, the terrible monster plucked the shaft from its scaly hide and cast it contemptuously upon the ground.

For the first time Thorgrim felt the grip of fear. With whispered words, he prayed to Shalya for deliverance this day.

ORC AND GOBLIN TURN FOUR

The Goblin fanatics that still besieged the Dwarf battleline made it impossible for the other Orc and Goblin regiments to do anything other than stand and watch. This they did happily, cheering on the fanatics and bellowing loud "yaaargh!" and "bleeeeagh" as the deranged gobbos smashed into the packed

stop him, Grotsnak had grabbed hold of the stone thrower's firing lever. "No, no, no!" said Grotsnak, "You don't want to do it like *that*, you want to do it like *this*... Oooops! Look boyz... the firing lever's come off in me hand. Ur... Boss, what are you doing with that cleaver? Boss... it was only a jok...(swish-chop-THUNK)." And with that poor old Grotsnak's head bounced off to join the pile of rocks he had, until recently, been in charge of. Completely distracted by the mayhem around the stone thrower, the doom diver launched from the single remaining catapult but despite a frantic flapping of his wings, he fell way off target.

On the opposite side of the battlefield Borzag took off from the hill and swooped back over the Dwarf lines to rejoin the the rest of the army. Almost immediately he began to feel the Waaagh! energy course through his body. He hadn't enough power to cast any spells yet, but soon he would have, and then he knew the pitiful Dwarfs would be doomed!

DWARF TURN 3

As more and more fanatics streamed forth from the Night Goblin units, the Dwarfs resolutely held firm, determined to give no inch of ground. With grim faces, the Dwarfs paid no heed to the appalling casualties inflicted by the gibbering, ball-wielding maniacs. Though sweat beaded many a proud Dwarf brow, not a warrior flinched as heavy metal death swept by, mere inches away. Dishonour was more terrible than death for these doughty fighters and so they anchored themselves to the spot, praying for a chance to get to grips with their jeering foes, determined to

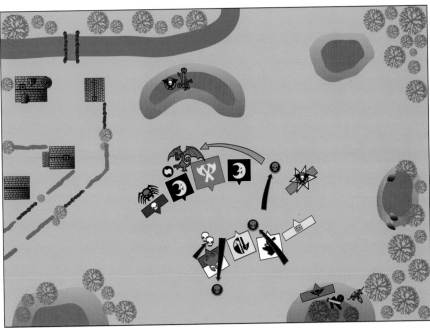

ORC TURN FOUR

BITTER HAND-TO-HAND FIGHTING ERUPTS BETWEEN THE TWO ARMIES.

Dwarf ranks. Now completely out of control, two of the fanatics crashed into each other, wrapping the balls and chains around their twisted and broken limbs – much to the amusement of the rest of the Boyz. Another one careered into the Iron Helms, killing another three Dwarfs and the fourth smashed into Thorgim's Guard from behind, killing four stout warriors. The Night Goblins added to the mayhem by firing at the Dwarfs with their short bows, and were rewarded for their persistance as one of the Borri's Iron Helms fell to their arrows. Even the Goblin doom diver was on target, smashing into the Dwarf Troll Slayers and killing two of them.

Borzag, determined to gather sufficient Waaagh! energy from the army, had moved to the centre of the Orc battle line. Surrounded on all sides by cheering Orc and Goblin warriors his body began to crackle with barely contained power.

Calling on the mighty Orc war gods Mork and Gork, he unleashed the pent up force, creating a gigantic glowing vortex of energy in the shape of a giant foot, ready to stomp down and crush his foes. But his cry of triumph quickly turned to one of despair and anguish, as the spell was dissipated by the magical resistance of the Dwarf warriors. The Orc shaman cursed and spit, but he knew their resistance couldn't save them forever. Mork would smile and he would destroy them all with his next spell!

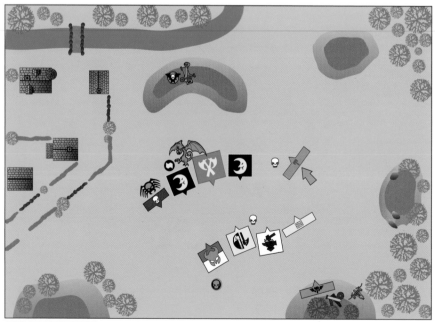

DWARF TURN FOUR

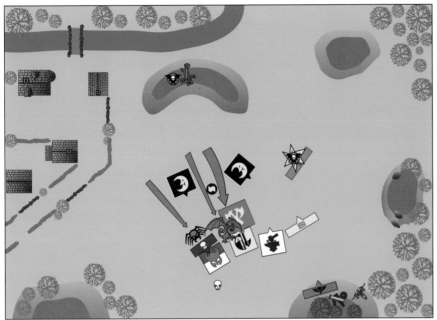

ORC TURN FIVE.

ORC AND GOBLIN TURN 5

As if realising that his job was now over, the last Goblin fanatic collapsed, his ball and chain wrapped firmly round his neck, leaving the path clear for the Orcs to attack. From high above the battlefield a doom diver made his screaming descent, crashing into the Troll Slayers and killing one of the doughty warriors.

Then, with a huge cry of "Waaaaaaaaaaargh!" Skargash and his Boyz, and the now furious Borzag on his wyvern, charged at the Oakshields. To their right, the trolls, urged on by Gorblum, also dashed forward into the shattered remnants of the once proud Iron Helms. The Night Goblins on each flank held their positions to

DWARF TURN 4

Hearts pounding and breath coming in heavy gasps, the Troll Slayers continued to jog towards their opponents. They gnashed their teeth, shook their fists and jeered at the wyvern as it fled to its perch amid the Goblin horde but were unable to close the distance. As they moved forward, Grunnir, their leader, spat a great moist gobbet of saliva in the direction of the approaching Night Goblin fanatic and gripped his axe. On Thorgrim's command the rest of the now depleted Dwarf army readied itself to receive the charge of the howling greenskins and their shambling troll lackeys.

For the first time in the battle the Thunderers discharged their weapons. A hail of iron cut down the fanatic who was now menacing the Troll Slayers. With a desolate scream, the dying Goblin fell to the ground. As he released his grip on the great metal ball, it arched towards the Troll Slayers, thudding into the ground near Grunnir's feet.

Back on the hill, the Crossbows attempted to cover their embattled brethren. Some of them killed the fanatic whizzing about in the open ground between the two armies, while a volley from the remainder only managed to cut down a solitary Night Goblin archer. Behind them, the commander of the bolt thrower took careful aim as he lined up his war machine on the Orc shaman. Quickly he performed the complex calculations of range on his fingers and then let fly. As the deadly missile flew straight and true, the triumphant Dwarf punched his fist into the air, only to have his hopes dashed to despair when the bolt glanced off the shaman's armour. Long and loud were the curses that scorched the air round the Dwarf war engine.

As if in answer to this close call the shaman raised his arms and howled an invocation to Gork and Mork. His eyes glowed green, a nimbus of light played round his body and his guttural words reverberated like thunder over the battlefield. An enormous scaly foot took shape over Thorgrim's unit and then began its inexorable descent. The runes on the Dwarf army standard glowed bright as the nightmare magic came down. For a moment the foot hovered there, like a multi-ton weight suspended from a crane, then it vanished in a disintegrating cloud of jade sparks.

protect the flanks of the Orcs and trolls.

The trolls were the first to reach the Dwarfs, their long legs carrying them improbably quickly for such large monsters. They crashed into the Iron Helms, killing two of the remaining Dwarf warriors with their powerful fists and clubs.

The Dwarfs who remained fought back ferociously – Troll Slayer blood must have run in their veins – and, although none of the trolls fell to the Dwarfs' swords and hammers, they did stop the charge in its tracks. For the merest moment the trolls hesitated and it seemed that they might break and run, but the presence of Gorblum and the soothing effects of his Crown of Command won the day, and the trolls returned to the fray.

The Orcs' charge was devastating. As his regiment charged the Dwarfs, Skargash swigged back his *Potion of Strength* and with one mighty blow slew Gharth One-Eye, cleaving him from head to groin. Borzag vented his frustration at the failure of his spells by smiting left and right with his *Blade of Darting Steel*, while his wyvern tore Dwarfs apart limb from limb.

The Dwarfs tried to hold the charge, but they didn't really stand a chance. Their formation shattered under the ferocity of the Orcs' attack and they were forced back. Faced by the twin

THE WYVERN DESTROYS THE OAKSHIELDS.

DWARF TURN 5.

overflowing with Waaagh! energy. His failure to use his magical abilities very nearly cost the Orcs and Goblins the battle...

DWARF TURN 5

Crossbow bolts hissed through the air and several of the hooded archers fell shrieking to their deaths. In the gathering darkness the Troll Slayers realised that they would soon get to grips with an enemy and let out a great howl of joy.

Ignoring the fleeing remnants of the Oakshields, Thorgrim and his Guards siezed their opportunity and charged into the flank of the Orcs. Thorgrim's mighty hammer crunched into the greenskins. Bones splintered and skulls were turned to jelly by the impact. Four howling Orcs died under its might, as the Dwarf general single-handedly tried to avenge his fallen kinsmen. Beside him his personal standard bearer hewed into the foe, protecting his leader's back and cutting down two more Orcs. In spite of their leader's brave example and the hatred they felt for their enemies, the rest of the Dwarfs failed to inflict a single casualty despite being locked in a bloody struggle to the death with the Orcs.

horrors of the war wyvern and the Skargash's *Shrieking Blade*, they broke and ran. The speed of the Dwarf collapse surprised even Skargash and his Boyz and they stumbled forward only a short distance in pursuit of their beaten enemies. But Borzag, wild with rage and goading his wyvern to a peak of bestial fury, tore into the fleeing Dwarfs and hacked them down to a man. The last thing on the shaman's mind was casting spells, even though his body was charged to

THORGRIM'S GUARDS ATTACK THE ORCS, AS THE IRON HELMS AND OAKSHIELDS BREAK AND FLEE.

Under the impact of the Dwarf charge the Orcs reeled back in confusion. Their magic weapons had availed them not. Their foes were terrible and their onslaught seemed irresistible. For a moment the Orcs wavered and, ignoring Gorblum's shouted commands, a few turned to flee. For an instant the scales of battle seemed about to tip in favour of the Dwarfs. Their stoic endurance was about to be rewarded. Then the Orcs caught sight of their army standard and their reverence for its crude symbol restored their faith. They would not leave it on the field to be captured by their foes. With renewed determination they threw themselves back into the fray. The moment of indecision had passed.

On the Dwarfs' left flank, the pitifiul remnants of the Iron Helms faced the shambling trolls. The few remaining Dwarfs were no match for the great misshapen monsters which had ripped their comrades asunder. Watching their comrades fall to the trolls' irresistible advance, the last three Iron Helms' nerve finally broke and they turned and fled, only to be pulled down by the loping monstrosities.

Darkness had almost fallen now. By the flickering light of the still-burning village, the Dwarfs saw a great scaly hand descend and cast the wyvern and shaman into the battle against Thorgrim's Guard. Sensing the battle was lost Thorgrim and his kinsmen closed ranks and made ready for a desperate last stand. Perhaps under cover of the darkness a messenger might win free and bring word of this terrible defeat to their clan. Singing their deathsongs the Dwarfs made ready to sell their lives dearly.

'ERE WE GO ,'ERE WE GO, 'ERE WE GO!
(Jervis Johnson)

For once things went almost like clockwork, and I must say that I was extremely happy with the way things worked out in the end. In Bill's favour it has to be pointed out that I was very lucky with my dice rolling for the Goblin fanatics. I never rolled less than seven on two dice, and my average roll was nine! With such dice rolls the fanatics did wonderfully well, killing nineteen Dwarfs and bringing Bill's attack to a complete standstill. None the less I did learn a number of valuable lessons which will certainly prove useful the next time I play with an Orc and Goblin army.

On the whole the troops I selected performed well and there isn't very much that I would change. However, the fact that Borzag needed to be within 12" of an Orc or Goblin unit to draw power cards meant that he couldn't cast spells in four out of the ten magic phases in the game. I therefore wasn't able use him as effectively as I would have liked. In future I may take an Orc general or Big Boss on the war wyvern who can concentrate on causing mayhem in hand- to-hand combat, and allow Borzag to fight on foot so that he can stay with the Boyz. All my other characters performed magnificently, especially Gorblum who kept the trolls well under control, and whose presence nearby (along with the army standard bearer) stopped my Orcs from routing on the last turn of the game!

I've already mentioned how well the fanatics did, but this needs to be measured against the lack of success of my artillery, which cost almost 300 points and managed to kill only five Dwarfs. This was partially down to my range estimation (which is usually quite good) consistently being about an inch short. Even taking this into account, my artillery did very badly considering the inviting massed targets that they were presented with. As it was, in this game it didn't matter too much, because the fanatics made up for it, and that was a very valuable lesson for me. In previous games I have sometimes used a lot of fanatics *or* a lot of artillery, but I have never used a lot of fanatics *and* a lot of artillery. Both troops types have the potential to win the game for you, but their effect can be a bit random. However, by increasing the numbers of these types of troops you can even out the odds, increasing the chance that one or more of them will do something decisive. In this game the fanatics did well, in the next game it may be the artillery that will do well, and I can't wait for the game where they *both* do well...

My 'elite' regiment of Orcs performed better than I could have hoped. However, if the unit had taken just a few more casualties earlier in the game, it's less certain that they would have managed to break the Oakshields. As a result, in future games, I will definitely increase the number of models in this regiment. I am also very tempted to get a unit of Black Orcs to perform in the role of shock troops, instead of ordinary Orc warriors. Not only do Black Orcs have a higher weapon skill and strength than ordinary Boyz, but they also don't suffer from animosity, which means that you can be sure that they will do what you want, when you want.

Turning my attention to the other side of the table, there is not much I can fault with Bill's tactics – he did the best he could under very difficult circumstances. I think his only real mistake was concentrating his missile fire on Borzag, who he had very little chance of wounding, let alone killing. If my Orcs had only take a few more casualties then they would not have automatically routed the Oakshields, and the game may have turned out rather differently. In any case, the next time I face Bill's army I am sure that it will have been strengthened by more artillery and crossbows, which will make it a much tougher nut to crack.

THORGRIM'S LAMENT
(Bill King)

Curse those Goblin fanatics and the greenskins that spawned them! May carrion birds feast on their entrails and may their spirits wander endlessly through the cold dark void until the end of time. Today they cost the Dwarf realms dear. A monumental defeat must be recorded in the Book of Grudges.

At first I thought this battle a disaster so humiliating that I was going to have to shave my head and become a Troll Slayer. But, after long hours of futile brooding and muttering, I have come to the conclusion that it was not my fault. It was those accursed fanatics that did for my proud warriors. Less astute readers might have come to the conclusion that I was comprehensively thrashed by a superior general, but let me assure that this was not so.

At first glance you might think that Jervis's plan of using large fear-inspiring forces like that band of Orcs was a brilliant masterstroke. I admit that it has a certain low cunning but you'll notice that it actually relies on his units outnumbering my units. Given the relative sizes of our forces this was actually not all that likely. My infantry blocks each had 20 warriors. After taking casualties from my cannon his Orcs only had 21. If I had killed a few more Orcs then his entire strategy would have been neutralised. Certainly without the casualties inflicted by the fanatics, the trolls would never have automatically broken the Iron Helms. It was the fact that his fanatics whittled my units down to size that enabled him to break the two units he did.

As it was, the fanatics inflicted most of the casualties I took during the course of the battle. They weakened my force to the point where it could be overcome in melee. I reckon this was just about the only way those sneaky gobbos could overcome my true-hearted Dwarf warriors.

The wyvern was a threat that I couldn't really do much about once it had eaten my cannon crew. Because of the beast's high toughness, the cannon was the only weapon that could have harmed it with any certainty. Destroying the cannon was another typically underhanded Orc trick. Jervis picked on the one thing on the battlefield aside from my general that had any real chance of hurting his pet. Where's the honour in that, I ask you? Afterwards, you'll notice, the slimy overgrown lizard kept well away from Thorgrim. And just as well for it, I might add.

I must admit I was a bit surprised by the way Jervis set up his troops. The bulk of his force faced the left flank of my army. This illustrates one of the major weaknesses of a Dwarf army – its complete lack of speed. Since the Troll Slayers could not really redeploy fast enough to meet the Orcs' advance, they effectively did nothing for the whole game. They spent most of the battle jogging towards the foe and never really got to take part in the fight.

I was also less than pleased with my missile troops. Perhaps if they had spent less time shooting ineffectually at the wyvern and more time shooting at the Orcs then the disaster that befell the Oakshields might have been avoided. On the other hand I can understand why they did it. The wyvern was large and threatening and seemed perfectly capable of rampaging anywhere on the battlefield. Also there was the little matter of avenging the loss of the cannon.

There were some things to give praise to Grungni for. The stalwart Dwarf infantry managed to soak up what would have been catastrophic casualties for almost any other army and still hang in there for a final melee they could have won. Thorgrim's Guard could easily have broken the Orc infantry in that last melee. Indeed the Orcs had to make a break test of 5 or less and they only succeeded because of their army standard allowing them a re-roll. If the Orcs had fled it would have been more or less down to the trolls and the wyvern versus Thorgrim's Guard. It's possible that breaking the Orcs could have caused the Goblins to flee in panic as well. This would have given me some much needed victory points. Well – we might have won.

In conclusion, this was rather a frustrating battle for me. Basically, my army absorbed incredible amounts of punishment for four turns and then went down to glorious defeat on the fifth. My missile troops were mainly ineffective mostly due to the fact that I concentrated their fire inordinately on the wyvern and its rider. I might have been better advised to shoot up the Orcs. Conversely, everything went right for Jervis. His fanatics performed awesomely well and the 5 or less leadership test that his Orc unit made in the final melee robbed Thorgrim of his one great moment of glory. Still, lessons were learned. Next time I will be prepared.

So, a tragic defeat is recorded in the great Book of Grudges. Thorgrim and his brave warriors have gone to join the ancestors. It matters not – in the end vengeance will be mine.

The final ringing echoes of steel on steel had faded. With a crash, the last burning building fell to the ground in a shower of smoke and sparks. Eisenhof was now a smouldering ruin. Only embers and ash remained to show that a town had once stood on this site. The last dwarfs had fallen. Their mutilated corpses lay in great heaps upon the ground. Perhaps a few had fled into the darkness or had been lost beneath the piled bodies. Borzag raised his clawed hand and fitful green light illuminated the scene. He bared his tusks in a satisfied snarl. He was well pleased with the day's fighting. He had claimed more stunty beards to be woven into his cloak. Thorgrim's army had been overcome.

Gorblum stood atop of one of the corpse mounds and ranted to his followers. A blood-spattered blue cloak ripped from the shoulders of one of the dwarf captains was draped round his shoulders. His voice was filled with mad self-confidence as he outlined his scheme for marching on the lands of men and overthrowing their cities. Only the trolls listened, hypnotised by the crown's glitter. Their eyes, great empty pits in which tiny pupils glittered, were turned on him with fixed idiot attention.

All around drunken orcs and goblins strutted and pranced. Many clutched jacks of ale and foul orc brew in their fists. Sleekid had a plundered stunty helm set askew upon his head. Here and there goblins fought mock duels with captured hammers. Borzag did not doubt by the time the night was over, some duels would be being fought for real. Tempers would flare and word would be said. Borzag had seen it all before. Two orcs wrestled in the mud, locked in a dispute over who would have possession of a captured gold chain. It was the way. To the strong went the best plunder. The weak got nothing.

From behind Borzag came a hideous gnashing of teeth and slobbering as the wyvern feasted on the last of the troll slayer corpses. Tonight it would sleep well, its belly filled with red dwarf meat. Tonight Borzag would have to be particularly careful of enemies within his own army's ranks. With the wyvern in digestive torpor, he would have one less protection against assassination.

Borzag had to admit that the stunties had fought well. He would not have expected them to hold out so long. He doubted that even black orcs would have stayed around after taking the casualties that the fanatics had inflicted. Borzag had inspected the jellied remains of one dwarf who had been hit with a steel ball. The resulting damage had been quite awesome.

Wa-Kurran emerged from the gloom. "Did you find him? Did you find the stunty boss?" Borzag asked. The goblin shook his head. Borzag gave him a taste of boot. So Thorgrim had escaped. Well, it did not matter. Borzag was sure their paths would cross again. He could kill the stunty chief another day. For now he was pleased. Word of this victory would spread through the woods and over the mountains to wherever orcs and goblins gathered. Soon they would flock to Gorblum's banner, and then Borzag would have an army that could trample the kingdoms of men and of dwarfs into the dust.

His day was coming. He knew it.

GOBLINS

Goblins fight in large units called Mobs. The bigger the Mob the better it fights, because the Goblins at the back push the others forward and the enemy is overwhelmed by sheer weight of numbers. The chances of succsses are vastly improved with the addition of a good Boss and a banner to follow.

GOBLIN WITH SWORD

GOBLIN CHAMPION

GOBLIN STANDARD BEARER

WITH SPIKED CLUB

WITH AXE

WITH SPEAR

WITH SPEAR

A REGIMENT OF GOBLINS WITH STANDARD BEARER AND CHAMPION

NIGHT GOBLINS

NETTERS

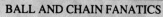

BALL AND CHAIN FANATICS

NETTER CLUBBERS

NIGHT GOBLIN DOOM DIVERS

SHAMAN

A SELECTION OF CAVE SQUIGS

SQUIG HUNTERS

NIGHT GOBLINS

LEADER

CHAMPION

GOBLIN WITH WAR GONG

BANNER BEARER

A COMPLETE SQUIG HUNTER TEAM

SQUIG HUNTERS

CAVE SQUIGS

RIVER TROLLS

River Trolls are amongst the most loathsome of all varieties of Troll found in the Old World. These enormous creatures inhabit dank, wet places such as rivers and marshes. River Trolls catch their prey by covering their bodies in ooze and slime and partially submerging themselves until a hapless victim comes within reach.

Despite their stupidity River Trolls are fearsome opponents and are easily driven into battle by evil creatures such as Orcs and Goblins with the prospect of a juicy titbit.

STONE TROLLS

A FEARSOME BAND OF ORCS AND STONE TROLLS

NIGHT GOBLINS POUR ACROSS A RIVER CROSSING

AN ORC WARBAND LINES UP FOR BATTLE

FOREST GOBLINS AND STONE TROLLS CLASH WITH AN ARMY OF WOOD ELVES

ORCS

ORC BOSS

CHIEFTAIN GORFANG ROTGUT

ORC BANNER BEARER

Gorfang Rotgut is the Chieftain of the Orcs of Black Crag, the ruined Dwarf stronghold at the western end of Death Pass. Gorfang lost an eye at the Battle of the Jaws, fighting against the Dwarfs of Karaz a Karak, and now wears an iron patch to cover the wound. Many of his battles have been fought against Dwarfs, including the siege of Barak Varr and the attack on Karak Azul. As a result of his long struggles, Gorfang has acquired a bitter and utter hatred of the Dwarf race.

DETAIL OF GORFANG

GORFANG ROTGUT LEADING A UNIT OF ORC BOYZ

ORC AND GOBLIN PAINTING GUIDE

Follow this stage-by-stage painting guide carefully and you can pick up useful tips about painting your own miniatures. The models shown are colourful examples of some of the most common troop types in an Orc and Goblin army, plus a finished leader model for that particular unit.

To start off, you will need to cover the entire model with an undercoat. Skull White was ideal for the Orc and the Forest Goblin. The Night Goblin is predominantly black and was therefore given an undercoat of Chaos Black.

Next, apply a basecoat to the models in the areas required. For example Orcs and Goblin skins are green so the skin areas are given a basecoat of Goblin Green. Try to be as neat as possible and concentrate on achieving a smooth and even coat of paint.

When the basecoat is dry, you can add some basic highlighting and shading. Areas of the model can be shaded by applying a wash of the most appropriate ink. The tunic on the Orc for example, was shaded using a wash of Plasma Red Ink. A lighter shade of the base colour was then used to highlight the raised features of the model. The final stage is to paint in any small, detailed areas such as the eyes and other markings and then to texture and paint the base.

The same technique applies to painting the skin areas. For example, the skin on the Night Goblin was painted Skull White, over the Chaos Black undercoat. A basecoat of Goblin Green was applied and then shaded with Waaargh! Green Ink. When this was dry, the raised areas, such as the nose, eyes, fingers and muscles were highlighted with a mixture of Goblin Green and Bad Moon Yellow. The eyes were painted using Blood Red paint, with a small dot of Sunburst Yellow for the pupil.

If you are painting a leader model, the techniques for painting the skin are the same as other troop types. The leader models here have been taken a step further, with more detailed shading and highlighting on areas such as the markings and insignia. It is a good idea to paint parts of the leader a different colour. This will distinguish him from the rank and file troops. The bright yellow hat on the Night Goblin leader is an example of how effective this is.

| STAGE 1 BASECOAT | STAGE 2 SHADING | STAGE 3 COMPLETE | GOBLIN CHAMPION |

| STAGE 1 BASECOAT | STAGE 2 SHADING | STAGE 3 COMPLETE | NIGHT GOBLIN CHAMPION |

| STAGE 1 BASECOAT | STAGE 2 SHADING | STAGE 3 COMPLETE | FOREST GOBLIN CHAMPION |

| STAGE 1 BASECOAT | STAGE 2 SHADING | STAGE 3 COMPLETE | ORC BOSS |

SAVAGE ORCS

Savage Orcs are wild fighters, whooping and screaming as they charge into the attack. They wear wild animal skins and cover their bodies in tattoos and warpaint, which they believe will protect them from enemy arrows and sword blows.

ARRER BOY

WITH SPEAR

WITH SPEAR

ARRER BOYZ

WITH CLUB

WITH STONE AXE

WITH SPIKY CLUB

WITH SPIKY CLUB

WITH STONE CLUB

ARRER BOYZ

SAVAGE ORCS PAINTING GUIDE

Savage Orcs have a wild, primitive look that is very different to the usual, heavily armoured Orc warriors. Their naked flesh is painted and tattooed with primitive designs, and decorated with bones, bangles and the shrunken heads of their enemies. Savage Orcs wield crude weapons, fashioned from wood and stones that have been roughly lashed together. The only clothes they wear are the skins of animals, which further adds to their fearsome appearance.

Units of Savage Orcs provide a colourful contrast to the usual metal-clad Orcs that make up most of the rank and file of an Orc and Goblin army. Their un-regimented appearance gives them a lively sense of action and they look very dynamic on the tabletop. These miniatures are covered in decoration and there is plenty of opportunity to invent creative colour schemes. There are also lots of areas of wood and fur on the models and it's best to paint these in strong bold colours to make them look wild and interesting.

Weapons and Furs

All of the weapons were given a base coat consisting of a mixture of Snakebite Leather and Blood Red paint. I then applied a wash of Skaven Brown ink and highlighted this with Hobgoblin Orange. The stone parts of the weapon were painted to resemble flint to make them look realistic and threatening. First of all, a base coat of Chaos Black was applied and then the sharp edges were picked out, initially in Elf Grey and then with Skull White. This gives the weapons a sharp and dangerous look but retains the primitive feel that is characteristic of the models.

The animal skins were painted in bright, strong colours with lots of distinctive markings. These were rendered in strong colours that contrasted well with the fur. The tiger skin is a good example. The whole pelt is first given a base coat of Spearstaff Brown, which is then shaded down with Rust Brown ink. The ink was applied towards the edges of the area, leaving the base coat showing in the centre. This was then highlighted with Skull White to pick out the fur texture. To create deeper shading in the furthest recesses, take a fine brush and apply Skaven Brown ink sparingly to the fur areas, then blend this into the fur with a second, slightly wet, brush. The stripes are painted on with Chaos Black, in broad bands tapering to a fine point. Try not to space the stripes too close together or add too many as you'll start to obscure the base colour and darken the overall effect.

The main type of decoration on the Savage Orcs are bones and teeth, often strung together to form crude necklaces or primitive clothing. These were painted by first applying a base coat of Skaven Brown ink mixed with Chaos Black in order to create some really sharp contrast. The main colour consisted of Bleached Bone mixed with a little Snakebite Leather to deepen the tone and finally this was highlighted with Bleached Bone and Skull White.

War Paint and Tattoos

The main features of the Savage Orcs which really give them character, are their warpaint and tattoos. Red and blue are the colours that work best as they provide the strongest contrast with the green colour of Orc skin. Even though all the models are individuals with no set uniform, they are visually linked together by the colour of the warpaint, weapons and shields.

As large portions of the faces are going to be covered with warpaint, its best to give only a basic highlight to the skin when it is first painted. Once the warpaint has been applied, it can then be highlighted in the same places as normal, across the cheekbones, the brows, nose, bottom lip and chin. The markings on the faces of our models consist of bold, geometric designs, such as triangles, bands and zig-zags. Be as inventive as you like and use bright colours and striking patterns.

The tattoos on the body are made up of pictograms repeated in a symmetrical pattern over the largest areas of the bare flesh. Skulls, bones, snakes and lightning bolts are fairly common patterns, but there are plenty of other suitable devices. It's best not to make them over-complex as they will become unrecognisable. It's a good idea to stick to one design on a model, any more and the overall effect will be lost. The main feature which gives the Savage Orcs their character is the strong, bold way in which they utilise colours and markings. Similar devices to the tattoos are also used on their shields, and even though each one has a different device and patterned rim, they are linked together by the connected colours.

GLYPHS

These are just a few examples of Orc and Goblin pictograms which are used to decorate their shields, banners, clothing and in the case of Savage Orcs, their bodies. These glyphs may also be used to make up new banner designs or embellish those shown elsewhere in this book.

ORC BESTIARY

ORCS

Orcs vary in height and their physical appearance more than humans – some are no taller than a man but most are substantially larger and the biggest Orcs stand well over seven feet tall. They are also much broader than humans, with big deep chests, massive shoulders and long, powerfully muscled arms. Orcs have large heads with huge jaws but tiny foreheads behind which lurk a thick skull and not very much brain.

Despite their apparent lack of intelligence Orcs are not stupid, although they are rather limited in the way they think and act. They are not the deepest thinkers in the world, but neither are they doubtful or divided. When an Orc wants to do something he simply does it, where a human might spend untold time weighing the alternatives.

The Orcs' single-mindedness is one of their greatest strengths, especially as they enjoy fighting more than anything else. When they're not actually at war, Orcs spend all their time fighting each other to establish rights of leadership. Orc leaders are known as Boss Orcs, but even Boss Orcs fight amongst themselves to decide which of them is the overall leader. This means there are innumerable layers in the Orc pecking order, from Boss to Big Boss, Warboss and Warlord.

A Warlord is an Orc who has established total supremacy over his rivals (having either killed them or driven them away) and now leads all the tribes in glorious conquest over other puny races such as Men, Elves and Dwarfs (Orcs call Elves skinnies and Dwarfs stunties). An Orc's life is therefore spent in constant battle either with his fellow Orcs or against some worthy opponent. This is regarded as a Good Thing by Orcs who are universally content with their lot, being ultimately happy to meet their end in battle so long as they get a chance of a good fight.

The more battles and the more kills an Orc has under his belt the more respect he earns from other Orcs, the more his enemies fear him, and the happier he will be.

Troop Type	M	WS	BS	S	T	W	I	A	Ld
ORC	4	3	3	3	4	1	2	1	7
BOSS ORC	4	4	4	4	4	1	3	2	7
BIG BOSS	4	5	5	4	5	2	4	3	8
WAR BOSS	4	6	6	4	5	3	5	4	9

Troop Type	M	WS	BS	S	T	W	I	A	Ld
SHAMAN	4	3	3	3	5	1	3	1	7
SHAMAN CHAMPION	4	3	3	4	5	2	3	1	7
MASTER SHAMAN	4	3	3	4	5	3	4	2	7
SHAMAN LORD	4	3	3	4	5	4	5	3	8

SPECIAL RULE

PANIC

Orcs expect Goblins to run away and it doesn't really surprise them when this happens. The sight of Goblins running in flight does not upset the Orcs, it simply reminds them why they are better! When a Goblin unit breaks or flees past during the turn, there is no need for the Orcs to test for panic. There is no way that big, tough Orcs are going to panic just because some weedy Goblins run off!

SAVAGE ORCS

There are so many tribes of Orcs that it is impossible to count them, especially as they are constantly breaking up and reforming under the leadership of new ambitious Orc Warlords. Most of these tribes are the common sort of Orc, but there are other kinds as well, including Savage Orcs.

Savage Orcs are not physically different to the great mass of Orcs, except that they like to wear tattoos and warpaint, but they are none-the-less quite distinct. They live in their own tribes and have their own ways of fighting which make them easily distinguishable.

Many hundreds of years ago all Orcs were savages with no means of manufacturing metal weapons, armour and war machines. These primitive Orcs used stone weapons, wooden clubs, and what other weaponry they could steal from more advanced races. When other Orcs began to learn about metal working from the Chaos Dwarfs, a few tribes either missed out or deliberately turned their back on these new ways. These Savage Orcs were happy to continue in their old ways, using metal weapons and armour on occasions when they could steal or trade it, but on the whole sticking to their ancient traditions. Over the years the Savage Orc tribes became increasingly distinct as their brother Orcs continued to develop, until eventually the two kinds were quite different.

Troop Type	M	WS	BS	S	T	W	I	A	Ld
SAVAGE ORC	4	3	3	3	4	1	2	1	7
BOSS ORC	4	4	4	4	4	1	3	2	7
BIG BOSS	4	5	5	4	5	2	4	3	8
WAR BOSS	4	6	6	4	5	3	5	4	9

Troop Type	M	WS	BS	S	T	W	I	A	Ld
SHAMAN	4	3	3	3	5	1	3	1	7
SHAMAN CHAMPION	4	3	3	4	5	2	3	1	7
MASTER SHAMAN	4	3	3	4	5	3	4	2	7
SHAMAN LORD	4	3	3	4	5	4	5	3	8

SPECIAL RULES

PROTECTIVE TATTOOS

Savage Orcs do not usually wear armour although they sometimes obtain it as war booty or trade it from wandering Goblin tribes. They do use shields and these are often made from animal hide. A Savage Orc without body armour will be protected by his unshakeable faith. This is comparable to wearing a mail shirt or breastplate, conferring a D6 saving throw of 6. If the Savage Orc has a shield as well then he has a saving throw of 5 or 6 just as if he had a mail shirt and shield.

Note that this saving throw is not strictly speaking because of armour, and the Orc always has a saving throw of 6 even if he is struck by a weapon that would normally have a saving throw modifier. For example, a two-handed axe deducts -2 from your armour save but a Savage Orc protected by his tattoos still gets a save of 6. This special protection is lost if the Orc wears body armour.

Savage Orcs persist in their savage ways to this day. They continue to sing the praises of the boisterous Orc gods Gork and Mork in their barbarous fashion, holding midnight feasts to consume gallons of Brew and to fight each other under the watchful eyes of their crude idols. In battle they believe so strongly in the power of the Orc gods Gork and Mork to protect them that enemy arrows and swords blows really can be deflected by the Orcs' aura of self-generated arcane power.

It is also possible that the tribal tattoos which Savage Orc Shamans paint onto the Orcs' bodies protect them in some way. This is a very mysterious and wondrous thing, and confirms the Savage Orcs' strong belief in their old and trusty ways. Other Orcs are completely puzzled by this, but the Savage Orcs maintain it is their undivided attention to the tried and tested Orc way of life and the veneration of their ancient gods. Perhaps this is why Savage Orcs are famous for the number and power of their skin-clad bone waving Shamans.

FRENZY

Savage Orcs are wild fighters, whooping and screaming as they attack, calling upon Gork and Mork to help them as they crash into the enemy ranks. Savage Orcs are therefore affected by the rules for *frenzy* described in the main rules. This means that they will charge enemy within reach, and fight with double attacks (two rather than one). See the Warhammer rulebook for details.

PANIC

Just like other Orcs, Savage Orcs expect Goblins to run away and it doesn't really surprise them when this happens. The sight of Goblins running in flight does not upset the Orcs, it simply reminds them why they are better!

When a Goblin unit breaks or flees past during the turn, there is no need for the Savage Orcs to test for panic. There is no way that big, tough Orcs are going to panic just because some weedy Goblins run off!

BLACK ORCS

Black Orcs are the biggest and strongest of all Orcs. They first appeared in the Old World during Sigmar's time, when a whole band crossed the Worlds Edge Mountains and conquered the other Orcs that lived in the hills to the northwest of Stirland. The great hero Sigmar first united the men of the middle Old World into the Empire, and to do so he had to drive out the Orcs and Goblins that lived there. The Black Orcs were the most difficult to defeat, because they were so warlike and determined.

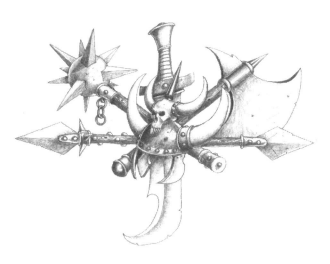

Black Orcs have skin which is black or extremely dark green. They are bigger than normal Orcs and pride themselves on being the best fighters of all. They take war much more seriously than other Orcs, and are usually better armoured and carry more or better weapons. Black Orcs prefer to fight at close quarters, where their brute strength and determination makes them very powerful. They often carry two weapons, one in each hand, rather than a shield, so they can strike their enemies two at a time.

Black Orcs regard other Orcs and Goblins as frivolous and not entirely trustworthy, especially Goblins, who are always running off in battle instead of standing and fighting. When they are not fighting in battle Black Orcs engage each other in head-butting contests to settle minor differences. Disputes which would lead to squabbling or disorganised fighting in other Orcs are therefore settled in a formal way, without causing any unnecessary disruption on the battlefield. Some other Orcs claim that this head-butting has seriously reduced what intelligence Black Orcs might have originally had, but Black Orcs have exceptionally thick skulls and, like all Orcs, they are very resilient.

SPECIAL RULES

ANIMOSITY

Black Orcs are not affected by the squabbling and infighting that characterises other Orcs and Goblins, and never test for animosity. Note that because Black Orcs don't suffer from animosity they cannot be the victims of animosity themselves. This is a new rule, and is different from the Warhammer rulebook.

LEADERS

Black Orcs don't think much of other Orc Bosses. If another Orc or Goblin character model joins the unit he will be allowed to fight with it, but the Black Orc unit will refuse to take much notice of him. This means the unit cannot test against the character's leadership as it normally would.

BLACK ORC LEADERS

Black Orc characters can join up with other Orc or Goblin units and lead them, exactly as described in the rules. Because the unit is led by a Black Orc it wouldn't dare start scrapping amongst itself and so doesn't suffer from the normal animosity rules. In fact, the unit is treated exactly like a unit of Black Orcs for animosity.

PANIC

Black Orcs think so little of other Orcs and Goblins that they do not have to take a panic test if they break or flee past them during the turn. Black Orcs expect other Orcs and Goblins to run away – when they do it merely confirms the Black Orcs' conviction that they are the best. This applies only to Black Orcs, not to units of other Orcs or Goblins being led by a Black Orc character.

Troop Type	M	WS	BS	S	T	W	I	A	Ld
BLACK ORC	4	4	3	4	4	1	2	1	8
BOSS ORC	4	5	4	5	4	1	3	2	8
BIG BOSS	4	6	5	5	5	2	4	3	9
WAR BOSS	4	7	6	5	5	3	5	4	10

BIG'UNS

Orcs have an unusual metabolism, and they can continue to grow throughout their lives. How large they grow has little to do with what or how much they eat, but more to do with their status among other Orcs. The more important the Orc the bigger he grows, and the bigger he grows the stronger and tougher he gets. As it is inevitably the biggest, toughest Orcs that become more important it goes without saying that it is the big Orcs who get bigger!

If a tough, pushy Orc grows fast he will soon come into conflict with an established equally big Orc. When this happens the two rival Orcs settle matters by fighting it out to decide which of them is best. In this way the number of huge and powerful Orcs is naturally regulated and every Orc knows his place amongst his fellows.

The biggest Orcs of all are the Warbosses and Warlords, but there are some almost equally big Orcs who consider themselves just one step down from the great leader himself. These are very important Orcs and they are known as the Big'uns. When the Warboss is killed or badly wounded, the Big'uns who fancy their chances fight each other for the leadership. The winner becomes the new Warboss. The other Big'uns continue to support the new Warboss because they know their chance will come one day.

The number of Big'uns in an Orc tribe is never very great, the natural process of growth and conflict ensures that there are always many more ordinary Orcs.

In battle the Big'uns fight together in a single mass. They are very strong and mean, and by far the best Mob of Orcs in the whole army.

	M	WS	BS	S	T	W	I	A	Ld
BIG 'UN	4	4	3	4	4	1	3	1	7

SPECIAL RULES

PANIC

Big'uns are not affected by Goblins that break or flee past them, in the same way as other Orcs.

GOBLINS

Like their big relatives the Orcs, Goblins vary in size although they are typically smaller than Orcs and usually smaller than a man. Goblins have quick, nimble fingers and small darting eyes, their teeth are tiny and very pointy. Compared to the large, powerful bodies of the Orcs, Goblins look rather thin and skrawny with gangly arms. Their voices are much higher pitched than those of Orcs, and they are extremely noisy and garrulous where Orcs are inclined to speak slowly and infrequently (considering the determined glare and comparison of fangs to be sufficient communication in most situations).

Goblins are more intelligent than Orcs and love nothing better that trading and bartering with their slow-witted relatives, because they always come out best. Goblin tribes are partly nomadic. They move about from plain to forest, or along the river valleys and in between the mountain passes where they buy, sell or steal things that they can re-sell to other Orcs or Goblins later on.

Goblin tribes are often accompanied by huge caravans of scrap metal, captured monsters in crude wooden cages, or even Men, Dwarfs or Elves that they have trapped and enslaved. Outriders mounted on huge slavering wolves patrol the area to the tribe's front, probing for enemies and scouting out small settlements that can be raided and pillaged.

Some Goblins become very wealthy by trading in this way and the tribe's King becomes exceedingly rich. Goblins like to show off their wealth. A really successful Goblin trader wears countless rings, ornamental daggers, swords, and the biggest helmet he can comfortably balance on his head. Others spend their ill-gotten gains on fast chariots which they race against each other, trying to outdo their rivals by having the fastest or flashiest machine. Goblins can acquire a great variety of weaponry as they travel about, either looted or traded with other Orcs and Goblins.

Troop Type	M	WS	BS	S	T	W	I	A	Ld
GOBLIN	4	2	3	3	3	1	2	1	5
BOSS GOBLIN	4	3	4	4	3	1	3	2	5
BIG BOSS	4	4	5	4	4	2	4	3	6
WAR BOSS	4	5	6	4	4	3	5	4	7

Troop Type	M	WS	BS	S	T	W	I	A	Ld
SHAMAN	4	2	3	3	4	1	3	1	5
SHAMAN CHAMPION	4	2	3	4	4	2	3	1	5
MASTER SHAMAN	4	2	3	4	4	3	4	2	5
SHAMAN LORD	4	2	3	4	4	4	5	3	6

SPECIAL RULE

FEAR

Goblins strongly dislike fighting Elves, partly because of the dire reputation of these formidable troops, but also because the natural aura of Elves incites unreasoning fear in Goblins. A unit of Goblins *fears* any unit of Elves which it does not outnumber by at least two to one. The unit is affected by fear as described in the Psychology section of the Warhammer rules.

NIGHT GOBLINS

Many years ago some Goblins took to living in the caves beneath the Worlds Edge mountains. Over the centuries these became distinct in type and are now known as Night Goblins.

Night Goblins have become so accustomed to the dark that when they come out into the open they prefer to move around at night and hide away during the day. Many of them wear long ragged cloaks, hooded coats, and dangling caps which cover their bodies and protect them from the sunlight.

Night Goblins raise special subterranean fungi deep beneath the mountains in their cool damp caves. They cultivate many types of fungus and are always searching for new ones to experiment with. Some fungus is used as food for the Night Goblins and their strange animals, but many are grown for their hallucinogenic or intoxicating properties or because they affect the Goblin metabolism in some other way. These fungi are traded with other Goblins for weapons and many of the other items the Night Goblins need. Night Goblin Shamans are expert at identifying, growing and using fungi, and they grow many special strains to use as poisons or even weapons.

When the Night Goblins prepare for battle they brew huge quantities of fungus beer to bolster their courage. As they get steadily more drunk they sing loudly so that their voices fill the tunnels of the Worlds Edge Mountains and echo through the Dwarf strongholds. When the time is right Shamans pick the special fungus and make the vile brew which sends the Fanatics crazy and turns them into uncontrolled whirling maniacs.

Night Goblins often take over abandoned Dwarf strongholds to live in, and much of the ancient Dwarf Empire is now infested with these creatures. Occasionally the Dwarfs will try to drive the Goblins out, or the Goblins will find some tunnel which leads them into the Dwarf tunnels, and the two races battle it out beneath the mountains. Due to this ancient enmity Dwarfs and Goblins are implacable foes and will often fight to the death rather than give an inch of ground to their enemies.

Troop Type	M	WS	BS	S	T	W	I	A	Ld
NIGHT GOBLIN	4	2	3	3	3	1	2	1	5
BOSS GOBLIN	4	3	4	4	3	1	3	2	5
BIG BOSS	4	4	5	4	4	2	4	3	6
WAR BOSS	4	5	6	4	4	3	5	4	7

Troop Type	M	WS	BS	S	T	W	I	A	Ld
SHAMAN	4	2	3	3	4	1	3	1	5
SHAMAN CHAMPION	4	2	3	4	4	2	3	1	5
MASTER SHAMAN	4	2	3	4	4	3	4	2	5
SHAMAN LORD	4	2	3	4	4	4	5	3	6

SPECIAL RULES

HATE DWARFS

Night Goblins *hate* their old rivals the Dwarfs so intensely that they will often fight to the death rather than run away. When fighting Dwarfs Night Goblins are affected by the rules for *hatred* as described in the Warhammer rulebook.

FEAR

Like other Goblins, Night Goblins strongly dislike fighting Elves. A unit of Night Goblins *fears* any unit of Elves which it does not outnumber by at least two to one. The unit is affected by fear as described in the Warhammer rulebook.

NIGHT GOBLIN FANATICS

Night Goblins cultivate many kinds of toxic fungi in their dark caves and they are constantly on the look-out for new and exotic varieties. The least noxious ones are eaten with great enthusiasm. Others are used by Shamans to make their foul potions and poisons. One particular variety, known as the Mad Cap, is used as the basis for an intoxicating brew whose effects are legendary amongst the Night Goblins. This is the brew which turns a Goblin into an ecstatic gibbering lunatic who is impervious to pain, almost completely unaware of his environment, hugely strong, and completely fearless into the bargain. It is the secret behind the powers of the Goblin Fanatics, probably the most dangerous Goblins of all.

Fanatics carry a huge ball and chain, a weapon so large that it would be impossible for a Goblin to pick up in normal circumstances, but the Fanatic's strength is boosted by fungus beer enabling him to swing the heavy ball round and round. The Goblin is almost completely unaware of what is happening around him, and he has to be carried into battle by his mates. His urge to leap about and start to swing his weapon is difficult to suppress, but his fellows manage this by grabbing him very tightly and sitting on him if necessary. Should the Fanatic start to whirl about anywhere near them they know they are in trouble!

The Goblins wait until the enemy are close by, and then push the Fanatic out towards the foe, giving him a good shove to start him off in the right direction. Free at last, the deranged Goblin starts to spin round crazily, swinging his ball and chain in a dizzy circle of death. Anything that gets in his way is smashed to pieces. Eventually the Goblin runs out of energy and collapses in an exhausted pile with a silly grin on his face, or he crashes straight into a tree or other obstacle and ends up throttling himself with his chain.

If the Goblin Fanatic manages to keep going then he quickly becomes disoriented, and will start to spin about the battlefield first one way and then another – which can be very disconcerting for all combatants! Despite the eager shouting of his Goblin mates, the Fanatic really has little idea of where he is going, and will happily plough through troops from his own side if they get in the way.

SPECIAL RULES

HIDE

Goblin Fanatics are not placed on the table at the start of the game like other troops. Instead you must note down where they are hidden. Up to three Fanatics can hide in each Night Goblin infantry unit – note down which units conceal Fanatics and how many. These Fanatics remain hidden, carried along by their fellows, until they are ready to be pushed out towards the enemy.

If the Night Goblin unit is routed then the Fanatics are carried along with their companions. If the Night Goblin unit is destroyed then the Fanatics are destroyed as well.

ATTACK

Goblin Fanatics are released as soon as enemy come within 8" of their unit. There is no choice here, all the Fanatics in a unit must be released as soon as enemy are within this distance. This often forms an exception to the normal turn sequence, because the enemy may move to within 8" during his turn. He may even be charging the Night Goblin unit, for example.

Whatever the situation, whether it is your turn or your opponent's, as soon as enemy approach to within 8" you declare that your Fanatics are coming out! All movement is halted immediately. If a moving enemy has triggered the Fanatics then the enemy unit is halted at 8" away. The Fanatics' attacks are worked out completely before the game proceeds any further.

MOVE

The Fanatics are shoved out of their unit towards the enemy. Take each Fanatic model and declare which direction it will be moving in. Now roll 2D6 for each Fanatic and move the model that number of inches. Obviously some models will move further than others, and the average roll is 7, so you have to do slightly better than average to hit your target.

Fanatics move straight through any troops in the way. They do not stop but keep whirling forwards oblivious to their surroundings. It is possible for a Fanatic to whirl through several enemy units if he is especially lucky!

FIGHTING

Fanatics don't fight hand-to-hand combat at all. Instead they cause immense damage as they whirl through their target. They cannot be attacked in hand-to-hand combat either – the only way to destroy a Fanatic is to shoot him or to wait and let him collapse from exhaustion.

If a Fanatic touches a unit as he moves, it automatically sustains D6 strength 5 hits from the spinning ball of death. It does not matter how many models the Fanatic spins through. If he hits one then he bounds about inside the unit, bouncing from foe to foe, until he spins out of the other side, leaving the enemy completely devastated.

No saving throws are permitted for armour from Fanatic attacks. Heavily armoured targets are therefore just as vulnerable to others – their armour is easily crushed by the huge ball while nimbler, more lightly armour individuals may actually be able to dodge and duck more easily.

	M	WS	BS	S	T	W	I	A	Ld
FANATIC	2D6	Special		5	3	1	-	D6	-

Work out all the damage from Fanatics as they emerge from their concealing units. If they cause very high casualties the enemy units may have to take a panic test in the same way as for missile casualties. In this case work out the result before continuing. This can be useful, as it allows Goblins to drive off charging enemy units with their Fanatics, and even enemy who are not panicked into fleeing away will be severely mauled.

FURTHER MOVEMENT

Once Fanatics are in place they move during their own turn at the beginning of the movement phase once charges have been declared. It is best to move Fanatics before doing other compulsory movement (such as fleeing units). For each Fanatic in turn roll a scatter dice to determine which direction it moves in – the Goblin is now so utterly disorientated that he moves in a random direction. Move the Fanatic 2D6 inches in the direction indicated by the arrow on the scatter dice.

If you roll a double on the 2D6 roll then the Fanatic has met with an accident, wrapping the chain around his neck, or perhaps his heart just gives out and he collapses to the ground. In any case, a double indicates the Fanatic has met his end and the model is immediately removed from the table. Note this only happens when moving randomly, not when the Fanatic emerges from his unit.

Work out damage on units the Fanatic touches as he moves. Of course, as he is moving in a random direction at a random speed, he is quite likely to whirl out of control and hit either side. Hopefully the initial push towards the enemy will ensure that the Fanatic hits the enemy more often than he hits his mates... but you can never be sure.

CHARGING THROUGH FANATICS

Fanatics are spinning circles of death, so it is not a good idea to move troops into them deliberately. If a charging unit is suddenly confronted by emerging Fanatics, leaving Fanatics in front of the chargers and between them and their target unit, then the chargers can either remain halted or complete their charge. This is up to the player.

If chargers move through Fanatics they have not already encountered then they sustain more damage as they hit the deranged Goblins. This may cause a panic test on the charging unit, but if they have already taken and passed a panic test due to Fanatic casualties that turn then they do not have to test again.

MOVING THROUGH FANATICS

Apart from chargers who are moving through emerging Fanatics, troops are not allowed to move through Fanatics. . Sometimes troops are forced to move into Fanatics, because they move randomly, or they are forced to flee through them for example. Such troops sustain damage as if hit by the Fanatics

OBSTACLES

If a Fanatic moves into an obstacle, wood, building, or into another Fanatic then he is slain. In the case of two Fanatics colliding both are slain. Splat!

PSYCHOLOGY

Fanatics are immune to all Psychology and cannot be beaten (or even fought) in hand-to-hand combat. They therefore have no leadership value – they are far too crazed to care!

NIGHT GOBLIN SQUIG HUNTERS

Night Goblins cultivate different kinds of fungus and moulds in their meandering caves and tunnels. They also descend into the deeper caverns to search for the wild and exotic funguses which they use to make powerful magic potions. Night Goblins are not the only creatures that like to eat fungus, so they have to be constantly on the look out for dangerous subterranean denizens. One of the most deadly of all these creatures is the elusive Cave Squig. These are hybrid creatures, part fungus and part flesh, with tough ball-shaped bodies and clumsy taloned feet. Cave Squigs have huge gaping mouths thronged with slashing teeth, and an enraged Cave Squig can bite a large creature clean in two and can easily swallow a Night Goblin whole.

Over the many hundreds of years that Night Goblins have lived in the tunnels they have become quite used to dealing with these fearsome creatures. Roasted Cave Squig is considered a great delicacy and captive Cave Squigs are kept as pets by Night Goblin Chieftains.

Night Goblins hunt Cave Squigs using long, sturdy forks called 'prodders' to goad the Squigs from their hiding places and to keep the enraged beasts at bay. Once a Squig has been provoked from its lair the Night Goblins throw nets over it then bash it senseless with large clubs so it can be safely dragged away. Some Night Goblins become very proficient Squig hunters and come to be quite nonchalant about the dangers involved. Famous

Squig hunters are happy to exhibit their skills with daring spectacles such as Squig wrestling, tunnel racing, Squig pit leaping, and bare-back Squig riding.

Squigs are often herded into battle by Night Goblins armed with prodders. The Squigs don't like daylight at all, and quickly become maddened by the sun. The Goblins herd the enraged Squigs towards the enemy where they gnash, bite and chew their way through the enemy's ranks.

	M	WS	BS	S	T	W	I	A	Ld
HUNTER	4	2	3	3	3	1	2	1	5
CAVE SQUIG	2D6"	4	0	5	3	1	5	2	2

SPECIAL RULES

MOVEMENT

A unit of Squig Hunters includes a number of Night Goblins armed with prodder forks plus a number of Cave Squigs. At the start of the battle there must be at least two Goblins in the unit to carry a prodder fork, and there must be at least five models in total. Although Goblins and Squigs have different movement rates, the whole unit keeps together moving at the speed of the Goblins.

FORMATION

A unit of Squig Hunters is always deployed in two ranks with all the Cave Squigs in the front rank and all the Night Goblins behind them.

HAND-TO-HAND FIGHTING

The Cave Squigs will attack any models in base contact except for the prodder-armed Night Goblins behind them.

Night Goblins armed with prodders can also attack enemy models they are touching. They are mounted two models to a base, and both models get their own attack. Both Goblins can fight if any part of their base is touching an enemy model. Prodder-armed Night Goblins can also use their long prodder to attack from behind their Squigs in a similar way to troops armed with spears. If the Cave Squig in front of the Goblins is fighting then both the Goblins carrying the prodder can fight too.

Goblins using a prodder receive a +1 strength bonus because the prodder is so big and heavy. Note that prodder-armed Goblins can fight from a rear rank even if they have moved – unlike spears which can only do so when stationary (see the Warhammer rulebook).

SHOOTING

When the enemy shoots at the Squig Hunter unit any hits are randomised between the Squigs and Goblins. For example if there are three Squigs and two Goblins roll a D6: 1-3 = a Squig hit, 4-5 = a Goblin hit, 6 = roll again. Remember that a pair of Goblins carrying a prodder is two Goblins not one.

LEADERSHIP AND CHARACTERISTICS

The whole unit uses the leadership value of the Goblins unless the Squigs go wild as explained below. The unit can be joined and led by an Orc or Goblin character, in which case you test leadership on the character's value. However, note that Squigs will attack *any* model that isn't a prodder-armed Night Goblin... so any character with the unit will have to be placed at the back to be safe!

GOBLIN CASUALTIES

The prodder-armed Goblins are mounted two to a base, so you will have to either remember or make a note if one of them is killed. Alternatively you can substitute an ordinary Goblin model if you have one. A single Goblin can continue to use the huge prodder to keep back the Squigs and fight, but he loses the +1 strength bonus as the prodder is exceptionally unwieldy. When Goblin casualties are taken any odd Goblins are always removed first, leaving as many complete pairs as possible.

FEAR

Goblins dislike fighting Elves and the usual rule for fear applies. The unit *fears* any unit of Elves it does not outnumber by at least two to one. The size of the unit is the number of Goblins plus the number of Squigs.

WILD SQUIGS

So long as the Squigs are successfully herded by the prodder-armed Night Goblins they are moved and fight just like any other unit. However, if the Goblins should be slain some or all the Squigs may break away and go wild. Each prodder can control up to three Squigs. If there are not enough prodders to control all the Squigs then any excess Squigs will go wild. Of course, if all the Goblins are slain then *all* the remaining Squigs will go wild!

Wild Squigs are moved individually along with other compulsory movement at the start of the movement phase. Each Squig moves 2D6" in a random direction. Use the scatter dice to determine the direction moved in the same way as for Goblin Fanatics. As the Squig escapes from the control of its Night Goblin herders it may burst through its own unit, but it does not cause any damage as it does so. However, if its movement carries it into any other target it charges into hand-to-hand combat and stops. The wild Squig fights whatever it hits, regardless of which side its opponent is on. Once in hand-to-hand combat the Squig doesn't move, but it will pursue a broken enemy and then continue to move randomly.

A wild Squig is far too angry to take any psychology or other leadership tests. It cannot be broken in hand-to-hand combat and is immune to the effects of psychology.

NIGHT GOBLIN SQUIG HOPPERS

Night Goblin Squig Hunters have a carefree attitude to the dangers posed by huge and hungry Cave Squigs. Most have impressive scars which they cheerfully exhibit to anyone foolhardy enough to express an interest. Drunken Squig Hunters often compete with each other to show off their most horrific injuries and tell (grossly exaggerated) tales of how they were earned. The most reckless Squig Hunters even ride Squigs into battle, grabbing hold of the Squig's tiny horns or ears, and bouncing along as the Squig leaps about. These bravados are called Squig Hoppers. Squig Hoppers don't fight in Mobs because individual Squigs move in an unpredictable manner while their riders hang on as best they can. A skilled Goblin can direct his Squig vaguely towards the enemy, but some Squigs prove almost impossibe to control and end up bouncing around on top of everybody.

	M	WS	BS	S	T	W	I	A	Ld
HUNTER	4	2	3	3	3	1	2	1	5
BOUNCING SQUIG	2D6"	4	0	5	3	1	5	2	2

SPECIAL RULES

MOVEMENT

Each Squig Hopper is moved randomly along with other compulsory movement at the start of the movement phase. Like Goblin Fanatics, Squig Hoppers are moved as individual models and do not fight in units. Begin by nominating the direction you wish the Squig Hopper to move in and then bounce it 2D6" in that direction. On the roll of a double the Squig moves the distance indicated but in an entirely random direction. Use the Scatter dice to establish the direction moved in the same way as for Goblin Fanatics.

Squigs bounce over intervening troops and scenery and land where indicated. They can therefore land directly on top of models, in the middle of a unit, etc. If a Squig lands on top of any other model it will attack as described below and then bounce off again! Nominate a direction once more and move the Squig Hopper again in the same way. Continue to bounce the Squig Hopper and continue to attack until it fails to land on a model.

If Squig Hoppers land in a river or lake the squig sinks like a stone, drowning both squig and rider! If a Squig Hopper bounces off the table it does not return.

PSYCHOLOGY

The Squig is literally hopping mad and certainly far too angry to take any psychology or other leadership tests. It cannot be broken in hand-to-hand combat and is immune to the effects of psychology. The Night Goblin just hangs on and has no effect upon the Squig's determination.

FIGHTING

When a Squig Hopper lands on any model the Squig will bite it. The Goblin may also strike a blow if you want, but does not have to (if you land on one of your own units, for example). The Squig and Goblin hit automatically – no roll to hit is necessary. Work out damage as normal. The enemy models may not fight back as they are too surprised to react in time to return blows.

CHARGING A SQUIG HOPPER

An enemy unit may charge a Squig Hopper and fight it in hand-to-hand combat exactly as if it were a normal cavalry model. Once engaged in hand-to-hand combat in this way the Squig Hopper is pinioned to the ground and does not move away. This means it fights exactly like any other model in hand-to-hand combat except that it is immune to psychology and does not take a break test. Should its enemies be destroyed or forced to flee the Squig is free to start bouncing again.

SHOOTING

Squig Hoppers are treated like any other cavalry when hit by missile fire. Work out the shot against the rider and remove the entire model if the rider is slain. A saving throw of 6 is permitted to take account of the Squig.

NIGHT GOBLIN NETTERS

The subterranean tunnels where the Night Goblins live are riddled with other, even older, passages and caverns. The deeper down a tunnel goes the more dangerous it is and the more likely it is to be inhabited by some terrible monster. Night Goblins find it necessary to occasionally descend into the chill depths in search of exotic funguses, so they know all too well what dangers await them. Night Goblin Netters and Clubbers fight together in order to immobilise and either destroy or capture dangerous creatures. On the battlefield they use their skills against the enemy, throwing their nets to entangle the foe while Clubbers bash the enemy senseless.

clubs and some with nets. Net-armed and club-armed Goblins fight in slightly different ways, so it is up to you to decide upon your ideal mix.

The Netter unit moves and fights just like any other Goblin unit. If the unit is arranged in several ranks then only models in base contact can fight (usually the front rank). This means the number of net-armed and club-armed models you have in your front rank is crucial. As casualties occur you can remove any of the models fighting and replace them with any models from a rearward rank – so you can change the ratio of nets to clubs by, say removing a club and replacing it with a net.

	M	WS	BS	S	T	W	I	A	Ld
NETTER	4	2	3	3	3	1	2	1	5

SPECIAL RULES

FORMATION

Night Goblin Netters fight in units of five or more models. Each Night Goblin is armed with either a net or a huge club. The unit can include as many net-armed and as many club-armed Night Goblins as you wish, and they can be mixed up in the ranks as you please. For example, you could have all your Night Goblins armed with nets, or all armed with clubs, or you can have some armed with

NETS

Goblins with nets receive a +1 initiative bonus and so always attack before club-armed Goblins. Work out the attack as normal. Hits do not cause any damage at all, instead make a note of the number of net hits caused. Each enemy hit by a net cannot attack back that turn assuming he has not already done so. In addition, any enemy hit by a net is a prime target for a club attack as explained below.

CLUBS

Club-armed Goblins receive a +1 strength bonus and so count as having a strength of 4. Work out the attacks as normal. Once you have established how many hits your clubs have caused add the number of enemy already netted that turn. In effect the club-armed Goblins get an extra free hit for every netted enemy. For example, if four enemy are already netted and the club-armed Goblins hit two enemy then 2+4 = 6 hits inflicted. All these hits are resolved with the +1 strength bonus. It doesn't matter how few clubbers are fighting so long as there is at least one. If there are no clubbers at all then any netted enemy are jumped on by the netters themselves, and damage is resolved with a strength of 3 as normal. Any netted model which are not slain free themselves automatically – they do not continue to count as netted.

SHOOTING

When the enemy shoots at a unit of Night Goblin Netters randomise any hits amongst the potential targets. For example, if there are four net-armed and two club-armed Night Goblins roll a dice: 1, 2, 3, 4 = a net; 5, 6 = a club.

FOREST GOBLINS

The dark forests of the Old World are home to many strange and dangerous creatures including marauding bands of Chaos Warriors, elusive Beastmen, Minotaurs and countless others even more ancient and hideous. In these gloomy forests also live the Forest Goblins.

Forest Goblins are not physically different from other Goblins. They are the same size, have the same green skin, and overall it would be hard to tell one from another were it not for their distinctive styles of dress and skin painting. Forest Goblins decorate themselves with colourful feathers, often sticking the quills directly into their skin as Goblins feel little pain. Different tribes often use different colours and combinations of feathers to identify themselves.

Metal ores are quite rare in the forests, so the Forest Goblins trade with other Goblin tribes, swapping captives and fungus for ores from the mountains. Because they don't have much metal at their disposal, Forest Goblins also like to use bones and teeth to make armour as well as for decoration.

Forest Goblins wear warpaint in broad bands of colour over their bodies. Bright red and blue are the most popular colours, and these are commonly applied to make V shaped chevrons over their face and arms.

The forests are full of all kinds of spiders, and the Forest Goblins are experts when it comes to capturing and finding uses for these creatures. Forest Goblins even eat certain species of spiders which they regard as especially succulent and superior to any other kind of flesh. The really gigantic spiders are sometimes captured and used as barter, but mostly these enormous creatures are avoided because they are too dangerous. Smaller spiders, about the size of a horse, are ridden by the Goblins, and smaller ones are kept as pets.

Forest Goblin Shamans keep small poisonous spiders in their mouths. These bite the Goblin on the tongue so that his body is always saturated with strange intoxicating poisons. This drives the Shaman a bit mad and makes his tongue swell up and turn a bright colour such as purple or blue, but it also stimulates the part of his brain that controls magic.

Forest Shamans are the chief figures in the Spider Cult which worships the forest spiders as the gods of the forest. Forest Goblin tribes have totem poles depicting Gork, Mork and the Spider, and this is where they meet before marching to raid a human farmstead or burn some woodcutter's house. Shields and banners often have spiders on them, and spider decorations are common designs for buckles, banner pole tops, and weapons

Troop Type	M	WS	BS	S	T	W	I	A	Ld
FOREST GOBLIN	4	2	3	3	3	1	2	1	5
BOSS GOBLIN	4	3	4	4	3	1	3	2	5
BIG BOSS	4	4	5	4	4	2	4	3	6
WAR BOSS	4	5	6	4	4	3	5	4	7

Troop Type	M	WS	BS	S	T	W	I	A	Ld
SHAMAN	4	2	3	3	4	1	3	1	5
SHAMAN CHAMPION	4	2	3	4	4	2	3	1	5
MASTER SHAMAN	4	2	3	4	4	3	4	2	5
SHAMAN LORD	4	2	3	4	4	4	5	3	6

SPECIAL RULE

FEAR

Like other Goblins Forest Goblins strongly dislike fighting Elves. A unit of Goblins *fears* any unit of Elves that it does not outnumber by at least two to one. The unit is affected by fear as described in the Warhammer rulebook.

SNOTLINGS

Snotlings are the smallest of the green-skinned races. They are not very intelligent and behave very much like extremely enthusiastic and uncontrollable puppies. They can fetch and carry for other Goblin or Orc races, and do other rather limited tasks, but they are little use for any real work.

Snotlings live around Orcs and Goblins, infesting their caves and huts, scavenging amongst their rubbish piles, and stealing anything they can get their hands on. Their larger relatives regard Snotlings with a certain amount of affection and treat them as wayward and rather mischievous pets. Sometimes an Orc or Goblin will capture a few Snotlings and train them to perform entertaining tricks, or to perform simple tasks.

Snotlings are great mimics and are fascinated by the activities of their larger relatives, which, although their actions are completely inexplicable to Snotlings, they will often cheerfully imitate. It is quite common to see an important Orc Boss strutting through the Orc camp followed closely by a tiny Snotling impersonating his walk and copying the Boss' every movement in an exaggerated comic fashion. This aping behaviour can be infuriating for Orc Bosses who like take themselves seriously, especially the Black Orcs, who are renowned for their lack of humour. When Orcs or Goblins march off to battle they invariably find themselves accompanied by a horde of Snotlings armed with bits of wood, broken spears, and weapons they have stolen or scrounged.

On the battlefield the Snotlings latch on to a unit of Orcs or Goblins, following them about and copying their actions. When their big friends get stuck into close combat the Snotlings throw themselves on the enemy, screaming and yelling crazily, waving their wooden clubs and biting the foes with their sharp teeth. The sheer mass of Snotlings can overwhelm or tie down an enemy unit even if the tiny creatures don't cause many casualties!

	M	WS	BS	S	T	W	I	A	Ld
SNOTLINGS	4	2	2	1	1	3	3	3	4

SPECIAL RULES

SNOTLING BASES

Snotlings are so small that they are modelled in multiples on a single large base. The base contains about nine Snotlings but is treated as if it were a single large monster with several wounds and attacks. The Snotling base fights at full effect until it has taken 3 wounds when it is removed.

MIMIC

Snotlings don't really think for themselves, they merely mimic the actions of Orcs and Goblins around them. A Snotling unit must always be within 12" of an Orc or Goblin unit and will move to within this distance during the movement phase if it finds itself further away. The Snotlings always do what the nearest unit of Orcs or Goblins does – cheerfully imitating their neighbours' actions.

If the nearest unit of Orcs or Goblins is engaged in hand-to-hand combat or declares a charge this turn then the Snotlings must charge the nearest enemy if they can. If they are too far away to charge the Snotlings move towards the nearest enemy as fast as they are able.

If the nearest unit of Orcs or Goblins is fleeing, or if it fails a break or panic test and so starts to flee, then the Snotlings pretend to flee as well! The Snotling unit is immediately broken and treated just like a unit broken in combat or fleeing following a failed panic test.

If the nearest unit is Savage Orcs fighting in a *frenzy* then the Snotlings also go frenzied if they are fighting hand-to-hand.

Otherwise the Snotlings will keep pace with their nearest neighbours, ensuring that they remain within 12".

So long as they have neighbours within 12" the Snotlings are not affected by the psychology rules and they do not need to take break tests when they are beaten in hand-to-hand combat. Because they copy their neighbours they will be affected by the results of these units' psychology tests, break tests, and so on. This means that Snotlings can be very frustrating to fight, because no matter how many are slain they keep fighting so long as their neighbours hold steady. A large powerful unit of enemy troops can be bogged down by Snotlings and overwhelmed, even though the Snotlings are unlikely to cause many casualties.

If Snotlings find themselves themselves further than 12" away from a unit of Orcs or Goblins, and if they cannot move to within 12" of a unit during that movement phase, then they mill around in a confused mass. The Snotlings will not move until they are able to move within 12" of a friendly Orc or Goblin unit, and if charged by enemy troops they are automatically broken as if they had failed a panic or fear test. If the Snotlings are not within 12" of a friendly Orc or Goblin unit they are affected by psychology as normal.

LEADERS

Snotlings cannot be joined by heroes or led by them – they fight as a big mass of their own kind and are far too excited to respond to even the simplest commands. Note that the animosity rules do not affect Snotlings – animosity only applies to Orcs and Goblins.

GIANT WOLVES

The Giant or Great Wolf of the Warhammer World is a fearsome monster with slavering fangs and huge claws. They are a great menace to humans and have been hunted to such an extent that the huge wolf packs that terrorised whole provinces are now a thing of the past. Only in the vast wastes of Kislev is it still common for entire villages to be raided and destroyed by marauding wolf packs, and for children to be stolen away or herds of domestic animals to be destroyed in a single night.

Attacked and driven out by men, Giant Wolves have allied with Goblin tribes. This partnership of Goblin and wolf has proved very successful. The Goblins protect and feed the wolves. In turn, Goblins are small enough to ride Giant Wolves, and also hitch them to chariots and carts in place of horses, who detest the smell of Goblin, and won't have anything to do with them. Wolves and Goblins seem to get along very well, and the two races have thrived together. Goblin wolf riders raid and pillage far afield, while outriders scour the surrounding countryside for any sign of enemy armies.

	M	WS	BS	S	T	W	I	A	Ld
GIANT WOLF	9	4	0	3	3	1	3	1	3

GIANT SPIDERS

The forests of the Old World are infested with all kinds of horrible creatures of which spiders are probably the most numerous. Most are no larger than the palm of a man's hand, but even spiders this small can have a deadly poisonous bite. Others are as big as dragons, great bloated monsters which can hardly move from their lairs and which are revered by the Forest Goblins as gods of the forest. There are all sorts and shapes of spider between these two extremes, including the creatures about the size of small ponies which Forest Goblins capture and ride. These are captured when still small and raised on tasty tit-bits until they are big enough to ride. As they are hand reared these spiders become accustomed to Goblins and quickly learn to accept a rider.

Spiders are good fighters, with gaping mandibles like steel pincers. Although they are not as fast as wolves or horses, spiders can move swiftly over obstacles or rough territory thanks to their eight legs.

SPECIAL RULE

MOVE

Spiders have eight hairy legs which enable them to move easily over obstacles and rough territory. In woodlands they can swing from tree to tree or scramble over the treetops to drop to the forest floor below. To represent this spiders are not slowed down by crossing difficult ground or obstacles.

	M	WS	BS	S	T	W	I	A	Ld
SPIDER	7	3	0	4	3	1	1	1	5

WAR BOARS

The war boar is a ferocious animal, as big as a horse, extremely strong, vicious, bad tempered, loudly flatulent, and its behaviour is in all respects dangerous and unpredictable. These are just the sort of qualities that Orcs really admire!

Orc war boar riders are rough, tough and very determined. Breaking in a war boar can be a long and dangerous business, but fortunately Orcs have thick skulls and don't feel pain much. In fact you never really train a war boar, you just learn to hang on better while the creature goes crazy, goring and stamping, twisting and biting, and generally causing as much damage as it can.

Thanks to their size, toughness, and extreme ferocity war boars make excellent mounts for Orc warriors. They can also be harnessed to pull chariots. Thanks to these admirable qualities war boars have earned themselves a place alongside Orcs, and most Orc settlements have one or more secure pens where the war boars are kept. War boars are evil minded creatures that will take every opportunity to maim, bite, and kick their Orc masters but this doesn't really bother the Orcs who are on the whole sensible enough to keep out of the way.

SPECIAL RULES

LEADERSHIP

War boars are really hard to control so when the boar decides to run off or charge madly out of control it is very difficult for the rider to do much about it. To represent this wildness a war boar rider always reduces his leadership value by -1 when taking any tests. So an Orc with a leadership of 7 will test with a leadership of 6, for example.

SAVE

War boars are obstinate, thick-skinned and very difficult to kill. A hit is likely to make the creature even more determined to fight on. A war boar rider therefore receives an extra bonus onto his save roll, +2 rather than +1 for other cavalry mounts such as horses and wolves. So, for example, an Orc rider wearing a chainmail shirt and carrying a shield has an armour save of 3+ compared to 4+ for a man wearing the same armour and riding a horse, and 5+ for the same Orc fighting on foot. This makes war boar riders very difficult to kill!

COMBAT BONUS

A charging war boar is a bad-tempered mound of bloody-minded muscle and bone with pointy tusks and sharp teeth. The impact of this slavering beast on an enemy formation is just as effective as that of a Knight with a lance. A charging war boar therefore receives a strength bonus of +2. This extra bonus applies only to the war boar and not to the Orc rider.

	M	WS	BS	S	T	W	I	A	Ld
WAR BOAR	7	4	0	3	4	1	3	1	3

TROLLS

Trolls are large and hideous creatures, bestial and foul with long gangling limbs and cold damp hides. Their warty, slimy and sometimes scaly skins can be almost any colour. There are many different kinds of Trolls – spines are not uncommon, while two headed Trolls have sometimes been sighted travelling with Chaos warbands.

Trolls are not very intelligent, but they are extremely strong, and can easily rip a man apart with their bare hands. Trolls are greatly feared because of their unthinking ferocity and indiscriminate appetite. They can and will eat anything – flesh and bone, wood, rocks, bits of metal. The stomach of a Troll contains some of the most powerful acids known in the Old World, and its digestive juices are highly valued by alchemists and wizards.

The other unusual and perhaps best known characteristic of Trolls is that their flesh is able to regrow almost as quickly as it is damaged. If a Troll's clawed hand is severed a fresh one will grow from the stump. You have to cause a great deal of damage to a Troll to stop it regenerating. The only thing that Trolls cannot survive is fire. If they are burned they cannot regenerate, so fire is the greatest ally of the Troll fighter.

Trolls can sometimes be persuaded to join Orcs or Goblins as they march to battle, although it is doubtful if they really understand what is going on. Left to their own devices, the chances are the Trolls will go wild or become soporific, but if led by a more intelligent creature they can often prove to be dangerous foes.

	M	WS	BS	S	T	W	I	A	Ld
TROLL	6	3	1	5	4	3	1	3	4

SPECIAL RULES

FEAR

Trolls are large and extremely repulsive monsters which cause *fear* as described in the Psychology rules.

STUPIDITY

Trolls are extremely stupid creatures that get confused very easily. Trolls are affected by the rules described for *stupidity*.

REGENERATE

Trolls can regenerate damage if they are not too badly hurt. Work this out as follows. When Trolls are attacked calculate the number of wounds the unit suffers as normal. Once both sides involved in the combat have made all their attacks the Trolls may try to regenerate. Roll a D6 for each wound suffered during the combat. If you roll a 4 or more that wound has regenerated. Any regenerated wounds are reinstated, and models removed as casualties are replaced if enough wounds are regenerated.

The results of combat are worked out after the Trolls have regenerated, and the number of wounds inflicted on them does not include any that are regenerated.

For example, three Trolls are fighting five Empire knights. The knights strike first and inflict 5 wounds, enough to kill one Troll and cause 2 further wounds. The remaining 2 Trolls inflict 3 wounds on the knights. The Trolls now test to regenerate and successfully regenerate 3 wounds. The 3 wounds are reinstated, the slain Troll is replaced, and the 2 wounds suffered are noted down. In this example the knights have scored only 2 wounds in the end while the Trolls have inflicted 3. Assuming no other combat bonuses apply the Trolls have won.

FIRE

Troll flesh cannot regenerate when it is burned. If a Troll sustains one or more wounds from flames then it cannot regenerate any wounds, not even those inflicted by ordinary weapons.

VOMIT

A Troll has a particularly unpleasant alternative method of attack which is to vomit the contents of its stomach over its enemy. Should a Troll elect to vomit it may make no other attacks in hand-to-hand combat that turn. The heaving Troll automatically inflicts 1 strength 5 hit on his enemy. The Troll's vomit is sticky and semi-liquid, so it penetrates through armour easily and even dissolves part of it away. No armour saving throw is therefore allowed against a vomit attack.

STONE TROLLS

Stone Trolls live in the rocky regions of the Old World, amongst the mountains and craggy hills. Like all Trolls they will eat anything and through force of circumstance they tend to eat a lot of rocks. Trolls tend to acquire physical attributes as a result of what they eat, and Stone Trolls are craggy with cracked flesh like weathered stone. Rocks and stones absorb sluggish Light magic, and because the Troll eats a lot of rocks his body naturally absorbs a large quantity of magical power. This makes Stone Trolls extraordinarily resistant to attack by magic.

If a spell is directed upon a unit of Stone Trolls it will be automatically dispelled on the D6 roll of a 4, 5 or 6. However, this applies to all spells for both sides, not just enemy spells. Ordinary dispels, rebounds and other magic cards may be used as normal to stop spells directed at the Trolls should their natural dispel fail to work. Their magical resistance does not affect magic weapons or other items, except for those which cast spells in the usual way.

RIVER TROLLS

River Trolls live in marshlands or bogs, and beside untamed rivers where the banks are broad and muddy. They are both slimy and scaly, with vile green-coloured skin and lank hair-like growths. The slime they exhude is obnoxious and slippery, and has the stench of rotting fish. The malodorous slime has the dual effects of choking anyone too near the Troll and also making it extremely hard for an attacker to land a blow.

All enemy must subtract -1 from any rolls to hit River Trolls in hand-to-hand combat, down to a minimum of 6 to hit. If the Troll would normally require 6 to be hit, if it is behind a low wall for example, then the slime makes no difference – it is hard enough to hit already. The Troll's slime has no effect on hits from shooting.

THE ARMY LIST

The Orc and Goblin Army list has been designed so that you can choose an army to a points value agreed by you and your opponent. There is no upper limit to the size of an army, but one thousand points is about the smallest size that will allow you to field a battleworthy force. Two thousand points is the usual size for battles that will last an entire evening, and three thousand points will give you enough troops for a battle that will take the best part of a day to fight. Most people prefer to collect their armies in blocks of a thousand or five hundred points, starting with say a one thousand point core force and adding five hundred points at a time. This allows you to conveniently plan your purchases and gives you time to paint the models and try them out on the tabletop before deciding what to add next.

It is usual for each side to begin with an equal points value of troops – say two thousand points a side. This means both players pick an army worth up to the agreed points value. The Orc and Goblin player uses the Orc and Goblin army list, while his opponent uses the list from the Warhammer Armies book for his army. The total value of a player's army may be slightly less than the agreed value, and will often be a few points short simply because there is nothing left to spend the odd point on.

THE ARMY

When you choose your army you can spend your points on five different types of troops: Characters, Mobs, War Machines, Monsters, and Allies. You are permitted to spend only a certain maximum proportion of your points on each each of these categories. For example, you can spend up to 25% of your army's points value on war machines. These limitations ensure that the army is reasonably representative and doesn't consist entirely of heroes, big monsters, or war machines. The list which defines the limitations for each category is given immediately before the army list itself.

Of the five different categories of troops all except for allies are covered by the list in this book. Allies are covered by the Warhammer Armies book for that race.

CHARACTERS

The portion of the army's points value which you are permitted to spend on characters includes the value of characters' armour and weapons, any magic items they have, a steed if they are mounted, a monster if they ride a monster, and a chariot and its crew if they ride a chariot.

Note especially that if a character rides a monster its points value is included in the Character point allowance and not the Monster point allowance. You still select the monster from the Monsters part of the list, but the points value is added to that of the character. The proportion of your army's points permitted for monsters is for monsters without riders, and this is quite separate. Similarly, if a character rides in a chariot then its points value including that of its crew is included in the Characters' point allowance.

One of the types of characters available to you is Bosses. Bosses are Orc or Goblin unit champions. Although they are characters they cannot move or fight on their own, because they are part of their Mob. You cannot include a Boss unless you also include his own Mob for him to fight with. Although the Boss always fights with his Mob he still counts as a Character and his points cost must be reckoned with the Character points allowance.

The characters in the lists do not have specific weapons. They can be equipped with any of the weapons or armour indicted by the Equipment List printed below. In principal, a character may be armed with any weapon or piece of equipment normally available to the Mobs, but this does not include special weapons such as a Fanatic's ball and chain, or a Squig Hunter's prodder for example. Bosses always have the same equipment as their Mob.

A character can carry appropriate magic items chosen from the magic item cards in Warhammer or Warhammer Battle Magic. It is also our intention to add more magic items at a future date, possibly as part of scenario supplements and also in White Dwarf magazine. The points value of magic items is indicated on the cards themselves. Characters are permitted no more than the number of magic items shown on the chart below.

Character	Maximum Number of Magic Items
HEROES	
Boss	1
Big Boss	2
Warboss	3
WIZARDS	
Shaman	1
Shaman Champion	2
Master Shaman	3
Shaman Lord	4

Note that some magic items are restricted to certain races or types of characters. Scrolls can only be used by wizards (ie, shamans), for example.

MOBS

The great mass of Orc and Goblin troops are covered by the Mobs section of the army list. Troops are organised into units which, in the case of Orcs and Goblins, are called Mobs. These units must be at least five models strong unless indicated otherwise. There is no upper limit to the size of a unit. The minimum of five models includes its leader, standard bearer, musician and champion if it has them.

All units are assumed to include a leader equipped in the same way as his troops and with identical characteristics. He costs the same points as an ordinary trooper. All units may include a standard bearer and/or musician, and these cost double the points value of an ordinary trooper.

Standard bearers and musicians are assumed to be equipped with the same weapons as the rest of the unit and fight just like ordinary troopers (see the Warhammer rulebook for a full description).

Some units are permitted magic standards. These are covered by the Warhammer Battle Magic supplement and are included as magic item cards. If you include a magic standard then its points value is included with the points value of the unit.

Units are permitted champions which in the case of Orcs and Goblins are called Bosses. Bosses are always equipped exactly as the rest of the unit, except that they are permitted one magic item in addition. A Boss may be the unit's leader, but does not have to be – you can have a separate leader and champion model if you wish. As we have already seen, the points value of a Boss, and any magic item he carries, comes from your Character points allocation.

WAR MACHINES

War machines includes all the artillery and other machines of war available to the Orc and Goblin army including Rock Lobbers, Doom Divers, and Snotling Pump Wagons. The War Machines section also includes chariots – note that this is different from some other armies where chariots may be included as part of their ordinary units.

MONSTERS

Monsters are beasts brought along to fight beside the army. They include captive monsters goaded into fighting and monsters which have been magically bound by spells of obedience. Monsters chosen as mounts for characters are NOT included in the points allocation for Monsters: they are included in the points for Characters instead.

ALLIES

The Orc and Goblin army may include a proportion of allies worth up to a quarter of its total points value. Allies are chosen from the Warhammer Armies book or books indicated. So, for example, your Orc and Goblin army could include up to a quarter of its points value as Dark Elves chosen from the Dark Elf list, or Chaos chosen from the Chaos list. There is nothing to prevent you choosing allies from several different lists if you wish. Including allies is a good way of expanding your miniature collection, and it also allows you to paint something different and still include it in your army.

When you choose allies you can spend your points freely on characters, regiments, and war machines (also Daemons in the case of Chaos allies). The normal army selection proportions do not apply, although other normal restrictions do (eg, you need an Orc unit to buy an Orc war machine). You cannot include monsters from your allies except for monsters ridden by characters.

You do not have to include a general model for your allies but you can do so if you wish. The allied general counts as a character in the normal way but he does not benefit from any of the special rules for generals. In effect the allied general becomes a subordinate character in the same way as other heroes.

PRESENTATION OF PROFILES

Profiles are given in the standard format and include all the characteristic values. They do not take into account movement reductions due to armour, as this may vary depending on how you choose to equip your troops. Saving throws are not included on the profiles for the same reason, as they may vary depending on what armour you choose to buy.

Cavalry have two profiles, one for the rider and one for the mount. As the mount will be either a war boar, giant spider or giant wolf their profiles have been included in full.

M = Movement

WS = Weapon Skill

BS = Ballistic Skill

S = Strength

T = Toughness

W = Wounds

I = Initiative

A = Attacks

Ld = Leadership

LIMITATIONS ON CERTAIN CHARACTERS/UNITS

The army lists presents the player with lists of troop types which can be included in the Orc and Goblin Army. In most cases there is no limit on the number of individual models, or the number of units, other than that imposed by the points values. However, some particular types of unit or character are limited. In some cases you can only include one character of a certain type in your army, or one of a specific unit. Any such limitations are clearly indicated in the lists. For example, you may only ever include one Warlord model.

SPECIAL CHARACTERS

The army list itself is intended to broadly represent an Orc and Goblin army. Provision has been made to include a general, but we do not specify that the general should be a particular Orc or Goblin warlord, the chieftain of a powerful tribe, or any given individual. We leave it up to you to invent a name and background as you feel appropriate for your own general and for any heroes you include in your army.

A separate section describing famous Orc and Goblin warlords has been included after the army list. These are, in effect, ready-made heroes and shamans, with their own unique characteristics, magic artefacts, and points values. You may include these characters in your army if you wish. The points cost of these special characters comes out of your Character points allowance in the normal way. So, for example, you can have Grom as your army's warlord if you wish.

ARMOUR

The saving throws for troops is not given on their profile because it can vary depending on the armour they wear. Saving throws are summarised below.

Armour	Save	Cavalry save
None	None	6+
Shield or light armour	6+	5+
Shield & light armour or heavy armour only	5+	4+
Shield and heavy armour	4+	3+
Cavalry with barding		adds further +1
Cavalry is war boar		adds further +1

For example, an Orc Boar Boy is cavalry wearing light armour and shield and riding a war boar, his save is therefore 3+ (4+ with a further +1 on account of the boar).

EQUIPMENT LIST

The following is a list of all the usual weapons in the Warhammer game. It has been included so that you can refer to it for comparative purposes, and so that you can choose equipment for character models without having to refer to the army list entries or the Warhammer rulebook. A character model may be armed with any weapons available to the troops themselves, subject to the usual restriction regarding weapon use – for example, it is impossible to wield a double-handed axe and a halberd as both require two hands to use. In the case of characters the models must actually carry the weapons ascribed to them. Note that regimental champions (Bosses) are always assumed to be armed and equipped exactly as the rank and file members of their regiment.

Items marked with an asterix (*) are not used by Orc or Goblin troops and are not therefore available to your army's characters. They have been included out of a sense of completeness.

EQUIPMENT LIST

HAND-TO-HAND COMBAT WEAPONS

A single sword, axe, mace
or other hand weapon .... Free

An additional sword, axe, etc. 1

A double-handed weapon,
including double-handed axe, sword, etc 2

Flail* 1

Halberd 2

Spear 1

A lance for a mounted warrior* 2

MISSILE WEAPONS

Bow 2

Short Bow 1

Long Bow * 3

Crossbow 3

Repeating Crossbow* 4

Javelin* 1

Sling* 1

Hand Gun* 3

Pistol* 2

ARMOUR

Shield 1

Light Armour 2

Heavy Armour* 3

Barding for steed* 4

ARMY SELECTION

Characters	**0-50%**	Up to half the points value of the army may be spent on characters. This includes the cost of a monster or chariot ridden by a character.
Mobs	**25%+**	At least a quarter of the total points value of the army must be spent on troops. This does not include the cost of champions or of chariots ridden by characters (both of these are paid for out of the Characters allowance).
War Machines	**0-25%**	Up to a quarter of the points value of the army may be spent on war machines.
Monsters	**0-25%**	Up to a quarter of the points value of the army may be spent on monsters. Note that this does not include monsters ridden by characters, which must be paid for from the Characters allowance.
Allies	**0-25%**	Up to a quarter of the points value of the army may be spent on allied troops chosen from any of the following list or lists: Chaos, Chaos Dwarf, Dark Elves, and Skaven.

CHARACTERS

Your army may include up to 50% of its points value as characters chosen from the list below. You must always include one Warlord, but apart from this you are free to choose as many or a few characters as you wish.

WARLORD .... Black Orc 140 points
Orc 110 points
Savage Orc 150 points
Goblin 50 points
Forest Goblin 50 points
Night Goblin 50 points

Your army must be led by a general and Orc and Goblin generals are called Warlords. The Warlord represents a great chieftain and leader of the Waaagh. He can be a Black Orc, an Orc, Savage Orc, Goblin, Forest Goblin or Night Goblin. Whichever race you choose, your army must always include at least one Mob of the same race. For example, if you have a Black Orc Warlord you must have at least one Mob of Black Orcs in your army.

WARBOSS	M	WS	BS	S	T	W	I	A	Ld
Black Orc	4	7	6	5	5	3	5	4	10
Orc	4	6	6	4	5	3	5	4	9
Savage Orc	4	6	6	4	5	3	5	4	9
Goblin	4	5	6	4	4	3	5	4	7
Forest Goblin	4	5	6	4	4	3	5	4	7
Night Goblin	4	5	6	4	4	3	5	4	7
War Boar	7	4	0	3	4	1	3	1	3
Giant Wolf	9	4	0	3	3	1	3	1	3
Giant Spider	7	3	0	4	3	1	1	1	5

EQUIPMENT: Sword.

WEAPONS/ARMOUR: The Warlord may be armed with any of the weapons or armour indicated on the Equipment List. See the separate Equipment List for summary and points values.

MAY RIDE: Orc and Goblin Warlords may ride either giant wolves, giant spiders, or war boars as shown on the chart below. Any Warlord may ride a monster (see separate Monster List for points values). A Warlord may ride in a chariot pulled by either war boars or giant wolves as described in the War Machines section of the list.

WARLORD	MAY RIDE	POINTS COST
Black Orc	War Boar	+8
Orc	War Boar	+8
Savage Orc	War Boar	+8
Goblin	Giant Wolf	+4
Forest Goblin	Giant Spider	+4
Night Goblin	None - may ride Monster or Chariot as normal	

MAGIC ITEMS: The Warlord is a Warboss character and is entitled to up to three magic items chosen from the appropriate Warhammer Battle Magic cards.

0-1 BATTLE STANDARD

Black Orc 92 points
Orc 83 points
Savage Orc 95 points
Goblin 65 points
Forest Goblin 65 points
Night Goblin 65 points

The army may include a Battle Standard together with its bearer if you wish. The Battle Standard Bearer may be of any of the Orc or Goblin races indicated. Whichever race you choose, your army must always include at least one Mob of the same race. For example, if you have a Forest Goblin as your Battle Standard Bearer you must have at least one Mob of Forest Goblins in your army.

STD BEARER	M	WS	BS	S	T	W	I	A	Ld
Black Orc	4	5	4	5	4	1	3	2	8
Orc	4	4	4	4	4	1	3	2	7
Savage Orc	4	4	4	4	4	1	3	2	7
Goblin	4	3	4	4	3	1	3	2	5
Forest Goblin	4	3	4	4	3	1	3	2	5
Night Goblin	4	3	4	4	3	1	3	2	5

EQUIPMENT: Sword and Battle Standard.

WEAPONS/ARMOUR: The Battle Standard Bearer may be armed with any of the weapons or armour indicated on the Equipment List. See the separate Equipment List for summary and points values.

MAY RIDE: Orc and Goblin Battle Standard Bearers may ride either giant wolves, giant spiders, or war boars as shown on the chart below. Any Battle Standard Bearer may ride a monster (see separate Monster List for more details). Any Battle Standard Bearer may ride in a chariot pulled by either war boars or giant wolves as described in the War Machines section of the list.

CHARACTER	MAY RIDE	POINTS COST
Black Orc	War Boar	+8
Orc	War Boar	+8
Savage Orc	War Boar	+8
Goblin	Giant Wolf	+4
Forest Goblin	Giant Spider	+4
Night Goblin	None - may ride Monster or Chariot as normal	

MAGIC ITEMS: The Battle Standard Bearer is a Boss character and is entitled to up to one magic item chosen from the appropriate Warhammer Battle Magic cards. This may be a magic standard, effectively turning the army's banner into a magic standard.

BIG BOSSES .... Black Orc 91 points
Orc 72 points
Savage Orc 98 points
Goblin 33 points
Forest Goblin 33 points
Night Goblin 33 points

BOSSES .... Black Orc 42 points
Orc 33 points
Savage Orc 45 points
Goblin 15 points
Forest Goblin 15 points
Night Goblin 15 points

The army may include as many Orc or Goblin Big Bosses as you wish within the normal limitations of the points available. You may choose from any of the Orc or Goblin races which are represented by Mobs in your army. For example, you can choose a Black Orc Big Boss only if your army includes at least one Mob of Black Orcs. Similarly you can only choose a Savage Orc Big Boss if your army includes at least one Mob of Savage Orcs.

Any regiment may include a Boss armed and equipped as the rest of the unit (see Equipment List for points values). A Boss is always the same race as the Mob to which he belongs.

BOSSES	M	WS	BS	S	T	W	I	A	Ld
Black Orc	4	5	4	5	4	1	3	2	8
Orc	4	4	4	4	4	1	3	2	7
Savage Orc	4	4	4	4	4	1	3	2	7
Goblin	4	3	4	4	3	1	3	2	5
Forest Goblin	4	3	4	4	3	1	3	2	5
Night Goblin	4	3	4	4	3	1	3	2	5

EQUIPMENT: A Boss is always armed and equipped in the same way as the rank and file members of his regiment (see Equipment List for points values).

MAGIC ITEMS: A Boss character is entitled to a single magic item chosen from the appropriate Warhammer Battle Magic cards.

BIG BOSSES	M	WS	BS	S	T	W	I	A	Ld
Black Orc	4	6	5	5	5	2	4	3	9
Orc	4	5	5	4	5	2	4	3	8
Savage Orc	4	5	5	4	5	2	4	3	8
Goblin	4	4	5	4	4	2	4	3	6
Forest Goblin	4	4	5	4	4	2	4	3	6
Night Goblin	4	4	5	4	4	2	4	3	6

EQUIPMENT: Sword.

WEAPONS/ARMOUR: A Big Boss may be armed with any of the weapons or armour indicated on the Equipment List. See the separate Equipment List for summary and points values.

MAY RIDE: Orc and Goblin Big Bosses may ride either giant wolves, giant spiders, or war boars as shown on the chart below. Any Big Boss may ride a Monster (see separate Monster List for points values and selection). Any Big Boss may ride in a chariot pulled by either war boars or giant wolves as described in the War Machines section of the list.

BIG BOSS	MAY RIDE	POINTS COST
Black Orc	War Boar	+8
Orc	War Boar	+8
Savage Orc	War Boar	+8
Goblin	Giant Wolf	+4
Forest Goblin	Giant Spider	+4
Night Goblin	None - may ride Monster or Chariot as normal	

MAGIC ITEMS: A Big Boss character is entitled to up to two magic items chosen from the appropriate Warhammer Battle Magic cards.

SHAMANS

Orc	Shaman .... 57 points
	Shaman Champion ...... 118 points
	Master Shaman .... 211 points
	Shaman Lord .... 287 points
Savage Orc	Shaman .... 59 points
	Shaman Champion ...... 122 points
	Master Shaman .... 219 points
	Shaman Lord .... 303 points
Goblin	Shaman .... 28 points
	Shaman Champion ...... 83 points
	Master Shaman .... 159 points
	Shaman Lord .... 253 points
Night Goblin	Shaman .... 28 points
	Shaman Champion ...... 83 points
	Master Shaman .... 159 points
	Shaman Lord .... 253 points
Forest Goblin	Shaman .... 28 points
	Shaman Champion ...... 83 points
	Master Shaman .... 159 points
	Shaman Lord .... 253 points

The army may include as many Shamans as you wish within the usual limitations of points cost. You may choose from any of the Orc or Goblin races which are represented by Mobs in your army. For example, you can choose a Night Goblin Shaman if your army includes at least one Mob of Night Goblins. Similarly, you can only choose a Savage Orc Shaman if your army includes at least one Mob of Savage Orcs. Note that there are no such things as Black Orc Shamans.

EQUIPMENT: Sword.

WEAPONS/ARMOUR: A Shaman may be armed with any of the weapons or armour allowed to any of the troop types in this list. See the Equipment List for separate summary and points values.

MAY RIDE: Orc and Goblin Shamans may ride either giant wolves, giant spiders, or war boars as shown on the chart below. Any Shaman may ride a Monster (see separate Monster List for points values and selection). Any Shaman may ride in a chariot pulled by either war boars or giant wolves as described in the War Machines section of the list. Note that the points value of a Shaman's chariot is included as part of his total points value.

SHAMAN	MAY RIDE	POINTS COST
Orc	War Boar	+8
Savage Orc	War Boar	+8
Goblin	Giant Wolf	+4
Forest Goblin	Giant Spider	+4
Night Goblin	None - may ride Monster or Chariot as normal	

MAGIC ITEMS: A Shaman is entitled to magic items chosen from the appropriate cards. A Shaman may have one magic item, a Shaman Champion may have two magic items, a Master Shaman may have three magic items, and a Shaman Lord may have four magic items.

ORC SHAMANS	M	WS	BS	S	T	W	I	A	Ld
Shaman	4	3	3	3	5	1	3	1	7
Champion Shaman	4	3	3	4	5	2	3	1	7
Master Shaman	4	3	3	4	5	3	4	2	7
Shaman Lord	4	3	3	4	5	4	5	3	8

GOBLIN SHAMANS	M	WS	BS	S	T	W	I	A	Ld
Shaman	4	2	3	3	4	1	3	1	5
Champion Shaman	4	2	3	4	4	2	3	1	5
Master Shaman	4	2	3	4	4	3	4	2	5
Shaman Lord	4	2	3	4	4	4	5	3	6

MOBS

Your army must include at least 25% of its points value as units chosen from the following list; it may include more if you wish. Orc and Goblin units are called Mobs, but in other respects they are exactly like the regiments of Men and Elves. In some cases you may only choose a maximum of one unit of a specific type, for example you can only have one Mob of Big'uns. There is no limitation on the size of a unit, other than units must consist of at least five models unless otherwise stated.

SAVAGE ORC BOAR BOYZ .... 25 points per model

Your army may include any number of Mobs of Savage Orc Boar Boyz – Savage Orcs riding war boars.

PROFILE	M	WS	BS	S	T	W	I	A	Ld
Savage Orc	4	3	3	3	4	1	2	1	7
War Boar	7	4	0	3	4	1	3	1	3

EQUIPMENT: Savage Orc Boar Boyz carry shields. They ride fierce war boars and are armed with a hand weapon.

SAVE: 3+ (A Savage Orc's protective tattoos give him a save equivalent to light armour.)

OPTIONS: Any Mobs of Savage Orc Boar Boyz may be equipped with spears at an additional cost of +2 points per model. Any Mobs of Savage Orc Boar Boyz may be equipped with bows at an additional cost of +4 points per model. One Mob of Savage Orc Boar Boyz Mob may carry a Magic Standard. This may be chosen from the appropriate magic item cards and its cost is indicated on the card itself (see Warhammer Battle Magic).

SPECIAL RULE: Savage Orcs are affected by the rules for *frenzy*, as described in the Warhammer rulebook.

ORC BOAR BOYZ .... 27 points per model

Your army may include any number of Mobs of Orc Boar Boyz – fierce Orcs riding equally fierce war boars. These are powerful troops, better fighters than normal Orcs, and potentially the equal to the best heavily armoured knights of the Empire or High Elves.

PROFILE	M	WS	BS	S	T	W	I	A	Ld
Orc	4	4	3	3	4	1	2	1	7
War Boar	7	4	0	3	4	1	3	1	3

EQUIPMENT: Boar Boyz wear light armour and carry shields. They ride fierce war boars and are armed with a hand weapon.

SAVE: 3+

OPTIONS: Any Mobs of Boar Boyz may be equipped with spears at an additional cost of +2 points per model. Any Boar Boyz Mob may carry a Magic Standard. This may be chosen from the appropriate magic item cards and its cost is indicated on the card itself (see Warhammer Battle Magic).

GOBLIN WOLF RIDERS .... 9 points per model

Your army may include any number of Mobs of Goblin wolf riders. Goblin wolf riders are among the fastest and most mobile of all troops. They are capable of moving rapidly across the battlefield in a very short time, either to intercept enemy or to harass static war machines. Swarms of wolf riders are often deployed ahead of the army's line of march to scout and block any route of escape.

PROFILE	M	WS	BS	S	T	W	I	A	Ld
Goblin	4	2	3	3	3	1	2	1	5
Giant Wolf	9	4	0	3	3	1	3	1	3

EQUIPMENT: Wolf riders carry a hand weapon and ride a giant wolf.

SAVE: 6+

OPTIONS: Any Mobs of wolf riders may be armed with spears at an additional cost of +1 point per model. Any Mobs of wolf riders may be armed with short bows at an additional cost of +1 point per model. Any Mobs of wolf riders may be equipped with light armour at an additional cost of +2 points per model. Any Mobs of wolf riders may be equipped with shields at an additional cost of +1 point per model.

FOREST GOBLIN SPIDER RIDERS .... 9 points per model

Your army may include any number of Mobs of Forest Goblin spider riders. Spider riders can move easily through woods and forests, scuttling over the treetops and through the dense foliage.

PROFILE	M	WS	BS	S	T	W	I	A	Ld
Forest Goblin	4	2	3	3	3	1	2	1	5
Giant Spider	7	3	0	4	3	1	1	1	5

EQUIPMENT: Spider riders carry a hand weapon and ride a giant spider.

SAVE: 6+

OPTIONS: Any Mobs of spider riders may carry shields at an additional cost of +1 point per model. Any Mobs of spider riders may be armed with spears at an additional cost of +1 point per model. Any Mobs of spider riders may be armed with short bows at an additional cost of +1 point per model.

0-1 MOB OF ORC BIG'UNS .... 6 1/2 points per model

PROFILE	M	WS	BS	S	T	W	I	A	Ld
Big'uns	4	4	3	4	4	1	3	1	7

Your army may include one Mob of Big'uns. These are especially large and fierce Orcs, the most powerful of all after the tribe's chieftain. They are often well armoured and likely to carry the pick of any wargear the tribe has.

EQUIPMENT: Hand weapon.

SAVE: None.

OPTIONS: The Big'uns may be equipped with shields at an additional cost of +1 point per model. The Big'uns may be equipped with light armour at an additional cost of +2 points per model. Big'uns may carry one of the following weapons: either spears (+1 point per model), or double-handed weapons (+2 points per model) or bows (+2 points per model). The Big'uns may carry a Magic Standard. This may be chosen from the appropriate Magic Item cards and its cost is indicated on the card itself (see Warhammer Battle Magic).

ORC BOYZ .... 5 1/2 points per model

Your army may include any number of Mobs of Orc Boyz. These are the mainstay of many an army – tough, reliable fighters able to hold a battleline against almost any enemy.

PROFILE	M	WS	BS	S	T	W	I	A	Ld
Orc	4	3	3	3	4	1	2	1	7

EQUIPMENT: Orc Boyz carry a hand weapon.

SAVE: None.

OPTIONS: Any Mobs of Orc Boyz may be equipped with light armour at an additional cost of +2 points per model. Any Mobs may be equipped with shields at a cost of +1 points per model. Any Mobs may be armed with one of the following weapons: either a double-handed weapon (+2 points per model), a halberd (+2 points per model), a spear (+1 point per model), or an additional hand weapon (+1 point per model). One Orc Boyz Mob may carry a Magic Standard. This may be chosen from the appropriate magic item cards and its cost is indicated on the card itself (see Warhammer Battle Magic).

ORC ARRER BOYZ .... 7 1/2 points per model

Your army may include any number of Mobs of Orc Arrer Boyz. These are Orc Boyz armed with bows or crossbows. Despite their armament they are equally good hand-to-hand fighters as other Boyz.

PROFILE	M	WS	BS	S	T	W	I	A	Ld
Orc	4	3	3	3	4	1	2	1	7

EQUIPMENT: Orc Arrer Boyz carry a hand weapon and bow.

SAVE: None.

OPTIONS: Any Mobs of Orc Arrer Boyz may be equipped with light armour at an additional cost of +2 points per model. Any Mobs may be equipped with shields at a cost of +1 points per model. Any Mobs may be armed with crossbows instead of bows at an additional cost of +1 point per model.

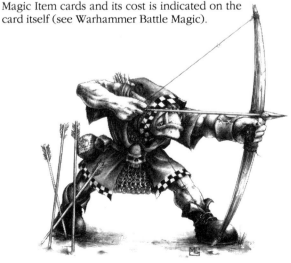

0-1 MOB OF BLACK ORCS .... 9 points per model

Your army may include one Mob of Black Orcs. Black Orcs come from the eastern side of the Worlds Edge Mountains and are bigger, stronger and tougher than ordinary Orcs. They are also more reliable, and don't fight amongst themselves like other Orcs and Goblins.

PROFILE	M	WS	BS	S	T	W	I	A	Ld
Black Orc	4	4	3	4	4	1	2	1	8

EQUIPMENT: Black Orcs wear light armour and carry a hand weapon.

SAVE: 6+

OPTIONS: A Mob of Black Orcs may be armed with one of the following: double-handed weapons (+2 points per model), halberds (+2 points per model), spears (+1 point per model) or an additional hand weapon (+1 point). A Mob of Black Orcs may carry a shield (+1 point). The Mob of Black Orcs may carry a Magic Standard. This may be chosen from the appropriate magic item cards and its cost is indicated on the card itself (see Warhammer Battle Magic).

SAVAGE ORCS .... 7 1/2 points per model

Your army may include any number of Mobs of Savage Orcs. Savage Orcs are barbaric and fierce, they wear no armour and fight with simply made weapons such as maces and clubs.

PROFILE	M	WS	BS	S	T	W	I	A	Ld
Savage Orc	4	3	3	3	4	1	2	1	7

EQUIPMENT: Savage Orcs carry a crude hand weapon, usually a club, mace or stone axe.

SAVE: 6+ due to protective tattoos.

OPTIONS: Any Mobs of Savage Orcs may carry a shield at an additional cost of +1 point per model. Any Mobs of Savage Orcs may be armed with one of the following weapons: either a double-handed weapon (+2 points per model) or an additional hand weapon (+1 point per model) or a bow (+2 points per model). One Mob of Savage Orcs may carry a Magic Standard. This may be chosen from the appropriate magic item cards and its cost is indicated on the card itself (see Warhammer Battle Magic).

SPECIAL RULES: Savage Orcs can *skirmish* as described in the Warhammer rulebook. Savage Orcs are affected by the rules for *frenzy*.

NB: *The points value of 7 1/2 is correct, and takes into account their frenzy and natural armour. The points value of 5 1/2 given in the Warhammer rulebook does not take these into account and is (as astute players have pointed out!) a mistake.*

GOBLINS .... 2 1/2 points per model

Your army may include any number of Mobs of Goblins. Goblins are numerous and fight most effectively in big Mobs with many ranks – this enables the Goblins to bowl over their enemy by sheer weight of numbers.

PROFILE	M	WS	BS	S	T	W	I	A	Ld
Goblin	4	2	3	3	3	1	2	1	5

EQUIPMENT: Goblins carry a hand weapon.

SAVE: None.

OPTIONS: Any Mobs of Goblins may carry shields at an additional cost of +1/2 point per model. Any Mobs of Goblins may wear light armour at an additional cost of +1 point per model. Any Mob may be armed with one of the following weapons: either double-handed weapons (+1 point per model), halberds (+1 point per model), spears (+1/2 point per model), or short bows (+1/2 point per model). One Mob of Goblins may carry a Magic Standard. This may be chosen from the appropriate magic item cards and its cost is indicated on the card itself (see Warhammer Battle Magic).

FOREST GOBLINS ...... 2 1/2 points per model

Your army may include any number of Mobs of Forest Goblins. Forest Goblins wear exotic war paint, carry war axes and are often decorated with colourful feathers.

PROFILE	M	WS	BS	S	T	W	I	A	Ld
Goblin	4	2	3	3	3	1	2	1	5

EQUIPMENT: Forest Goblins are armed with a hand weapon – often a war axe or club.

SAVE: None.

OPTIONS: Any Mobs of Forest Goblins may carry shields at an additional cost of +1/2 point per model. Any Mobs may be armed with one of the following weapons: either double-handed weapons (+1 point per model), spears (+1/2 point per model), or short bows (+1/2 point per model). One Mob of Forest Goblins may carry a Magic Standard. This may be chosen from the appropriate magic item cards and its cost is indicated on the card itself.

NIGHT GOBLINS .... 2 1/2 points per model

Your army may include any number of Mobs of Night Goblins. Night Goblins live in the tunnels and caverns beneath the mountains, and dress in black or dark cloaks and hoods.

PROFILE	M	WS	BS	S	T	W	I	A	Ld
Night Goblin	4	2	3	3	3	1	2	1	5

EQUIPMENT: Night Goblins are armed with a hand weapon.

SAVE: None.

OPTIONS: Any Mobs of Night Goblins may carry shields at an additional cost of +1/2 point per model. Any Mobs may be armed with one of the following weapons: either double-handed weapons (+1 point per model), halberds (+1 point per model), spears (+1/2 point per model), or short bows (+1/2 point per model). One Mob of Night Goblins may carry a Magic Standard. This may be chosen from the appropriate magic item cards and its cost is indicated on the card itself (see Warhammer Battle Magic).

SPECIAL RULES: Each Night Goblin Mob may include up to three hidden Night Goblin Fanatics.

0-1 MOB OF SQUIG HUNTERS

8 points per hunter team
20 points per cave squig

If your army contains at least one Mob of ordinary Night Goblins then it may include a single Squig Hunter Mob too. A Squig Hunter Mob must contain at least five models (a Squig Hunter team counts as two) and may include Cave Squigs as well as Hunters armed with long prodders. A Mob must have at least one Hunter team for every three Cave Squigs in order to control the Squigs properly.

PROFILE	M	WS	BS	S	T	W	I	A	Ld
Night Goblin	4	2	3	3	3	1	2	1	5
Cave Squig	2D6"	4	0	5	3	1	5	2	2

EQUIPMENT: Night Goblin Squig Hunters are armed with long handled squig prodders.

SAVE: None.

SPECIAL RULES: See the Orc Bestiary rules section of this book for a full description of how Squig Hunters work.

BOSS. As Squig Hunter teams normally carry one prodder between two models a Boss can be armed with a sword, axe or any other kind of hand weapon rather than with a prodder. This is an exception to the normal rules – normally a champion/boss is armed in the same way as his unit.

0-1 MOB OF NETTERS .... 3 1/2 points per model

If your army contains at least one Mob of ordinary Night Goblins then it may include a single Netter Mob too. A Netter Mob contains five or more models like any other Mob, but unlike other units it can contain both net- and club-armed Night Goblins. The ratio of net- to club-armed Netters is entirely up to you: you could have all clubs, all nets or a mixture of the two. If a Netter Mob has a Boss he may be armed with a club at a cost of +1 point.

PROFILE	M	WS	BS	S	T	W	I	A	Ld
Night Goblin	4	2	3	3	3	1	2	1	5

EQUIPMENT: Night Goblin Netters are armed with either nets or clubs.

SAVE: None.

SPECIAL RULES: See the Bestiary section in this volume for a full description of how Netters work.

BOSS. A Mob of Netters may have a Boss armed with a club, they may not have a Boss armed with a net. (What's the point of being the Boss if you don't get to bash things?)

NIGHT GOBLIN FANATICS .... 30 points per model

Each unit of Night Goblins in your army may include up to three hidden Night Goblin Fanatics. Only Night Goblin Mobs may include Night Goblin Fanatics. Night Goblin Netter and Night Goblin Squig Hunter units may not include Fanatics.

PROFILE	M	WS	BS	S	T	W	I	A	Ld
FANATIC	2D6	special		5	3	1	-	D6	-

EQUIPMENT: Ball and chain.

SAVE: None.

SPECIAL RULES: See the Orc Bestiary rules section.

SQUIG HOPPERS .... 25 points per model

Your army may include up to five Squig Hoppers for each Night Goblin Mob it contains (including Squig Hunter and Netter Mobs). They are *not* part of the Mobs (as are Fanatics) but quite independent. Squig Hoppers are not organised into formal units. Each Squig Hopper moves and fights as an individual model and as such they never have champions, standards, musicians, etc.

PROFILE	M	WS	BS	S	T	W	I	A	Ld
Night Goblin	4	2	3	3	3	1	2	1	5
Bouncing Squig	2D6"	4	0	5	3	1	5	2	2

EQUIPMENT: Each Night Goblin rider carries a hand weapon such as a club or axe.

SAVE: 6+

SPECIAL RULES: See the Squig Hopper rules in the Bestiary section of this volume for a full description of how Squig Hoppers work.

GIANTS .... 200 points per model

Giants are big and not very bright creatures. Although they do not need it to fight they are usually armed with a big club made from a tree trunk.

PROFILE	M	WS	BS	S	T	W	I	A	Ld
Giant	6	3	3	7	6	6	3	special	6

OGRES .... 40 points per model

Ogre bands are attracted to Orc armies by the prospects of loot. Orcs respect them partly because of their great strength but mostly because Ogres are bigger than them.

PROFILE	M	WS	BS	S	T	W	I	A	Ld
Ogre	6	3	2	4	5	3	3	2	7

EQUIPMENT: Hand weapon.

SAVE: None.

OPTIONS: Any units of Ogres may be equipped with one of the following: an additional hand weapon at a further +1 point per model, a double-handed weapon at +2 points per model, or a halberd at +2 points per model. Any unit may be equipped with light armour at an additional cost of +2 points per model.

TROLLS .... 65 points per model

Your army may include any number of Trolls, of which there are three types: Trolls, Stone Trolls and River Trolls. Trolls must be organised into units of the same type, but the number of Trolls in a unit can be less than the normal minimum of five models. If your army includes up to five Trolls these form a single unit. For example you could have just one Troll in your army and it will count as a unit on its own. If your army includes six to ten Trolls these may be organised into either one unit or into two as near as possible equally sized units.

For example, if you have seven Trolls these could be organised into one unit of four and one unit of three. If your army includes eleven to fifteen Trolls these may be organised into either a single unit, two as near as possible equally-sized units, or three as near a possible equally-sized units. If your army includes sixteen or more Trolls then the possible number of units goes up by 1 for every extra 5 models, eg 16-20 Trolls = up to 4 units, 21-25 Trolls = up to 5 units, 26-30 Trolls = up to 6 units and so on.

PROFILE	M	WS	BS	S	T	W	I	A	Ld
Troll	6	3	1	5	4	3	1	3	4

EQUIPMENT: Trolls do not require weapons to fight but often carry a big club.

SAVE: None.

SPECIAL RULES: See the Bestiary section for details.

SNOTLINGS .... 15 points per base

Your army may include any number of Snotling bases. If your army includes up to five Snotling bases these form a single unit. For example, if you have just one Snotling base in your army it will count as a unit on its own. If your army includes six to ten Snotling bases these may be organised into either one unit or into two as near as possible equally sized units. If your army includes eleven to fifteen bases these may be organised into either a single unit, two as near as possible equally-sized units, or three as near as possible equally-sized units. If your army includes sixteen or more Snotling bases then the possible number of units goes up by one for every extra five bases.

PROFILE	M	WS	BS	S	T	W	I	A	Ld
Snotling	4	2	2	1	1	3	3	3	4

WAR MACHINES

Neither Orcs nor Goblins are particularly technically minded, but they build fast and strong so their devices usually work even though they may appear crude in comparison to human constructions. Your army may include up to 25% of its points value as war machines chosen from the following list.

ROCK LOBBERS

Small Rock Lobbers 66 1/2 points each
Big Rock Lobbers 96 1/2 points each

If your army contains at least one Mob of Orcs (including Big'uns) it may also include any number of stone throwers, which Orcs call Rock Lobbers. Each machine has three Orc crew to operate and defend it.

PROFILE	M	WS	BS	S	T	W	I	A	Ld
Rock Lobber	-	-	-	-	7	3	-	-	-
Crew	4	3	3	3	4	1	2	1	7

	RANGE	STRENGTH	SAVE	WOUNDS PER HIT
Big Rock Lobber	60"	10	none	D6
Small Rock Lobber	48"	7	none	D3

EQUIPMENT: The crew are armed with hand weapons.

SAVE: None.

OPTIONS: Rock Lobber crew may wear light armour at an additional cost of +2 points per model.

BOLT THROWERS .... 46 1/2 points each

If your army contains at least one Mob of Orcs (including Big'uns) it may also include any number of Bolt Throwers. Each machine has a crew of three Orcs to operate and defend it.

PROFILE	M	WS	BS	S	T	W	I	A	Ld
Bolt Thrower	-	-	-	-	7	3	-	-	-
Crew	4	3	3	3	4	1	2	1	7

	RANGE	STRENGTH	SAVE	WOUNDS PER HIT
Bolt Thrower	48"	5-1 per rank	none	D4

EQUIPMENT: The crew are armed with hand weapons.

SAVE: None.

OPTIONS: Rock Lobber crew may wear light armour at an additional cost of +2 points per model.

SNOTLING PUMP WAGON .... 40 points each

If your army includes at least one Goblin Mob then it may include any number of Snotling Pump Wagons. Each machine is crewed by a stand of Snotlings.

PROFILE	M	WS	BS	S	T	W	I	A	Ld
Pump Wagon	2D6"	-	-	7	7	3	1	-	-
Crew	-	2	2	1	1	3	3	3	4

93

DOOM DIVER
CATAPULT .... 100 points each

If your army contains at least one Goblin Mob then it may include any number of Doom Diver Catapults. Note that this must be an ordinary Goblin Mob – not a Night Goblin or a Forest Goblin Mob. Each Doom Diver Catapult is assumed to have an infinite supply of Doom Divers ready and waiting to be catapulted into the air.

PROFILE	M	WS	BS	S	T	W	I	A	Ld
Catapult	-	-	-	-	7	3	-	-	-
Doom Diver	4	2	3	3	3	1	2	1	5

	MAX. RANGE	STRENGTH	SAVE	WOUNDS PER HIT
Direct Hit	Anywhere on the tabletop	10	None	D6
Other Hits	Anywhere on the tabletop	5	-2	1

Special Rules: See elsewhere in this volume for special rules for the Doom Diver Catapult.

ORC BOAR
CHARIOTS .... 81 points per model

If your army includes at least one Mob of Orcs (including Big'uns) it may also include any number of Orc boar chariots. Chariots fight as individual models as described in the Warhammer rulebook. Each chariot has a crew of two Orcs and is pulled by two war boars.

PROFILE	M	WS	BS	S	T	W	I	A	Ld
Orc	4	3	3	3	4	1	2	1	7
War Boar	7	4	0	3	4	1	3	1	3
Chariot	-	-	-	7	7	3	1	-	-

EQUIPMENT: The Orcs carry swords and wear light armour.

OPTIONS: Any chariots may have up to two additional crewmen each at a cost of 7 1/2 points each. Any chariot crew may be equipped with shields at an additional cost of +1 point per crewman. Any chariot crew may be given short bows at an additional cost of +1 point per crewman. Any chariots may have scythed wheels at an additional cost of 20 points per chariot. One Orc boar chariot may carry a Magic Standard. This may be chosen from the appropriate magic item cards and its cost is indicated on the card itself (see Warhammer Battle Magic).

GOBLIN WOLF
CHARIOTS .... 65 points per model

If your army contains at least one Goblin Mob then it may include any number of Goblin wolf chariots. Chariots fight as individual models as described in the Warhammer rulebook. Each chariot has a crew of two Goblins and is pulled by two giant wolves.

PROFILE	M	WS	BS	S	T	W	I	A	Ld
Goblin	4	2	3	3	3	1	2	1	5
Giant Wolf	9	4	0	3	3	1	3	1	3
Chariot	-	-	-	7	7	3	1	-	-

EQUIPMENT: The Goblins carry swords and wear light armour.

OPTIONS: Any chariots may have up to two additional crewmen each at a cost of 3 1/2 points each. Any chariot may have an additional giant wolf to pull it at a cost of +4 points. Any chariot crew may be equipped with shields at an additional cost of +1/2 point per crewman. Any chariot crew many be given short bows at an additional cost of +1/2 point per crewman. Any chariots may have scythed wheels at an additional cost of 20 points per chariot. One Goblin wolf chariot may carry a Magic Standard. This may be chosen from the appropriate magic item cards and its cost is indicated on the card itself (see Warhammer Battle Magic).

MONSTERS

DRAGON

Dragon .... 450 points

Great Dragon .... 600 points

Emperor Dragon .... 750 points

May be used by any armies.

Profile	M	WS	BS	S	T	W	I	A	L
Dragon	6	6	0	6	6	7	8	7	7
Great Dragon	6	7	0	7	7	8	7	8	8
Emperor Dragon	6	8	0	8	8	9	6	9	9

CHIMERA .... 250 points

Profile	M	WS	BS	S	T	W	I	A	L
Chimera	6	4	0	7	6	6	4	6	8

COCKATRICE .... 150 points

Profile	M	WS	BS	S	T	W	I	A	L
Cockatrice	4	3	0	4	4	2	4	3	6

GRIFFON .... 150 points

Profile	M	WS	BS	S	T	W	I	A	L
Griffon	6	5	0	6	5	5	7	4	8

HIPPOGRIFF .... 145 points

Profile	M	WS	BS	S	T	W	I	A	L
Hippogriff	8	5	0	6	5	5	6	3	8

HYDRA .... 225 points

Profile	M	WS	BS	S	T	W	I	A	L
Hydra	6	3	0	5	6	7	3	5	6

GIGANTIC SPIDER .... 50 points

Profile	M	WS	BS	S	T	W	I	A	L
Gigantic Spider	5	3	0	5	4	4	1	2	7

MANTICORE .... 200 points

Profile	M	WS	BS	S	T	W	I	A	L
Manticore	6	6	0	7	7	5	4	4	8

WYVERN .... 180 points

Profile	M	WS	BS	S	T	W	I	A	L
Wyvern	6	5	0	5	6	4	4	3	5

GIANT SCORPION .... 50 points

Profile	M	WS	BS	S	T	W	I	A	L
Giant Scorpion	5	3	0	5	4	4	1	2	7

SWARMS .... 100 points

Profile	M	WS	BS	S	T	W	I	A	L
Rats	6	3	0	3	2	5	1	5	10
Frogs	4	3	0	3	2	5	1	5	10
Lizards	4	3	0	3	2	5	1	5	10
Bats	8	3	0	3	2	5	1	5	10
Serpents	3	3	0	4	2	5	1	5	10
Insects/Spiders	4	3	0	3	2	5	1	5	10
Scorpions	4	3	0	4	2	5	1	5	10

SPECIAL CHARACTERS

AZHAG
THE SLAUGHTERER .... 130 points

Wyvern: +180 points

Your army may be led by Azhag the Slaughterer. If you decide to do this, Azhag is the Warlord of your army and therefore replaces the Warlord described in the main army list. If your army is led by Azhag the Slaughterer it must include at least one unit of Orcs.

Azhag was one of the most dangerous Orc Warlords of recent history, and his campaigns of destruction throughout the Empire almost brought the eastern provinces to their knees. After defeating countless Orc and Goblin tribes from the Worlds Edge Mountains he led his horde into Ostermark and looted several towns destroying the Temple of Sigmar at Nachtdorf in the process.

Azhag possessed a strange iron crown which appeared to give him sorcerous powers. After his final defeat by a large Empire army this crown was taken by the Grand Theogonist of Sigmar and locked away forever.

Azhag rode to battle on the back of a large wyvern, often harrying his retreating enemies from the air after a battle.

Profile	M	WS	BS	S	T	W	I	A	Ld
Azhag	4	6	6	4	5	3	5	4	10
Wyvern	6	5	0	5	6	4	4	3	5

WEAPONS/ARMOUR: Azhag wears a suit of light armour and carries a shield.

MAY RIDE: Azhag rides a wyvern.

MAGIC ITEMS: Azhag may carry up to three magic items in total but the first magic item he has must always be the Crown of Sorcery. Azhag does not have to have the Crown of Sorcery, but if he has any magic items the Crown of Sorcery must be among them. Other items may be chosen freely from the Warhammer Battle Magic cards.

SPECIAL RULES

ANIMOSITY

No Orc or Goblin units within 12" of Azhag the Slaughterer are affected by animosity. They just don't dare. Units within 12" of Azhag therefore don't test. Units more than 12" away from Azhag at the start of your turn are affected exactly as normal.

GORFANG ROTGUT .... 90 points

You may include Gorfang Rotgut in your army as an Orc Big Boss or as a Warlord if you wish, but if you take him your army must include at least one unit of Orcs.

Gorfang Rotgut is the chieftain of the Orcs of Black Crag, the ancient Dwarf hold taken over by Orcs many years ago. Over the centuries many tribes have fought over and occupied Black Crag, and the most powerful tribe has always taken the crag as its homeland. Gorfang's tribe, the Red Fangs, is currently the most powerful Orc tribe in the whole of the area around the western end of Death Pass. Gorfang has subjugated most of the local Orc tribes but his neighbours are the Night Goblins of Karak Eight Peaks whose leader is the old and infamously cunning Skarsnik. The two leaders enjoy an uneasy alliance, with Skarsnik controlling the mountains around Karak Eight Peaks and the eastern end of Death Pass, while Gorfang controls the western end of Death Pass and the adjoining area.

Gorfang is an immensely strong Orc. He lost an eye at the Battle of the Jaws, and wears an iron patch to cover the wound. Many of his battles have been fought against Dwarfs, including the siege of Barak Varr and the attack on Karak Azul. As a result of his long struggles Gorfang has acquired an unreasoning hatred of the Dwarf race.

When Gorfang attacked Karak Azul he broke into Lord Kazador's throne room and captured many of the Dwarf Lord's kinsfolk. Some were taken back to the dungeons of Black Crag where they remain to this day, to the anger of Kazador. The Dwarf Lord's son, Kazrik, was not taken captive but was shaved, and his head tattooed with a crude Orc glyph representing Gorfang, and then firmly nailed to Kazador's own throne. Although Kazrik survived, the experienced has unhinged him somewhat. Lord Kazador has sworn vengeance and awaits the day when he can crush the Orc chieftain.

Profile	M	WS	BS	S	T	W	I	A	Ld
Gorfang	4	5	5	5	5	3	4	3	8
War Boar	7	4	0	3	4	1	3	1	3

WEAPONS/ARMOUR: Gorfang Rotgut wears light armour and carries a shield. He is armed with a huge sword.

MAY RIDE: Gorfang Rotgut may ride a war boar (+8 points), or a monster (see separate Monster List), or he can ride a chariot pulled by either war boars or giant wolves as described in the War Machines section.

MAGIC ITEMS: Gorfang Rotgut may carry up to two magic items chosen from the appropriate Warhammer Battle Magic cards.

SPECIAL RULES

HATES DWARFS

Gorfang Rotgut really hates Dwarfs – he just can't stand stunties. He is therefore affected by the rules for *hatred* as described in the Warhammer rulebook.

GROM THE PAUNCH OF MISTY MOUNTAIN .... 80 points

Niblit: +65 points with Battle Standard

Chariot: +62 points

Axe of Grom: +50 points

Your army may be led by Grom the Paunch of Misty Mountain. If you decide to do this, Grom is the Warlord of your army and therefore replaces the Warlord described in the main army list. Grom is accompanied by his Goblin assistant Niblit who also carries the army's battle banner. Niblit replaces the normal battle standard bearer option in the army list. Your army must include at least one unit of Goblins if it is led by Grom.

Grom is a hugely obese and extremely fierce Goblin Warlord. According to legend he once ate a plate of raw Troll meat which is regenerating within him all the time. As a result he is very fat and suffers from constant agony due to chronic indigestion, which may explain why he is so fierce. He rides a massive chariot pulled by three wolves, and swings his mighty axe Elf-Biter. He is accompanied by his assistant Niblit the Goblin who carries the army's battle standard. As a result of eating the troll flesh he has developed several troll-like traits and has an almost trollish resistance to injury.

Grom the Paunch

Profile	M	WS	BS	S	T	W	I	A	Ld
Grom	4	5	6	4	4	3	5	4	7
Niblit	4	3	4	4	3	1	3	2	5
Chariot	-	-	-	7	7	3	1	-	-
Giant Wolf	9	4	0	3	3	1	3	1	3

WEAPONS/ARMOUR: Grom wears a suit of light armour, and is armed with the huge Axe of Grom. Grom rides a chariot pulled by three giant wolves and is accompanied by his Goblin attendant Niblit who carries the army's battle standard.

MAGIC ITEMS: Grom may carry up to three magic items including the mighty Axe of Grom. The magic item card for Grom's axe is included in the Warhammer game itself. Other magic items may be chosen from the cards in Warhammer Battle Magic as usual. Niblit may carry a single magic item chosen from Warhammer Battle Magic.

SPECIAL RULES

REGENERATE

Grom can regenerate wounds in the same way as a Troll. This works as follows. If Grom suffers one or more wounds from shooting, combat, or whatever, he can try to recover these wounds at the end of the phase in which they are inflicted. Roll a dice for each wound. If you roll a 4 or more that wound has regenerated. Any regenerated wounds are reinstated. If Grom is slain he may still try to regenerate wounds suffered, and if successful he is not killed after all. Like Trolls, Grom cannot regenerate wounds suffered from flames or burning. If he sustains one or more wounds from flames then he loses his ability to regenerate, and he won't even be able to regenerate wounds inflicted by ordinary weapons.

GORBAD IRONCLAW .... 120 points

Morgor the Mangler: +125 points

Your army may be led by Gorbad Ironclaw. If you decide to do this, Gorbad is the Warlord of your army and therefore replaces the Warlord described in the main army list. Your army must include at least one unit of Orcs if it is led by Gorbad Ironclaw.

Gorbad Ironclaw was one of the most successful Orc leaders of all time. In his day the Empire almost crumbled, the Emperor Sigismund was slain, and the region of Solland turned into a wasteland. At the battle of Solland's Crown Gorbad slew Eldred, the last Count of Solland, and captured both his crown and sword, one of the ancient Runefangs of the Empire. Even today, almost a thousand years after his death, the name of Gorbad Ironclaw is feared in the Empire and his memory is kept alive by the Orc Warlords that have succeeded him. Perhaps none will ever be as great again – he is the greatest of all Orc heroes and an inspiration to all Orc-kind.

Profile	M	WS	BS	S	T	W	I	A	Ld
Gorbad	4	6	6	4	5	3	5	4	10
War Boar	7	4	0	3	4	1	3	1	3

WEAPONS/ARMOUR: Gorbad Ironclaw wears light armour. He is armed with a huge battle axe, Morgor the Mangler. Gorbad Ironclaw rides a huge war boar.

MAGIC ITEMS: Gorbad Ironclaw may carry up to three magic items including the mighty battle axe Morgor the Mangler. Other magic items may be chosen from the cards in Warhammer Battle Magic as usual.

MORGLUM
NECKSNAPPER .... 150 points

Your army may be led by Morglum Necksnapper. If you decide to do this, Morglum is the Warlord of your army and therefore replaces the Warlord described in the main army list. Your army must include at least one unit of Black Orcs if it is led by Morglum Necksnapper.

Black Orcs come from the east, from the Dark Lands and the Mountains of Mourn where the land lies under a cloud of black volcanic dust. Some Black Orc tribes have undertaken the arduous journey across the Dark Land into the west, where they have conquered Orc and Goblin tribes. The most feared of these tribes is the Necksnappers under their ambitious chieftain Morglum.

Most Orcs are loud and quarrelsome, but Black Orcs are quiet and stern, strong and silent. This is especially true of Morglum who appears to be almost entirely fearless. Morglum is renowned for his short, to the point battle cries and terse tactical observations. At the Battle of Death Pass he led his Black Orcs, Orcs and Goblins to a convincing victory against an errant Bretonnian army. As the Bretonnian duke and his knights galloped frantically out of Death Pass towards the setting sun, pursued by hordes of Goblins, Morglum Necksnapper made his famous pronouncement "Let 'em tell da King. Da east belongs to da Orcs. Da east belongs to Morglum. Da east is green."

Profile	M	WS	BS	S	T	W	I	A	Ld
Morglum	4	7	6	5	5	3	5	4	10
War Boar	7	4	0	3	4	1	3	1	3

WEAPONS/ARMOUR: Morglum wear light armour and carries an axe in each hand.

MAY RIDE: Morglum Necksnapper may ride a war boar (+8 points), or a monster (see separate Monster List for points), or he can ride a chariot pulled by either war boars or giant wolves as described in the War Machines section of the list.

MAGIC ITEMS: Morglum may carry up to three magic items chosen from the Warhammer Battle Magic cards.

> *The only good stunty is a dead stunty, and the only thing better n' a dead stunty is a dyin' stunty who tells yer where to find 'is mates.*
>
> Morglum Necksnapper

SPECIAL RULES

IMMUNE TO PSYCHOLOGY

Morglum Necksnapper is immune to all psychology. He cannot be affected by fear, terror, panic or any other psychology tests. He must still take break tests if defeated in hand-to-hand combat.

OGLOK
THE 'ORRIBLE .... 90 points

You may include Oglok in your army as an Orc Big Boss or as a Warlord if you wish. Your army must include at least one unit of Orcs if you decide to include Oglok.

Oglok's Orc tribe lives in the Bad Lands and was defeated by Morglum Necksnapper's Black Orcs. Oglok was so overawed by the Black Orc leader that he decided to throw in his lot with Morglum. Since then he has fought in many battles alongside the Black Orcs, leading his Orc Boar Boyz against the Bretonnians at the Battle of Death Pass and against the Dwarfs of Karak Azul. Oglok is a gnarled old Orc whose craggy head bears the scars of many years fighting. His powers of leadership are second only to Morglum himself.

Profile	M	WS	BS	S	T	W	I	A	Ld
Oglok	4	6	5	4	5	2	4	4	9
War Boar	7	4	0	3	4	1	3	1	3

WEAPONS/ARMOUR: Oglok wears light armour and carries a shield.

MAY RIDE: Oglok may ride a war boar (+8 points), or a monster (see separate Monster List for points), or he can ride a chariot pulled by either war boars or giant wolves as described in the War Machines section of the list.

MAGIC ITEMS: Oglok may carry up to two magic items chosen from the Warhammer Battle Magic cards.

SKARSNIK, WARLORD OF THE EIGHT PEAKS .... 80 points

+ 75 points Prodder

+ 50 points Gobbla

Skarsnik is the chieftain of the Crooked Moon tribe and the most powerful Night Goblin Warlord in the whole of the southern Worlds Edge Mountains. All the other Goblin and Orc tribes acknowledge his overlordship of the mountains around the ruined Dwarf hold of Karak Eight Peaks.

Since the Dwarfs returned to reoccupy their ancient hold, Skarsnik has virtually kept the Dwarfs prisoner within their tiny citadel. When Dwarfs try to enter or leave Karak Eight Peaks he hunts them down and hangs their beard scalps on long poles within sight of the citadel walls. He is remarkably cunning and is constantly luring the Dwarfs into ambushes and traps. At the battle of East Gate he managed to surround a Dwarf relief force and virtually destroy it, forcing the remnants to flee back into the citadel itself.

Skarsnik is accompanied by a huge Cave Squig which he calls Gobbla. Gobbla is enormous, very smelly, and mindlessly vicious but seems totally loyal to his master. Skarsnik feeds Gobbla on Dwarfs and any Goblins careless enough to stray too close.

Skarsnik carries a huge magical weapon called a Prodder. This enables him to throw blasts of magic about the battlefield.

Profile	M	WS	BS	S	T	W	I	A	Ld
Skarsnik	4	5	6	4	4	3	6	4	9
Gobbla	-	6	0	6	4	3	6	4	2

WEAPONS/ARMOUR: Skarsnik wears light armour.

MAY RIDE: Skarsnik can ride a chariot pulled by either war boars or giant wolves as described in the War Machines section of the list.

MAGIC ITEMS: Skarsnik may carry up to three magic items including Skarsnik's Prodder. Other items may be chosen from the magic item cards. See Warhammer Battle Magic.

SPECIAL RULES

MOVEMENT

Gobbla is chained to Skarsnik and so always moves together with him. The two models are placed side by side. Should Skarsnik be slain Gobbla will bite through his chains and act like a large monster that has lost its rider. See the Warhammer rulebook (PP68-69) for the Monster Reaction Table. Gobbla moves 2D6" per turn once free of Skarsnik.

HAND-TO-HAND FIGHTING

Gobbla will not bite Skarsnik but he may attack other Orcs or Goblins if given half a chance. If there are any enemy in base contact he will always bite enemy models in preference to friends. If there are no enemy in base contact he may bite other Orcs, Goblins, etc if they are touching. This tends to happen if Skarsnik joins a Mob and fights with it. Roll a dice at the start of the hand-to-hand combat phase. On the roll of a 6 Gobbla will attack whatever is touching him. Work out Gobbla's attack as normal. No break test is necessary for friends due to Gobbla's indiscretions.

SHOOTING

When the enemy shoots bows or other missiles at Skarsnik any hits are randomised between Skarsnik and Gobbla. Roll a D6: 1-3 = Skarsnik hit, 4-6 = Gobbla hit.

GOBBLA

Gobbla does not test psychology separately from Skarsnik. The two models are treated as a single entity and Gobbla always follows Skarsnik. Should Skarsnik be killed Gobbla reacts as described on the Monster Reaction Table in the Monsters section of the Warhammer rulebook. Gobbla does not react like an ordinary wild Squig as described under the Squig Hunter rules. If Skarsnik is killed Gobbla becomes so enraged that he takes no psychology or other leadership-based tests; he cannot be broken in hand-to-hand combat and is immune to the effects of psychology.

ORC AND GOBLIN
MAGIC ITEM CARDS

We have provided a number of magic items for you to make up into Warhammer Magic cards. To assemble your cards first photocopy the appropriate pages.

Using a thin layer of gum, paste or other glue suitable for paper, glue each photocopied sheet to a piece of thin card. The card from a cereal packet is just fine. Once the glue is thoroughly dry cut out your cards with scissors. It is not necessary to provide a back for these cards, but if you wish to do so you can use the accompanying sample card back design.

MAGIC ITEM   POINTS VALUE: 25

GORK'S WAR BANNER

As the ladz stride beneath Gork's own war banner their hearts swell with pride. When they charge they launch themselves upon the foe with deadly vigour, tearing and rending at their helpless enemy.

The unit adds +1 to its strength value when it charges into hand-to-hand combat. This bonus only applies when the unit charges and not at other times. It applies to all models in the unit including any characters with it.

Gork's War Banner may be carried by a permitted Orc or Goblin unit of any type including Savage and Black Orcs, and Forest and Night Goblins.

ORCS & GOBLINS ONLY

MAGIC ITEM   POINTS VALUE: 10

THE EVIL SUN BANNER

Troops carrying the Evil Sun are guided carefully by its strong magic, turning aside any thoughts of petty vengeance and dissension.

A unit carrying this standard may re-roll any failed Animosity test.

RE-ROLL ANIMOSITY TEST
NIGHT GOBLINS ONLY

MAGIC ITEM   POINTS VALUE: 65

MORK'S WAR BANNER

Mork's War Banner drips with the raw Waaagh energy of the great god Mork. While the ladz march beneath its awesome shadow they enjoy the protection and favour of Mork.

The unit is so suffused with magic that any spells directed against it are absorbed by the troops and turned into raw Waaagh energy. Spells cast upon the unit are dispelled on the D6 roll of a 4, 5 or 6, including any Waaagh spells cast by your own side. If any wizard or shaman touches the unit Waaagh energy will flow into him, overloading his mind and killing him instantly. No spell can be cast by the unit, including spells associated with magic items. Other magic items will work normally.

ORCS & GOBLINS ONLY

MAGIC ITEM   POINTS VALUE: 35

THE BAD MOON BANNER

The Bad Moon Banner is a creation of the Night Goblin shamans. The banner shrouds the unit carrying it in darkness, making it difficult to shoot at and confusing to fight in hand-to-hand combat.

A unit carrying this standard makes a difficult target due to the enveloping shadow that surrounds it. All shots at it count -1 to hit. War machine shots are not affected if they do not normally make a D6 roll to hit. In hand-to-hand fighting the unit always strikes first, even if it has been charged and irrespective of relative initiative values. If both units are entitled by magic to strike first then the highest initiative goes first; if these are equal roll a dice to decide.

NIGHT GOBLINS ONLY

MAGIC ITEM   POINTS VALUE: 10

THE SWORD OF BORK

Though gnarled and bitten with centuries of fighting, the magic of the Sword of Bork is still effective and its serrated edge glints with power. Orcs will follow any leader who carries the sword.

If a unit's leader carries the Sword of Bork it automatically ignores its first animosity failure – after it has failed its animosity test once any further Animosity applies as normal.

The sword may be carried by an Orc or a Savage Orc.

**IGNORES
FIRST ANIMOSITY FAILURE
ORCS & SAVAGE ORCS ONLY**

MAGIC ITEM

MAGIC ITEM

MAGIC ITEM   POINTS VALUE: 35

SPIDER BANNER

Under the gaze of their Spider god's magic the Forest Goblins fill with Waaagh energy, their eyes glint with power and anticipation of the slaughter.

A unit carrying the Spider Banner doubles all of its attacks during its first turn of hand-to-hand combat of the game. This bonus only applies once, after which its energy is dissipated. The extra attacks apply to all models fighting with the unit including characters.

**DOUBLE ATTACKS FIRST TURN
FOREST GOBLINS ONLY**

MAGIC ITEM   POINTS VALUE: 50

THE COLLAR OF ZORGA

The spiked collar enables its wearer to enter the mind of monsters and overpower or bind them to his will.

The wearer is immune to the hand-to-hand combat attacks of all Monsters. An enemy Monster in base contact will not attack the character or any other model that turn. This applies to Monsters being ridden as well. The wearer may attempt to take over any enemy Monsters in base contact at the end of any hand-to-hand combat round which his side has won. Roll 2D6, if the dice score is equal to or less than the character's leadership value then he has temporarily taken over the Monster. The Monster may immediately make an additional move and fight an additional hand-to-hand combat as normal. This additional move/combat happens immediately. A rider on top of a Monster which is taken over is helpless to stop it, but the Monster will not attack its rider. The Monster is taken over only briefly and reverts to its own player's control immediately afterwards.

ORCS & GOBLINS ONLY

MAGIC ITEM   POINTS VALUE: 125

MORGOR THE MANGLER

An Orc wielding the axe Morgor the Mangler adds +1 to his weapon skill, +1 to his toughness, and +1 to his strength. In addition he always strikes first. If both the wielder and his opponent are entitled to strike first the highest initiative takes priority, otherwise roll a dice to decide. Normal armour cannot protect against Morgor the Mangler, so no armour saving rolls are allowed unless the enemy is wearing magic armour, which saves as normal. Only an Orc, Savage Orc or Black Orc may use Morgor the Mangler.

MAY BE USED BY ORCS ONLY

MAGIC SPELL / ITEM   POINTS VALUE: 75

SKARSNIK'S PRODDER

The Night Goblin Chieftain Skarsnik had this Prodder enchanted by Night Goblin Shamans.

Skarsnik's Prodder fights in combat like an ordinary Squig Prodder (+1 strength). In the magic phase the Prodder may be used to unleash Waaagh energy in the form of one or more magic blasts. Each blast has S4 and hits the first model in its path in the same way as a Fireball spell. No armour save is allowed, even for magic armour. Skarsnik's Prodder may fire one blast for each Orc or Goblin unit within 12", plus one extra blast for each of these units in hand-to-hand combat. Orc units must be at least 10 strong to count, Goblin units 20 models strong. The maximum range of the blast is 24" and the blast can also be used against any opponents in base contact.

**WAAAGH NUMBER S4 BLASTS
NIGHT GOBLINS ONLY**

Below Azhag the great green horde advanced. As the shadow of his wyvern fell upon his troops they looked up, gazing skyward with a mixture of awe, fear and brute stupidity in their red eyes. On the left of the column were the mighty Orc warriors of Ghor's Renders, each a towering giant whose yellow tusks gleamed proudly in the sunlight. To the right were Jhorg's trolls, huge blue-skinned monsters eating the miles with their long loping strides. Behind them, stretching for mile upon mile, came Goblin tribe after Goblin tribe and Orc Mob after Orc Mob. The enormous bulks of stone throwers towered over the mass, each drawn by a sweating team of gobbo slaves.

Spider-riding chieftains led clans of stunted Forest Goblins across the open plain. Black-garbed Night Goblins shuffled and limped along in the bright sunlight. Here and there amid their lines Azhag could see sweating gobbos carrying the great ball and chains of their fanatic brethren. At the head of the army rode the boar riders, controlling their surly bristle-snouted mounts with blows and grunts. Far off in the distance Azhag could see the long grey line of the wolf rider scouts who spearheaded the horde's advance into man territory.

Azhag tugged on the wyvern's reins and the great beast swooped down over the mass of troops, sending panicked Goblins scuttling for cover. In their midst a few doom divers preened themselves and flapped their artificial wings, as if they wanted to leap into the air and join him. With its great banners fluttering in the chill wind the horde was like an endless river of colour flowing across the plains of the eastern Empire. Where it marched the long grass was beaten flat. A long muddy trail of despoilation stretched out behind the army.

Even from this height, hundreds of feet above the army, the din was immense, a hellish cacophony born from the beat of manskinned drums, the bellowing of beasts and the sounding of great bronze trumpets. The high pitched voices of the Goblins mingled with the deep sullen grumbling of the Orcs. The trolls emitted confused grunts and howls as the Orcs leading them poked them with sharp sticks. The soft eight-legged thud of spider legs competed with the weird giggling and screaming of the cave squigs.

Dozens of Orc regiments sang their battlesongs, each trying to drown out their neighbours' chants and make themselves heard above the din. Occasionally they would stop singing to hurl abuse at the regiments marching alongside. Mostly this was good natured, but Azhag knew that it could easily turn vicious and nasty. It was the way of things, and he could no more change it than he could stop himself from eating when he was hungry or cuffing his henchmen when he was annoyed.

From this height Azhag could see the different banners and remember where each unit had joined the Waaagh. He had not always led such a mighty force. Once he had been a simple Orc Boss leading his folk against their many enemies in the Troll Country. That had been before he had discovered his crown in the ruins of that vast abandoned mancity, before the strange evil dreams had come to trouble his sleep, before the foul dust of ancient days had filled his soul. Even now as he thought of it, he felt an urge to rummage through his saddle bags and look at the old rune-encrusted crown. The crown had granted him strange powers and given him a vision of conquered realms. It made him feel invincible and it granted him great cunning. Despite this there was something about its slumbering evil that troubled his simple soul. There were still days when he wished that he had never taken it from the dead troll's hoard.

No, that was foolish. The crown had lifted him above the ordinary Orc rut of eating and fighting and given him vision. It had shown him the path of conquest. Soon he had been leading his tribe down through Kislev. He had fought many battles with the horse warriors of the Ice Queen and the Dwarfs of the mountains. Mostly he had won, and more and more greenskinned followers had flocked to his banner.

After battling the Kislevites on the frozen lake of Tura, where stone thrower rocks had crashed through the ice drowning dozens of fleeing horsemen, Jhorg and his trolls had emerged from the snow-encrusted pine forest. After he had burned the Kislevite town of Petragrad, the boar riders had ridden up to take part in the plundering. Once he had given their leader Urgruk a good kicking they had volunteered to join the Waaagh.

Since then Orcs and Goblins had flocked to his banner from every deep forest and cave lair. Night Goblins had journeyed from Red Eye Mountain bringing cave squigs and their herders with them. Sensing the growing power of the Waaagh Goblin shamans had hastened to the fast growing army. Forest Goblins had joined them almost as soon as they had left the mountains. It was as if some silent call had summoned them to join this vast migration. Sometimes Azhag wondered about that....

The warning hornblast from the wolf riders drew him from his reverie. He glanced towards the horizon and saw the great grey wolves were loping back towards the main bulk of the army. In the distance, he could see a dark line moving to meet his army. It looked as if another group of men had gathered to try and slow his army's progress. Good, thought Azhag. His boyz would win. There would be more plunder, and word of this mighty victory would spread through the forests and hills and draw ever more warriors to his side. His great plan of conquest was advancing apace.

* * * * *

The human army deployed quickly and efficiently, as Azhag had expected it would. The humans had chosen to fight on the edge of the plain where the grass was shorter and fields of fire were easier to maintain. On their left flank, secured by the river and its marshy banks, was a great mass of heavily armoured infantry. *Reiksguard,* the crown's evil voice whispered into his mind. Near them were halberdiers and a huge number of poorly armoured spearmen. *Peasants, hastily pressed into service,* said the malignant voice. In the centre of the Imperial force were the knights, each heavily armed and armoured and mounted on a barded horse. They had massed under the banner of the Count of Ostland, their hereditary lord. Count von Raukov himself was there. As Azhag watched, the man strung his mighty enchanted bow.

On his right flank, Azhag's left, war engines were deployed: a cannon and a volley gun. Beside them several regiments of archers. As Azhag watched a line of Kislevite horsemen took up a skirmish position in front of the

Imperial army. Even at this distance Azhag thought he recognised their banner. The Northerners had obviously followed him, seeking vengeance for their ruined homes.

Azhag turned his attention to his own force. The column swiftly spread out into a long battleline. The boarboyz held the centre. Their bad tempered mounts grunted loudly and pawed the earth impatiently, as if they could not wait to get to grips with the foe. Beside them, on either side, were the Orcs, each regiment keen to get on with the fight. As Azhag watched Ghor's Renders started jeering and spitting at Nhaga's Choppers, taunting the rival unit and telling them that they were going to be left behind in the charge. Nhaga's boyz responded with obscene gestures and crude taunts. Azhag watched them carefully, knowing that it was possible that they might forget about the foe and come to blows among themselves if left unsupervised.

On the left wing of the Orc army, on a slight rise in the moor, were the rock lobbers. Each mighty catapult arm was being hastily winched into place. Sweating Orcs quickly loaded huge rocks for firing. Beside the lobbers were the great catapults of the doom divers. A long line of winged lunatics wound up the slope to the launchers. Some hopped and gibbered with excitement. Others rushed about, wings outstretched, making whooshing noises and pretending to be already airborne. On the brow of the ridge one doom diver licked his forefinger then extended it, testing the wind. He turned and shouted something to the doom divers behind him. Azhag assumed it was favourable because they let out a whooping cheer and began to bounce up and down on the spot excitedly.

In front of the ridge were a seething mass of Night Goblin archers. The squinting little gobbos unleashed arrow after arrow into the distance although the range was far too great for them to hit anything. Soon their leaders had to rush among them and knock a few heads together in order to get them to stop wasting their ammunition. Massed beside the archers, next to the Orcs, were all those spear-armed Night Goblins who could not be trusted with bows. They stood howling abuse at their archer brethren and sneakily spitting in the general direction of the Orcs when they thought their larger kin weren't looking. If an Orc cast an eye in their direction the gobbo who had spat hastily pointed to the next spearman in line. Here and there behind the Night Goblins a few fanatics lay writhing on the ground, foaming at the mouth, their jaws working steadily on great wad of hallucinogenic mushrooms. Soon they would move from a state of torpor to one of maniacal exaltation and then they would be ready to be unleashed against the foe.

Here and there among the Night Goblin lines net teams took up position. Azhag would have found them funny had he not seen the teams in action previously. The netters would quickly entangle their chosen enemy then the clubbers would swarm over them, wacking the trapped foes with their big spiky bludgeons. Working together the teams could deal with a foe many times their own size.

To the Orcs' right was a herd of cave squigs and their handlers. The massive spherical monstrosities threatened to wander off and rampage through their own lines and were restrained from doing so only by the efforts of the herders. The handlers had to work frantically with their great poking forks to keep their unruly charges in line. One squig broke away and waddled towards the trolls on

their right. The trolls turned their stupid blank-eyed gaze towards it. Before its handlers could stop it the squig scuttled over to a troll. Jaws like a mantrap closed and the squig took a great bite out of the troll's leg. Ignoring the great hole in its body the troll casually bludgeoned the squig to the ground with the ease of an Orc swatting a fly. The squig exploded with a horrid squelching noise. Azhag watched in fascination as the troll's flesh began to grow back.

On the trolls' right, almost abutting the river, were the Forest Goblins. Tribe after tribe lined up clutching their weapons and pushing their leaders forward into the front rank. Azhag counted the banners. The Goblins of the Gaping Maw were present along with the Horned Skulls and the Forest Scuttlers. At each end of the line were the shamans. Grimbog, the most powerful, was mounted on a spider. He scuttled into position down by the river. His apprentice, Morglum, stood by the Night Goblins where the vast tides of orky energy the army would soon generate could not overwhelm him. Already Azhag could sense the power that flowed over his force. Soon the humies would feel it too. Ahead of the army the wolf riders had formed up in a thin skirmish line ready to match the Kislevites. All in all it was an impressive force, thought Azhag, climbing into the special padded throne on the back of his wyvern.

The mighty creature surged under him. With a snap it unfurled its huge leathery wings. Azhag felt serpentine muscles coil beneath him as the beast prepared to leap into the air. The crown pulsed on his brow, feeding him its dark energy. Soon it would be time. His plans were laid. Every Orc boss and Goblin chieftain had his instructions. They would carry them out to the letter or feel his wrath. The crown's prompting told him it was time for a few inspiring words before the battle. Unholy energy pulsed through him as he raised his enchanted blade high above his head and let out a loud bellow. Thousands of pairs of red eyes turned to look at him.

"Right ladz," he shouted. "Letz give dem stinkin' humies a good seein' to."

His speech made he applied his spurs to the wyvern's flanks. The great reptile lurched skyward. Exaltation filled Azhag as the ground dropped away beneath him and the rushing wind whipped his face. Soon his force had dwindled till it seemed like an army of ants. He could see the blocks and squares that were both sides' units laid out like a diagram below him. He felt god-like, omniscient, filled with power, exalted by speed and distance.

He brought the wyvern round in a great spiral and forced the creature down. Left to its own devices he did not doubt that it would flap all the way to the distant mountains. As he watched, his boyz began to move forward, chanting and singing and brandishing their weapons at the foe. He felt proud, certain that the inexorable green tide would soon flow over his enemies.

Curses, what was that? A great ruck had broken out between Ghor's boyz and Nhaga's. As he'd feared, the rivalry between the forces had overstepped the bounds of good sense. As the two Mobs had begun to advance they had crashed into each other, perhaps by accident, perhaps by design. He swooped down till he could see the battle, frantically howling curses and imprecations at both sides equally. He saw that the Renders and the Choppers were both getting stuck in. Ghor and Nhaga moved among their warriors, bashing heads together and stopping the brawl turning into a full scale bloodbath.

Coming to a quick decision, Azhag decided that he could not wait. Much as he disliked the idea he would have to trust the two Orc bosses to settle the affair and carry on with his original plan. He had seen his boyz mown down by a volley gun before and did not intend to let it happen again. His stomach lurched as the monster banked and raced towards the enemy artillery. Azhag ducked his head as a doom diver whipped past. The thing's gibbering cries filled his ears and then faded as the gobbo receded into the distance. Even as Azhag watched it plunged into the ground next to the Imperial cannon. A moment later a second doom diver whizzed by him and crunched right into the cannon's barrel with its head, spiking it. Hearing a crunch off to his right Azhag glanced round. A giant boulder from the rock lobber had landed among the Imperial knights, crushing one of them. The other mounted warriors struggled to control their rearing mounts.

Azhag descended right by the volley gun. His padded saddle barely absorbed the shock of impact. Frantically the men tried to swivel the weapon to bear. The wyvern bit one of their heads off. Blood fountained into the air. Droplets of the red stuff ran down Azhag's cheek. He licked the blood off even as he leaned low in his saddle and chopped the other gunner down with his sword. Such was the power the blade lent him that he barely felt the shock of impact as his weapon bit into the man's flesh. Vertebrae snapped as he was cut in two. With a buffet of its wing the wyvern sent the volley gun tumbling into the mud. The nearby human archers stood pale faced. One coward had fainted clean away. A bold sergeant hastily bellowed orders to his men to turn and fire. Azhag opened his mouth and roared with laughter.

The crown pulsed and dark knowledge filled his mind. He howled the words of the Blade Wind spell. A dark, glittering cloud of enchanted scimitars swept out from his hand towards the sergeant. The man desperately tried to parry the ensorcelled weapons but there were too many of them. His friends watched horrified as he was cut to tiny pieces by the hovering swords. Sensing a shift in the winds of magic Azhag looked over at the knights. A mounted human sorcerer sent a bolt of lightning hurtling towards the oncoming Forest Goblins. The gobbos howled and capered as they fried, eyes popping from their sockets. Another wizard began to gesture and point at the Orc warlord. The crown instantly provided Azhag with the words of a counterspell and he dissipated the storm of mystic energy before it had even begun to form.

Azhag risked a glance at his own warriors. Seen from his position within the human line their advance certainly looked impressive. It was as if a seething green sea swept over the plain. Already shaken by the loss of their war engines the human line was panicky. Undaunted, the Kislevites swept out towards the wolf riders, and unleashed a hail of arrows at the wolfboyz. A few fell, arrows protruding from their throats and eyes. The rest turned about and fled.

"Cum bak yer yellow-bellied skum!" Azhag bellowed, but if the wolf riders heard him they pretended not to notice. A hail of fire from one of the human archer regiments encouraged them on their way. The archers who had turned to face Azhag opened fire. With a flickering movement of his hand the Elector Count unleashed three arrows from his enchanted bow. Azhag raised his magical shield to protect his face and ignored the arrows that pattered off his armour and the wyvern's scales. Suddenly the wyvern gave out an irritated screech. Looking up Azhag saw an arrow protruding through the thin membrane of its wings.

A loud roar from the humans indicated that at least part of their army was advancing. Spells scorched the air between the armies but the magical influences seemed balanced and neither side took any harm.

Azhag applied the spurs once more and the wyvern leapt skyward. From on high he had a good vantage point for the coming struggle. The human spearmen and knights were advancing behind the screen of Kislevites. The gap between the two armies had almost closed. The fleeing wolf riders were blocking the charge of the boarboyz. Ghor and Nhaga had finally got their ladz moving. The Night Goblins lurched closer to the Kislevites and suddenly three screaming Fanatics hurtled out of their ranks. Although they had been expecting it the speed of the attack took the Kislevites by surprise and one fell under the impact of a massive wrecking ball. Arrows from the advancing Night Goblins and Forest Goblins fell ineffectually on the Imperial force. A huge rock landed just in front of the Reiksguard knights, sending clods of muddy earth spurting into the air.

Suddenly the Elector Count and his knights saw their opportunity as the wolf riders surged past the boarboyz. The human horses moved from a canter to a charge and the lancers swept into the boarboyz, skewering several with their lances. The air around the Elector Count glittered as his enchanted blade bit deep. *Runefang*, whispered the Crown's lurking spirit. *ancient blade from the time of thrice-accursed Sigmar*. The surge of hatred that passed through him when the crown mentioned Sigmar made Azhag howl. For a moment it looked as if the boarboyz might hold. Their surly war hogs tried to gore the horses and their leader Buzhak shouted curses and threats at any lad who might retreat. But then the Runefang bit deep, severing Buzhak's head and sending it flying. The boarboyz turned and fled.

Azhak cursed loudly. Even as he watched, the knights pursued and careered straight into Ghor's Renders. Over by the river the Reiksguard infantry and the halberdiers advanced towards the Forest Goblins. They marched with disciplined precision, every stride in time with the beat of their great drums. At the last second they broke into a charge and threw themselves against the Forest Goblins. With a crash like a steel wave breaking on an iron shore the two forces clashed. Soon man and Goblin were fighting breast to breast in a turbulent maelstrom of death.

Clouds of arrows from the Imperial archers cut down the unleashed Fanatics. Several fell among the main Night Goblin unit throwing them into confusion and disarray. Magical energy made the air over the two armies shimmer and ripple. The tides of power made Azhag's skin tingle. Looking down he saw a bright green glow surround Grimbog's head. Suddenly with an enormous bang the Goblin shaman's head exploded sending green brains splattering over the combatants surrounding him. The human warriors seemed to take heart and fight on with renewed fury.

The entire battle hung in the balance. It actually seemed that through sheer courage and gobbo cowardice the humies might win. Azhag invoked the Blade Wind once more, sending the blades dancing down at the Elector Count himself. Before they could reach him a brilliant golden glow surrounded the Imperial war banner. The shafts of light struck the dark magical blades and the weapons faded like mist in morning sunlight. Azhag bellowed in frustration. Now he was just going to have to sort this out the old fashioned way, by hand.

Shrieking his battlecry he sent the wyvern into a steep dive, catching the Reiksguard knights in the flank. The Count tugged on his horse's reins forcing the terrified animal round to face the wyvern. For a moment even the Reiksguard's iron discipline wavered. Attacked from the side by the enormous wyvern their hearts quailed. Ghor's Renders took new heart at the sight of Azhag's charge and their foes' discomfiture. Ghor swigged down his enchanted potion and the muscles of his arms swelled with new found monstrous strength. He bellowed out a cheerful greeting to Azhag.

The Elector Count lashed out with the Runefang. Frantically Azhag parried. The writhing of the wyvern and the rearing of the warhorse made any sort of skilled fencing impossible and it was more a case of luck as to who hit who. Azhag bit back a howl of pain as the Runefang slashed his forearm. Pain seared up his arm and he almost dropped his sword. Fighting back the agony he lashed out at the Elector Count. His blade bit deep in return, cutting through the man's armour like a butcher's cleaver going through a piece of meat. The Elector was driven backwards by the sheer force of Azhag's blow.

Meanwhile the wyvern had reached forward with its long neck and caught a barded warhorse between its huge jaws. In an awesome display of its incredible strength it lifted the armoured beast up into the air, rider and all, then hurled the kicking and screaming creature to the ground with bonebreaking force. The shock of the impact and the weight of its armoured rider broke the animal's back, killing it instantly. The trapped knight was chopped to bits by the resurgent Orcs.

Ghor crashed through the melee like a daemon of elemental fury. With one back-handed swing of his scimitar he cut through the Count's standard and its bearer's arm. The severed limb flopped to the ground and twitched for a moment like a decapitated snake. It was all too much for the surviving knights. Forming up around the wounded Elector they turned and retreated. Their horses enabled them to outdistance the Orcs. Half blind with pain, Azhag tried to make the wyvern follow but it was too busy slobbering down chunks of the dead warhorse.

Azhag looked round blearily. In the distance he could see half a dozen surviving Reiksguard infantry cut down nearly an entire regiment of Forest Goblins. The stunted ones' nerve had broken and they had turned to flee, presenting their backs to the Imperial soldiers. The close packed mass of panicking gobbos tried to flee in every direction, tripping over each other in their confusion and getting in each other's way. All the humans had to do was run among them, trampling them under foot and hacking them in their undefended backs. In mere moments most of the Goblins were dead. The humans were chopping one down with every ill-aimed stroke. The greenskins were so close that the men couldn't miss. Azhag bellowed to Nhaga to sort it out. The Orcs charged in. The grossly outnumbered humans prepared for their last stand.

Azhag nearly allowed himself to slump in the saddle. The battle was almost won. The best of the human army was almost in full retreat. No, he decided he would not rest. Not when he had a blade in his hand and a fight before him. He dug his spurs into the wyvern's flanks, forcing the gorged creature to flap slowly into the air. There were still archers to slay and warriors to cut down.

* * * * *

Azhag looked down on the boy's body and tried to understand what had brought one so young so far only to be killed. He felt that if he could understand that then he would understand his enemies and find final victory. Humans were not like his followers, he knew that. The crown had given him sufficient insight to see. Humans were not warlike in the same way as Orcs. The big greenskins lived to fight. They might be momentarily overcome by panic in the heat of battle when all around was confusion, but death held no terrors for them. Orcs lived to fight and eat and plunder. Azhag looked at his boyz as they stomped around over the battlefield, rolling drunk on firewater and chanting their victory songs till it seemed the heavens would shake. Tonight they had grasped victory. Tomorrow they would go in search of another.

No, humans were not like Orcs. They feared to die. To an Orc death was something that just happened, a bit of bad luck, like breaking a tooth when you bit into stonebread. Death was not something an Orc looked forward to with any apprehension. Orcs knew their lot was to fight and die. They complained about it no more than a tree complained about the wind and rain. Humans were not like that. They were weak; they sought things other than ceaseless warfare, and the prospect of death frightened them.

Yet humans were not like Goblins either. They were not sly, avaricious, cowardly little creatures who had to be bullied by a powerful leader or ensorcelled or drugged before they would face a foe in battle. Looking at the gobbos slinking round the Orc warriors, sneakily stealing scraps of food and plunder, Azhag felt a surge of contempt. Goblins could be cruel and malicious but they rarely overcame their fear. Azhag found it hard to imagine any Goblin holding his ground unless they greatly outnumbered their foes. Goblins were not brave.

The human had been brave, Azhag thought. He had known fear and he had overcome it. He had held his ground in the face of certain death and tried to hold Azhag back while his wounded comrades fled. It had been a selfless thing to do, and all the more selfless because he had been afraid. Azhag shook his head. Such behaviour was almost beyond his comprehension. Still he had the time. The world was his to conquer.

All around the Orcs sang their victory songs. As if unaware of all the death and disaster about them they played like children in the wreckage of the battle. For a moment, Azhag felt alone. In all the screaming mob he seemed the only one to have stopped and thought about the future. It was that which separated him from the rest.

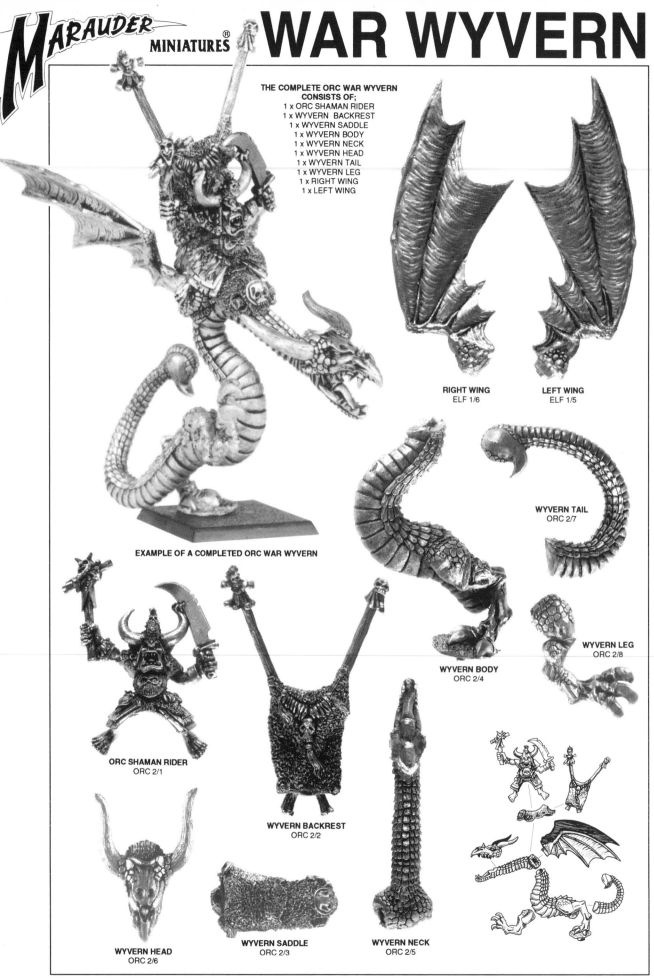

THE COMPLETE ORC WAR WYVERN
CONSISTS OF;
1 x ORC SHAMAN RIDER
1 x WYVERN BACKREST
1 x WYVERN SADDLE
1 x WYVERN BODY
1 x WYVERN NECK
1 x WYVERN HEAD
1 x WYVERN TAIL
1 x WYVERN LEG
1 x RIGHT WING
1 x LEFT WING

RIGHT WING
ELF 1/6

LEFT WING
ELF 1/5

WYVERN TAIL
ORC 2/7

EXAMPLE OF A COMPLETED ORC WAR WYVERN

WYVERN LEG
ORC 2/8

WYVERN BODY
ORC 2/4

ORC SHAMAN RIDER
ORC 2/1

WYVERN BACKREST
ORC 2/2

WYVERN HEAD
ORC 2/6

WYVERN SADDLE
ORC 2/3

WYVERN NECK
ORC 2/5

ORC ROCK LOBBER

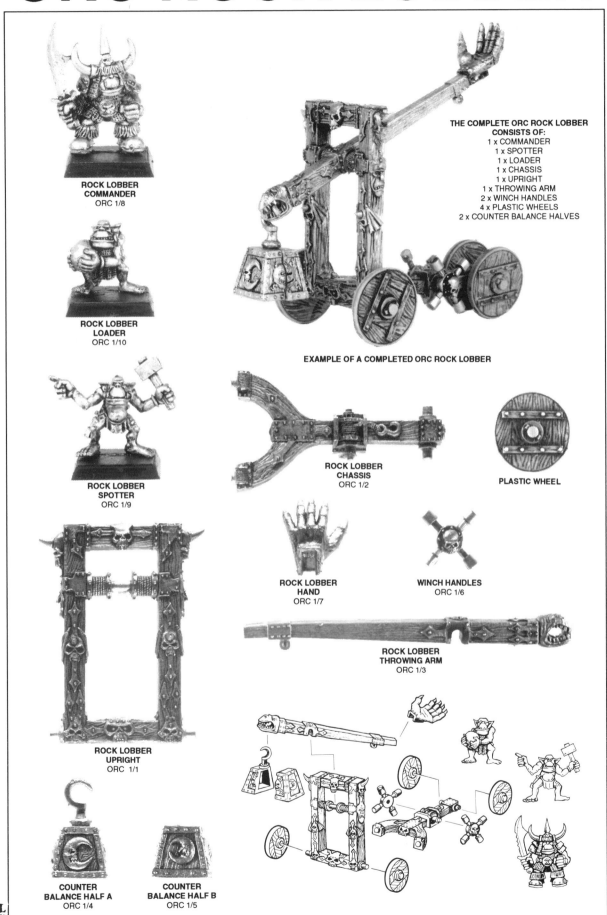

ROCK LOBBER COMMANDER
ORC 1/8

ROCK LOBBER LOADER
ORC 1/10

ROCK LOBBER SPOTTER
ORC 1/9

ROCK LOBBER UPRIGHT
ORC 1/1

COUNTER BALANCE HALF A
ORC 1/4

COUNTER BALANCE HALF B
ORC 1/5

THE COMPLETE ORC ROCK LOBBER
CONSISTS OF:
1 x COMMANDER
1 x SPOTTER
1 x LOADER
1 x CHASSIS
1 x UPRIGHT
1 x THROWING ARM
2 x WINCH HANDLES
4 x PLASTIC WHEELS
2 x COUNTER BALANCE HALVES

EXAMPLE OF A COMPLETED ORC ROCK LOBBER

ROCK LOBBER CHASSIS
ORC 1/2

PLASTIC WHEEL

ROCK LOBBER HAND
ORC 1/7

WINCH HANDLES
ORC 1/6

ROCK LOBBER THROWING ARM
ORC 1/3

Designed by Kev Adams and Norman Swales

ORCS

ORC COMMAND GROUP

CHAMPION 1
075235/1

STANDARD BEARER 1
075235/3

DRUMMER 1
075235/2

GORFANG ROTGUT

CHIEFTAIN
075240/1

ORC BIG'UNS

**BIG'UN
WITH SPEAR 1**
075230/1

**BIG'UN
WITH SPEAR 2**
075230/2

**BIG'UN
WITH SPEAR 3**
075230/3

**BIG'UN
WITH SWORD 1**
075230/4

**BIG'UN
WITH SWORD 2**
075230/5

**BIG'UN
WITH AXE**
075230/6

**BIG'UN
WITH MACE**
075230/7

**BIG'UN
WITH BOW**
075230/8

Designed by Kev Adams

ORCS

ORC BOYZ

ORC WITH
AXE AND DAGGER 1
075220/1

ORC
WITH SWORD 1
075220/2

ORC
WITH AXE 1
075220/3

ORC
WITH SPIKY CLUB 1
075220/4

ORC
WITH SWORD 2
075220/5

ORC
WITH SWORD 3
075220/6

ORC
WITH SWORD 4
075220/7

ORC
WITH SWORD 5
075220/8

ORC
WITH SWORD 6
075220/9

ORC
WITH SWORD 7
075220/10

Designed by Kev Adams

SAVAGE ORCS

SAVAGE ORC COMMAND GROUP

SAVAGE ORC BIG BOSS
075250/2

SAVAGE ORC BOSS
075250/1

SAVAGE ORC SHAMAN
075250/3

SAVAGE ORC HORN BLOWER
075250/4

SAVAGE ORC BANNER BEARER
075250/5

SAVAGE ORC BOYZ

SAVAGE ORC WITH SPEAR 3
075200/9

SAVAGE ORC WITH SPEAR 4
075200/10

SAVAGE ORC WITH SPIKED CLUB 3
075200/11

SAVAGE ORC WITH STONE HAMMER 2
075200/12

SAVAGE ORC WITH STONE HAMMER 3
075200/13

SAVAGE ORC WITH STONE HAMMER 4
075200/14

SAVAGE ORC WITH STONE HAMMER 5
075200/15

SAVAGE ORC WITH STONE HAMMER 6
075200/16

THESE MINIATURES ARE SUPPLIED WITH APPROPRIATE PLASTIC SHIELDS AS STANDARD

Designed by Alan Perry

SAVAGE ORCS

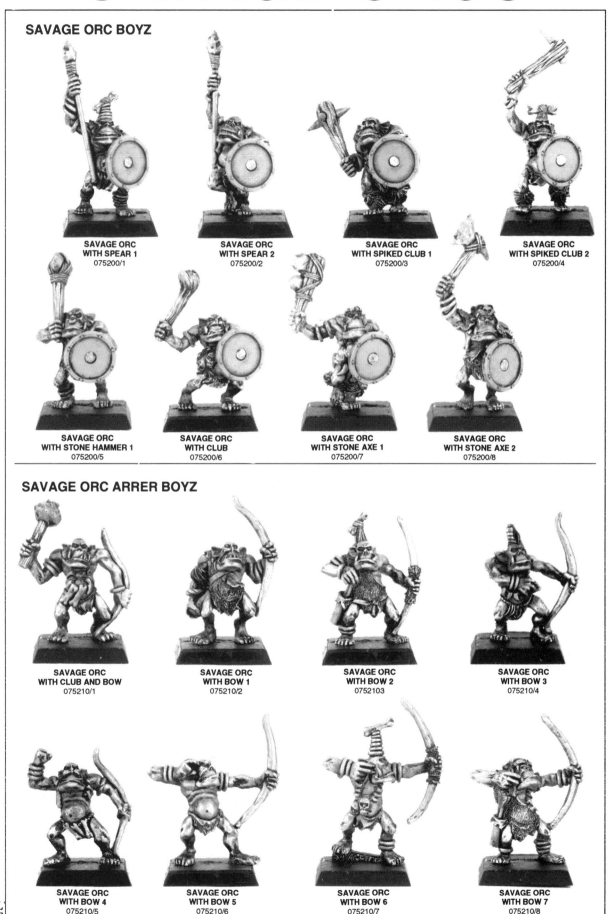

SAVAGE ORC BOYZ

SAVAGE ORC WITH SPEAR 1
075200/1

SAVAGE ORC WITH SPEAR 2
075200/2

SAVAGE ORC WITH SPIKED CLUB 1
075200/3

SAVAGE ORC WITH SPIKED CLUB 2
075200/4

SAVAGE ORC WITH STONE HAMMER 1
075200/5

SAVAGE ORC WITH CLUB
075200/6

SAVAGE ORC WITH STONE AXE 1
075200/7

SAVAGE ORC WITH STONE AXE 2
075200/8

SAVAGE ORC ARRER BOYZ

SAVAGE ORC WITH CLUB AND BOW
075210/1

SAVAGE ORC WITH BOW 1
075210/2

SAVAGE ORC WITH BOW 2
0752103

SAVAGE ORC WITH BOW 3
075210/4

SAVAGE ORC WITH BOW 4
075210/5

SAVAGE ORC WITH BOW 5
075210/6

SAVAGE ORC WITH BOW 6
075210/7

SAVAGE ORC WITH BOW 7
075210/8

Designed by Alan Perry

TROLLS

STONE TROLLS

**STONE TROLL
WITH TWO HANDED AXE**
075398/8

**STONE TROLL
WITH STONE AXE AND BONE CLUB**
075398/9

**STONE TROLL
WITH ROCK**
075398/7

STONE TROLL HEAD 1
075398/4

STONE TROLL HEAD 2
075398/5

STONE TROLL HEAD 3
075398/6

THE COMPLETE STONE TROLL
CONSISTS OF:
1 x STONE TROLL BODY
1 x STONE TROLL HEAD

EXAMPLES OF COMPLETED STONE TROLLS

THE THREE STONE TROLLS BELOW ARE ONE PIECE MODELS

**STONE TROLL
WITH AXE**
075398/2

**STONE TROLL
WITH STONE HAMMER**
075398/1

**STONE TROLL
WITH BONE CLUB**
075398/3

Designed by Michael Perry

TROLLS

RIVER TROLL BODY 2
075385/2

RIVER TROLL BODY 1
075385/1

RIVER TROLL BODY 3
075385/3

RIVER TROLL HEAD 1
075385/4

RIVER TROLL HEAD 2
075385/5

RIVER TROLL HEAD 3
075385/6

THE COMPLETE RIVER TROLL CONSISTS OF:
1 x RIVER TROLL BODY
1 x RIVER TROLL HEAD

EXAMPLES OF COMPLETED RIVER TROLLS

Designed by Michael Perry

FOREST GOBLINS

COMMAND GROUPS

FOREST GOBLIN
BOSS 1
075480/4

FOREST GOBLIN
SHAMAN
075480/1

FOREST GOBLIN
BOSS 2
075480/6

FOREST GOBLIN
BANNER BEARER 2
075480/3

FOREST GOBLIN
DRUMMER 1
075480/2

FOREST GOBLIN
BANNER BEARER 3
075480/5

FOREST GOBLIN
WITH BOW 1
075470/1

FOREST GOBLIN
WITH BOW 2
075470/2

FOREST GOBLIN
WITH BOW 3
075470/3

FOREST GOBLIN
WITH BOW 4
075470/4

FOREST GOBLIN
WITH AXE 1
075470/7

FOREST GOBLIN
WITH AXE 2
075470/8

FOREST GOBLIN
WITH SPEAR 1
075470/5

FOREST GOBLIN
WITH SPEAR 2
075470/6

FOREST GOBLIN
WITH SWORD 1
075470/9

FOREST GOBLIN
WITH SWORD 2
075470/10

FOREST GOBLIN
WITH SWORD 3
075470/11

FOREST GOBLIN
WITH SWORD 4
075470/12

THESE MINIATURES ARE SUPPLIED WITH THE APPROPRIATE PLASTIC SHIELDS

Designed by Kev Adams

FOREST GOBLINS

SPIDER RIDERS

**FOREST GOBLIN
SPIDER BODY 2**
075490/3

**FOREST GOBLIN
SPIDER BODY 1**
075490/2

**FOREST GOBLIN
SPIDER RIDER BANNER BEARER**
075490/6

**FOREST GOBLIN
SPIDER RIDER 2**
075490/7

**FOREST GOBLIN
SPIDER RIDER 1**
075490/4

**FOREST GOBLIN
SPIDER LEGS**
075490/1

**FOREST GOBLIN
SPIDER RIDER BOSS**
075490/5

**FOREST GOBLIN
SPIDER RIDER 3**
075490/9

**FOREST GOBLIN
SPIDER RIDER LEADER**
075490/8

**THE COMPLETE SPIDER RIDER MINIATURE
CONSISTS OF:**
1 x SPIDER BODY
1 x SPIDER LEGS
1 x SPIDER RIDER

EXAMPLES OF COMPLETED SPIDER RIDERS

THESE MINIATURES ARE SUPPLIED WITH THE APPROPRIATE PLASTIC SHIELDS

Designed by Kev Adams

NIGHT GOBLINS

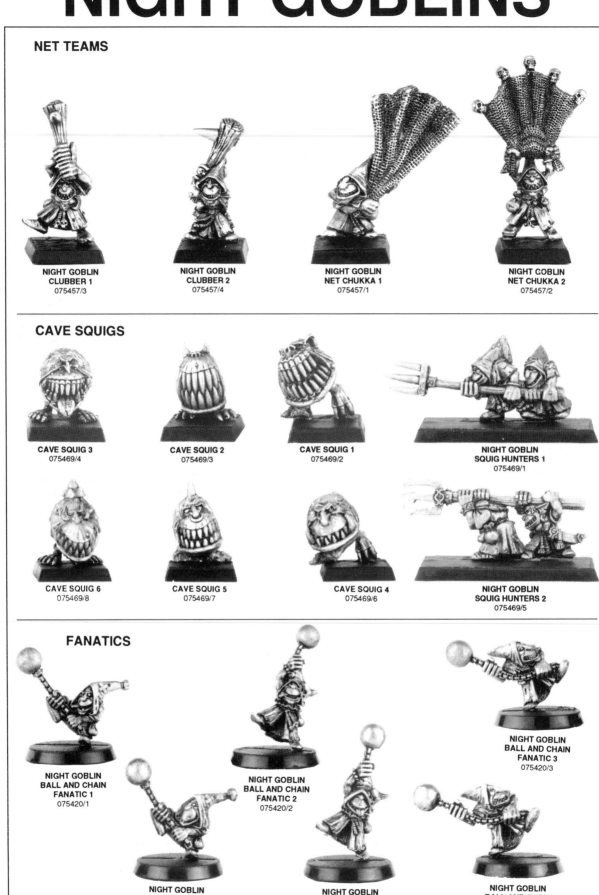

NET TEAMS

NIGHT GOBLIN
CLUBBER 1
075457/3

NIGHT GOBLIN
CLUBBER 2
075457/4

NIGHT GOBLIN
NET CHUKKA 1
075457/1

NIGHT GOBLIN
NET CHUKKA 2
075457/2

CAVE SQUIGS

CAVE SQUIG 3
075469/4

CAVE SQUIG 2
075469/3

CAVE SQUIG 1
075469/2

NIGHT GOBLIN
SQUIG HUNTERS 1
075469/1

CAVE SQUIG 6
075469/8

CAVE SQUIG 5
075469/7

CAVE SQUIG 4
075469/6

NIGHT GOBLIN
SQUIG HUNTERS 2
075469/5

FANATICS

NIGHT GOBLIN
BALL AND CHAIN
FANATIC 1
075420/1

NIGHT GOBLIN
BALL AND CHAIN
FANATIC 2
075420/2

NIGHT GOBLIN
BALL AND CHAIN
FANATIC 3
075420/3

NIGHT GOBLIN
BALL AND CHAIN
FANATIC 4
075420/4

NIGHT GOBLIN
BALL AND CHAIN
FANATIC 5
075420/5

NIGHT GOBLIN
BALL AND CHAIN
FANATIC 6
075420/6

Designed by Kev Adams

NIGHT GOBLINS

COMMAND GROUPS

NIGHT GOBLIN LEADER
075418/6

NIGHT GOBLIN CHAMPION 1
075418/2

NIGHT GOBLIN CHAMPION 2
075418/5

NIGHT GOBLIN WAR GONG 1
075418/3

NIGHT GOBLIN WAR GONG 2
075418/7

NIGHT GOBLIN BANNER BEARER 1
075418/1

NIGHT GOBLIN SHAMAN 2
075418/9

NIGHT GOBLIN SHAMAN
075418/4

NIGHT GOBLIN BANNER BEARER 2
075418/8

NIGHT GOBLIN WITH AXE 1
075405/9

NIGHT GOBLIN WITH AXE 2
075405/14

NIGHT GOBLIN WITH AXE 3
075405/17

NIGHT GOBLIN WITH MACE 1
075405/10

NIGHT GOBLIN WITH SWORD 1
075405/13

NIGHT GOBLIN WITH SPEAR 1
075405/4

NIGHT GOBLIN WITH SPEAR 2
075405/5

NIGHT GOBLIN WITH SPEAR 3
075405/6

NIGHT GOBLIN WITH SPEAR 4
075405/16

NIGHT GOBLIN WITH SPEAR 5
075405/15

NIGHT GOBLIN ARCHER 1
075405/11

NIGHT GOBLIN ARCHER 2
075405/12

NIGHT GOBLIN ARCHER 3
075405/1

NIGHT GOBLIN ARCHER 4
075405/2

NIGHT GOBLIN WITH FLAIL 1
075405/8

NIGHT GOBLIN WITH CLUB 1
075405/7

THESE MINIATURES ARE SUPPLIED WITH THE APPROPRIATE PLASTIC SHEILDS

Designed by Kev Adams

GOBLINS

GOBLIN DOOM DIVERS

**DOOM DIVER
CATAPULT CABLE**
075444/2

**THE COMPLETE GOBLIN DOOM DIVER
CONSISTS OF;**
1 x GOBLIN DOOM DIVER
1 x DOOM DIVER CATAPULT
1 x DOOM DIVER CATAPULT CABLE

**GOBLIN DOOM
DIVER 1**
075444/3

**GOBLIN DOOM
DIVER 2**
075444/4

**DOOM DIVER
CATAPULT**
075444/1

**GOBLIN
STANDARD BEARER 1**
075432/16

**GOBLIN
STANDARD BEARER 2**
075432/17

**GOBLIN
STANDARD BEARER 3**
075432/18

**GOBLIN WITH
SPEAR 10**
075432/1

**GOBLIN WITH
SPEAR 11**
075432/2

**GOBLIN WITH
SWORD 21**
075432/6

**GOBLIN WITH
SWORD 22**
075432/7

**GOBLIN WITH
SWORD 23**
075432/8

**GOBLIN WITH
SWORD 24**
075432/9

**GOBLIN WITH
SWORD 25**
075432/10

**GOBLIN WITH
SWORD 26**
075432/11

**GOBLIN WITH
SWORD 27**
075432/12

**GOBLIN WITH
SWORD 28**
075432/13

**GOBLIN WITH
CLUB 1**
075432/15

**GOBLIN WITH
CLUB 2**
075432/3

**GOBLIN WITH
MACE 1**
075432/5

**GOBLIN WITH
AXE 4**
075432/4

**GOBLIN WITH
AXE 5**
075432/14

THESE MINIATURES ARE SUPPLIED WITH THE APPROPRIATE PLASTIC SHIELDS

Designed by Kev Adams

 # GOBLINS

GIGANTIC SPIDER RIDERS

EXAMPLE OF COMPLETE GIGANTIC SPIDER RIDER AND SPIDER

GIGANTIC SPIDER HEAD
MM35/2

GIGANTIC SPIDER BODY
MM35/1

THE COMPLETE GIGANTIC SPIDER RIDER CONSISTS OF:
1 X GIGANTIC SPIDER BODY
1 X GIGANTIC SPIDER HEAD
1 X SPIDER RIDER SHAMAN OR CHAMPION
(The Champion Spider Rider includes one banner pole)

SHAMAN
MM35/3

CHAMPION
MM35/4

SPIDER RIDER CHAMPION'S BANNER POLE
MM35/5

Designed by Trish Morrison

SNOTLINGS

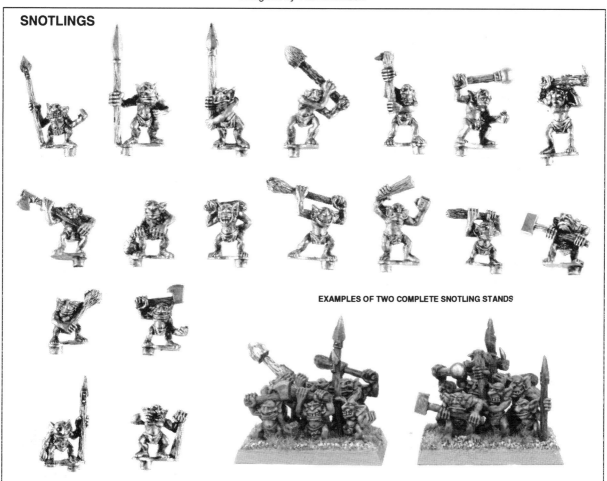

EXAMPLES OF TWO COMPLETE SNOTLING STANDS

MARAUDER SNOTLINGS ARE SUPPLIED IN PACKS OF NINE MINIATURES.

EACH PACK CONTAINS A RANDOM SELECTION OF MINIATURES AND WE TRY TO ENSURE THAT THERE ARE NO DUPLICATES IN EACH PACK.

Marauder Miniatures are supplied unpainted. Banners not included.

Designed by Colin Dixon

Warning! These miniatures contain lead which may be harmful if chewed or swallowed. Marauder Miniatures are not recommended for children under 14 years of age.

PLASTICS

PLASTIC ORC WARRIOR AND ARCHER SPRUE

THE PLASTIC ORC SPRUE IS SUPPLIED
WITH A VARIETY OF DIFFERENT SHIELD DESIGNS

PLASTIC GOBLIN SPEARMAN AND ARCHER SPRUE

THE PLASTIC GOBLIN SPRUE IS SUPPLIED
WITH A VARIETY OF DIFFERENT SHIELD DESIGNS

JOHN BLANCHE